WILEY
EXECUTIVE
MBA
Strategies, Skills, Solutions

MASTERING BUSINESS IN ASIA

HUMAN RESOURCE
MANAGEMENT

WILEY
EXECUTIVE
MBA
Strategies, Skills, Solutions

MASTERING BUSINESS IN ASIA
HUMAN RESOURCE
MANAGEMENT

Reiji Ohtaki
Hugh Bucknall

MERCER
Human Resource Consulting

John Wiley & Sons (Asia) Pte Ltd

Other Wiley Editorial Offices
John Wiley & Sons, Inc., 111 River Street, Hoboken, NJ 07030, USA
John Wiley & Sons Ltd, The Atrium, Southern Gate, Chichester PO19 BSQ, England
John Wiley & Sons (Canada) Ltd, 22 Worcester Road, Rexdale, Ontario M9W ILI, Canada
John Wiley & Sons Australia Ltd, 33 Park Road (PO Box 1226), Milton, Queensland 4046, Australia
Wiley-VCH, Pappelallee 3, 69469 Weinheim, Germany

Library of Congress Cataloging-in-Publication Data:

0-470-82113-2 (paperback)

Typeset in 11/15 point, Berkeley by Red Planet
Printed in Singapore by Saik Wah Press Pte Ltd
10 9 8 7 6 5 4 3 2

Contents

About the Contributors

TAKAO AIHARA

Takao Aihara is Executive Vice-President and Representative Director of Mercer Human Resource Consulting Japan. He is widely experienced in providing strategic direction for multiple areas of HRM development including performance management and compensation systems. He has worked with many Japanese and multinational companies. His more recent projects include renovating and developing HRM systems, developing assessment systems for people management, conducting corporate culture diagnostics and facilitating managerial development sessions.

Prior to joining Mercer, he was a consultant at a leading Japanese management consulting firm. Takao has authored and co-authored several Japanese language HRM books in the areas of competency development and application in Japan, and strategic human resource revolution.

He has a BA in Business and Commerce from Keio University. He is also a Director of Japan Society for Human Resource Management (JSHRM).

ILYA BONIC

Ilya Bonic is the Head of Mercer Human Resource Consulting's Global Information Services business in the Asia Pacific region. Ilya works with clients across 14 geographies, providing them with human resource information solutions, with a focus on the design of compensation systems, the development of broad-branding career structures, and the design and implementation of incentive programs.

HUGH BUCKNALL

Hugh is a Worldwide Partner of Mercer Human Resource Consulting and the Asia leader for Mercer's Performance, Measurement and Rewards practice. In his current role, he sets the strategic direction for the business in Asia and provides technical leadership for major projects across Asia.

He has worked extensively in Asia and Australia in the areas of reward strategy, job classification, team building, group facilitation, assessment centers, performance management, organization review, and job design. His wide client base includes multinationals and domestic companies across a number of industry sectors such as health, hi-tech, retail, and the public sector. Hugh has spoken at a number of international forums and client events on the topic of Asian HRM trends.

Prior to joining Mercer, Hugh worked for 14 years in major organizations such as Myer Stores, BHP, the Australian Public Service Board, The Australian Bureau of Statistics and the Victorian Department of Conservation.

Hugh has been involved in major projects such as designing to improve organization effectiveness, restructuring personnel practices, developing new pay structures, identifying organizational strategy and structures, and introducing talent and performance management systems.

Hugh has a Bachelor of Science in Psychology and a Graduate Diploma in Data Processing from Monash University, Melbourne, Australia.

NITIN DHEER

Nitin Dheer is a senior consultant at Mercer Human Resource Consulting's New Delhi office and part of the Performance, Measurement, and Rewards practice. His current responsibilities include working across industries, in consulting and in business development. His focus areas are performance management systems, training for enhancing organizational effectiveness, talent management, competency profiling, and development of competency-based applications. Nitin has worked with clients across a diverse group of industries in the areas of competencies, organization structuring, performance management, and reward management. His clients come from a variety of private-sector organizations including companies in the engineering, automobiles, pharmaceuticals, IT, and services industry. Nitin started his career in a large Indian company in the operation and HRM arena. He also worked in another multinational consulting firm prior to joining Mercer.

Nitin's area of interest is in the deployment of technology-enabled HRM processes and employee engagement in organizations. He has recently published a research paper on eHR.

Nitin has an MBA with a specialization in Human Resources Management from XLRI Jamshedpur. He has an Honors in Chemistry from Delhi University.

JACK LIM

Jack is Performance Measurement and Rewards Practice Leader of Mercer Human Resource Consulting's East China Operation. He leads a team of consultants who helps clients develop solutions to business problems by aligning people strategies, policies, procedures, and actions with business strategy and the external environment. His team assists clients on a broad range of human capital projects, including HRM strategy, organization clarification, performance measurement and management, compensation and benefits, change management, sales force effectiveness, competency modeling, and executive compensation. Jack has extensive experience in the development and implementation of organization-wide programs such as performance management systems, reward systems, competency modeling, and assessment, as well as leadership development. He has led consulting projects for large MNCs and SOEs, including SMBC, Marykay, Unilever, China Telecom, Baosteel Group, Yangzi Petrol, and Hua Tai Securities. Prior to joining Mercer, Jack was a senior consultant of another global human resource consulting firm.

Jack obtained a Masters degree in Engineering from Shanghai Jiao Tong University and an MBA from Massey University, New Zealand.

DR REIJI OHTAKI

Dr Ohtaki is the Managing Director of Mercer Human Resource Consulting (Asia). He is a director of the board, and the chairman of Mercer Japan. He has 20 years of experience in HRM consulting in the Asian marketplace. He specializes in developing and implementing HRM strategies, organizational strategies, and various human resources programs for multinational companies. He has consulted for a wide selection of organizations, including Japanese multinationals (such as Canon, Komatsu, and Kao) and American multinationals (such as

IBM, AIG, AFLAC, and GE). Reiji Ohtaki is a board member of EDB (Economic Development Board) of Singapore.

Dr Ohtaki travels between Singapore and Tokyo, and is actively involved in many of Mercer's regional projects. He helps clients succeed by providing them creative HRM solutions. Prior to joining Mercer, Dr Ohtaki was a senior consultant at a compensation consulting firm and a semiconductor researcher at Toshiba.

Dr Ohtaki received his Bachelor of Science degree in Engineering from Tohoku University. He has a PhD in Applied Physics from the University of California in San Diego. He is a keen author on HRM issues in Japan and has written several books. They are: *Purasu-shiko no Amerika-jin, Mainasu-shiko no Nippon-jin* (Positive/Proactive Americans vs Negative/Contemplative Japanese), Japan Times, 1997; *Competency-model de kaimeisuru Eigyo Professional. kogyoseki no hiketsu* (Competency Model for High Performing Sales People), Diamond Inc., 1996; and *21-seiki no Jinseisekkei – Ari ga warautoki, kirigirisu ga warautoki* (Life/Career Planning for the 21st Century), Fuso Publishing Inc., 2001.

RICHARD PAYNE

Richard is a Worldwide Partner of Mercer Human Resource Consulting. He is also Director of MercerHR.com, Mercer Human Resource Consulting's global corporate website. He has lived and worked in Asia for 20 years and is now based in San Francisco. Richard has developed and led projects involving organization analysis and design, performance management, competency profiling, and compensation management. Richard joined Mercer Human Resource Consulting in November 1998 with the acquisition of Corporate Resources Group. He had previously worked for Business International Corporation (Now part of The Economist Group) for almost 10 years in Washington, DC, Hong Kong, and San Francisco.

Prior to Richard Joining Mercer Human Resource Consulting, his positions included Research and Editorial Director (Asia), Director, Human Resources Services (Asia Pacific), and Vice- President (Western North America). He subsequently relocated to Australia and later worked with Mercer's Performance & Reward practice. Richard is the author of numerous articles and books. Among them are *The Asian Manager: Recruiting, Training and Retaining Executives* and *The Asian Expatriate: Strategies for Recruitment, Training and Re- entry*.

Richard has a Bachelor of Arts in Asian studies from the State University of New York at Albany and a Master of Arts in International Relations from John Hopkins University School for Advanced International Studies in Washington, DC. He has studied, lived, and worked in India, Japan, Hong Kong, Australia, and Singapore.

LU QIANG

Lu Qiang currently heads Mercer Human Resource Consulting's Shanghai office in China. He has over 10 years of wide-ranging human resource consulting experience, with particular expertise in organizational effectiveness and in restructuring employees' total remuneration. He has worked extensively with many local and foreign companies in China. Lu Qiang has completed consulting work with leading Japanese Corporations in China. His clients include Fujitsu in China, Kao Corporation (Shanghai), SMBC, UFJ, JVC, Suntory Holding (China), and Itochu (China)

In China, his clients include SOEs, such as Baosteel Group. China International Electronic Commerce Center, Huabei Pharma, and China Duty free Group, as well as some private firms including, Openet Information Technologies. Prior to Joining Mercer, Lu Qiang served as director of a board, was General Manager of Shanghai JTU Resource Consulting LTD, an affiliate of Shanghai Jiao Tong University. Lu Quiang earned a Master's in Industrial Foreign Trade from Shanghai Jiao Tong University. Prior to this, he received a Bachelor's degree in Industrial Management Engineering. He is a Certified Consultant of the Shanghai Consultancy Association. He is fluent in English and Mandarin.

LAUREL QIN

Laurel Qin is a senior analyst at Mercer Human Resource Consulting's Global Information Service in Mercer Beijing. She specializes in job analysis, compensation, and benefit analysis, as well as HRM benchmarking. She has been in the Accounting and HRM field for nearly seven years. Laurel has been involved in remuneration system design, HRM practice review for mergers and acquisitions, benefits auditing, and compensation competitiveness analysis among others. Some of the more recent clients she has worked with include

Matsushita Communication, Pfizer, SK&F, Fournier, Takeda, and DaimlerChrysler.

Prior to joining Mercer, Laurel worked in a large telecommunications company as a HRM professional. Laurel has a Bachelor's degree in Economics and an MBA.

SUNIT SINHA

Sunit is a senior consultant at Mercer Human Resource Consulting's New Delhi office and part of the Performance, Measurement, and Rewards practice. His current responsibilities include working across industries, both in an implementation and business development role. His focus areas are organization design and restructuring, talent management, competency profiling, and development of competency- based
applications.

At Mercer, Sunit has been working with clients across a diverse group of industries in the areas of competencies, organization structuring, manpower optimization studies, role analysis and position evaluation, performance management (including implementation of Balanced Scorecard), and reward management.

His area of interest is in the deployment of business strategy through organization design and HRM processes. Some of his major clients are Eli Lilly, Yamaha, MTNL, Hindustan Times, Maruti, Sony, CARE, Ericsson, IKEA, Dabur, and the BBC.

Sunit has an MBA specializing in HRM (electives in strategy and change management) from XLRI Jamshedpur. Prior to that he graduated from Delhi University with Honors in History and was at the School of International Studies, JNU.

He is also a permanent visiting faculty member with IIM Kozhikode. He has recently written a research paper on emerging HRM service delivery models. This was published by the Bombay Management Association.

RICHARD WEN

Richard is currently a senior consultant and the office head of Mercer Human Resource Consulting's Guangzhou Office, China. He is responsible for Mercer's operation in Southern China excluding Hong Kong.

Richard has over eight years of HRM experience. He has a background in human consulting, including organization design, position clarification, position evaluation, reward strategy, performance management, and competency management.

Richard is spearheading Mercer's Guangzhou human capital consulting to both multinationals and state/private companies across different industries to address their specific business challenges during China's economic transformation.

Prior to joining Mercer, Richard was a national human resources manager of Quaker China. He also worked for Pepsi China as a human resource manager. Richard holds a Bachelor of Arts in Literature.

GUO XIN

Guo Xin is the managing director for Mercer Human Resource Consulting's greater China sub-region. In his current position, he directs Mercer's activities in the design and implementation of innovative compensation programs for clients. Guo Xin's expertise includes developing total reward strategies, process, and organization effectiveness. His broad experience covers both Chinese and US multinationals across both continents. Prior to joining Mercer, Guo Xin was a senior manager for a large multinational consulting company. In that capacity he managed numerous large engagements in China. He has worked in the United States for 10 years, both as consultant and as a practitioner. He has also previously owned his own consulting firm, providing services in the areas of business process improvement and reengineering and organization effectiveness. His clients included corporations in the fast-moving consumer goods, IT, and banking sectors. As a practitioner, Guo Xin has held several positions in Fortune 500 companies as Director of Organization Effectiveness and Project Leader of e-Commerce.

Guo Xin holds a Bachelor's degree in Mechanical Engineering and a Masters in Industrial Engineering from a leading university in China. He also has an MBA from the University of San Francisco.

CINDY YI

Cindy is a consultant in Mercer Human Resource Consulting's Beijing office. She is focused on organization review work, designing and implementing innovative compensation programs, and performance/talent management systems. Cindy has in-depth experience working with state-owned enterprises. The companies she has done projects for include: Daqing Shiyoushicai, Sino Trans, Sinoair, Guangdong HuangPu Warehouse, Tianhong, and Vantone.

Prior to joining Mercer, Cindy was a strategy consultant and manager of Samsung Opentide China. She was in charge of the Securities and Insurance Industry. She has strong background knowledge in the financial industry and has built good relationships with many securities companies. Before joining Samsung, she was a consultant at Bexcel.

Cindy is a Certified Management Consultant, holding an MBA from the Economics & Management School of the Tsinghua University. She holds a Bachelor of Science in Ship Building from the Tianjin University.

CHAPTER

1

Introduction

A sia is an enigma still waiting to be unraveled. A major paradox about Asia is that it is just as mysterious to the average Asian as it is to the outside world. The vast canvas that makes up the Asian landscape defies most attempts to define what Asia is all about. What is stark about Asia is its diversity. Defining human resource management in Asia cannot be complete without looking at this multi-textured canvas that makes up Asia. One observation aptly describes the state of understanding of Asia: "Asians are just as ignorant about Asia as outsiders are."

This book is an attempt to understand some of the human capital dynamics that are unfolding and shaping Asia. The concept of human resource management (HRM) may have existed in various shapes in Asia over time, but it is still a concept short of maturity in most parts. Its impact is largely unresearched, uncatalogued, and unmeasured. What we have done is to try and capture some of the HRM developments we have experienced across the Asian topography, so they can be illustrative and useful for the everyday HRM manager and business leaders.

This is a defining moment. Most parts of Asia have just been through an economic catharsis. Asia's fall from grace has come hard and fast. For the first time in decades, Asia feels truly vulnerable to the vagaries of foreign capital and the painful side-effects of globalization at its doorstep. Our HRM stories from Asia often present the multiple challenges experienced by companies faced with globalization.

This is a book for Asians as well as Westerners seeking to understand issues HRM managers face in a region that is both dynamic and confusing. The different levels of economic development seen in Asia make the task of managing human resources much more complex for those trying to manage the region as if it were a "single bloc." Each chapter has elements that focus on people and organizational diversity, and should provide tips for the HRM practitioner, the business manager, and the business leader to move from.

The contributors to this book comprise Asians and Westerners. All have lived and worked in Asia for a combined total of over 100 years. They work in 11 Asian countries and are at different career stages. This diversity of experience reflects the vibrancy that is part of the Asian region.

Three major themes will surface throughout this book. These themes are highly relevant to Asian-based enterprises seeking to take the next leap into the globalized world. These three themes have appeared time and again as our experts speak to Asian-based managers across Asia – how can Asian enterprises go global; what can Asian HRM do differently to make the difference; and how can we unlock more value from our Asian employees?

The pressures are mounting for organizations in Asia that are seeking to create wealth in a complex operating environment. We maintain that the answers for the boardroom, and for HRM, need not be complex. These are the basic building blocks – first, embrace professionalism; second, focus on value creation; and third, adapt rather than import wholesale.

Our journey starts with a reflection of the cultural, economic, and social values that have shaped Asia's past and contribute to what we know as Asia today. What should HRM managers know about Asia and what differences exist in Asia?

Next we delve into the indelible mark globalization has left on Asia and other patterns that are unfolding. One major phenomenon from globalization is the transient nature of jobs and the high mobility of human assets. There are more Asian expatriates in Asia than Western expatriates. A mobile workforce is a reality in Asia and HRM's challenge is to find the right programs to attract, retain, and develop Asia's talent pool.

Set against this global scene is an Asia divided by economic wealth. Japan, Korea, Singapore, and Hong Kong have risen from the post-World War 2 economic uncertainties to amass great collective wealth. In this geography called Asia live some of the world's poorest. At one end of the table sit the rich of Asia (Japan, Korea, Singapore, Hong Kong, and Taiwan) and at the other end the poor (India, Indonesia, the Philippines, Vietnam, and, to a lesser extent, Malaysia and Thailand).

Chapter 4 will zoom into business issues faced by organizations in these two groups of countries. For Japan, South Korea, Hong Kong, and Singapore, the wealth of their nations has grown to the extent that they are rich but vulnerable and stalling economically. Individual workers are so well rewarded that those countries no longer can compete on the price of labor. Productivity, reform, and inventiveness are now the modern mantra to unlock more value in the workforce.

Will "Rich Asia's" organizations and HRM models go through this same cycle – mimic the best of the West, unbundle the design, reengineer, and then progressively take on the rest of the world? We will highlight examples of how Japanese, Korean, and Singapore organizations are coming to terms with dealing with some of the changes taking place in the business operating environment and why HRM needs to be cognizant of the organization's business challenge in adopting HRM programs for the future.

Poorer countries such as China, India, Indonesia, Thailand, and the Philippines have burgeoning economies. Cheap labor, a large pool of workers, and rising education levels are creating economic momentum. New jobs are being created as finance, capital, and careers are exported from Japan, Singapore, and Hong Kong to other parts of Asia. Will this group of countries mimic the path their richer neighbors took 30 years ago? How can they do things better by being smart, as well as using the force of numbers at low cost? Two chapters – on China and India – will demonstrate that HRM may be at its genesis in these two locations. Quantum leaps will be made as the pressure to globalize will force organizations to adopt and repackage HRM to serve these rapid growth economies, which have the distinct advantage of cheap labor. However, management of human capital presents its distinct set of challenges.

We dedicate Chapter 8 to the economics of compensation in Asia as salary issues will be an axis from where HRM policies will be driven. HRM managers need to be aware of the trends in compensation. The challenge is to achieve pay equity within the organization, as well as to meet the market's rate. The use of economic modeling can be a way forward to predict labor market demand, as this chapter will show.

Next, we take you into the boardrooms, the executive suites, and the HRM departments of businesses. A peek at the CEO's room – Chapter 9 – unveils what people-issues confront decision-makers in Asia. How do Asian conglomerates (the *Hongs, chaebols, keiretsus*), as well as tightly held family concerns, manage their people? We provide examples of HRM issues that CEOs in Asia need to confront.

Chapter 10 deals with HRM management set against an economically turbulent time. Does HRM have the mandate to build programs for the business? We help answer what business questions HRM professionals must ask to be effective. Now more so than ever the HRM function will have to invent a new relevance as a strategic partner to top management.

In Chapter 11 we look at some leadership models in Asia and present examples of what has shaped leadership values and variables, and how successfully managing leadership can greatly enhance an organization's effectiveness.

And after all the ambitious HRM programs have been implemented, does HRM have a true and tested method to measure the efficacy of such programs? In the final chapter, we deal with the paradox that most companies face – companies make the biggest single expenditure in their people programs, but have the least information about the return from these programs.

After reading this book, if you walk away with one or two major learnings about HRM in Asia, then it will have done its job. Our consultants did not set out to write a book based on academic findings, nor is this book written in the inimitable style of serious management books. Rather, we hope to illustrate through useful case examples and "war stories" the challenges HRM has faced in the region and how HRM has morphed in different parts of Asia. We hope, depending on which part of Asia you are interested in, that you will find useful nuggets as you travel into this space called Asia.

CHAPTER

2

Asia: Magic, Myths, Mysteries, and Mayhem

Hugh Bucknall, Reiji Ohtaki

*A*sia's HRM practices have been vastly imported from the West. Like its economic metamorphosis, Asia's HRM practices will change over time. As global companies introduce such practices to Asia, there are a few things to be mindful of. Asia's diversity does not suite a one-size HRM program. Although there isn't any overwhelming evidence of a collective set of "Asian" values that can be applied consistently across the region, there appears to be some convergence in attitudes among workers in Asia on how they view their work in a global world. HRM will go through some form of "Asianization" as a new breed of Asian managers rise to the challenge of importing Western HRM practices that will be adapted to suit local needs. Hence, global HRM needs to be much more comfortable with the concept of greater customization and localization.

OLD ASIA: REGIONALIZATION AND GLOBALIZATION IN THE OLD WORLD

Great civilizations have sprouted and disappeared in Asia over centuries. Some empires fell into obscurity, surviving only as legends or in history books. One example is the kingdom of Langkasuka, which disappeared abruptly without leaving much behind. Where Langkasuka is, is still the subject of modern historical debate – the toss being between northern Malaysia or in Thailand. Langkasuka could be for us an interesting example of an economy or an organization that lost its reason to exist, or an economic force that is no longer competitive against its peers. There is a new imperative for some economies in Asia to reposition themselves in the new economy or to fade to irrelevance.

Similarly, during the zenith of its reign in the ninth and tenth centuries, the Srivijayan empire (said to be located in southern Sumatra in Indonesia today) controlled the Straits of Malacca and maritime trade routes between China and India.[1] But it did not survive the ravages of competition, falling into the hands of the Cholas of India in 1025.

The adage "knowledge is power" has served many ancient rulers. But not being able to sustain the knowledge to keep a competitive position can be detrimental, as the ancient Khmers have experienced. The Khmers held expert knowledge of waterworks and were able, through the technology of irrigation, to cultivate large rice fields to feed a massive labor force for the development of the monumental Angkor Wat. The glory of Angkor ended in 1431 when the Thai army invaded the kingdom. Reasons abound as to why the Khmers lost their position. One theory from historians centers on the Khmer's diversion of focus from the Mekong River into the hinterland, weakening the empire's traditional position of power along the Mekong River. Similarly, the ancient kingdom of Champa, located in what we now know as Vietnam, had its moment of glory when trade in spices and silk flourished before Champa's annexation by the Vietnamese in 1470.

Old Asia between the fourteenth and eighteenth centuries was a center of maritime trade. There was a healthy mix of traders crisscrossing the globe, passing through the Straits of Malacca and the Malabar Coast in India. Prior to the settlement of Australia by the British, in the seventeenth century, the Macassan traders from Indonesia's Sulawesi island traveled to the northern coast of Australia at Arnhem Land to harvest *trepang* or sea cucumber for sale as a delicacy to the Chinese markets.[2]

Global or regional trade as we know it today was conducted on a grand scale in old Asia. Old Asia was a magnet for a hodgepodge of talent ranging from astute traders to boat builders and related maritime service providers. Today's Asia hosts a similar blend of technical experts and expert managers from around the world.

In search of Asian models: Why did Asia lose its way?

Asia had the makings of an economic superpower in China and if that had transpired, HRM as we know it today might look vastly different. Decades before Christopher Columbus found the New World, a Chinese Muslim eunuch, Zheng He, led a fleet of 300 ships and 28,000 men in search of trade and goods for China. Historians believe he sailed as far as Africa. Between 1405 and 1433, Zheng He led seven major expeditions, commanding the largest armada the world would see for the next five centuries. Not until World War 1 did the West mount anything comparable. Zheng He's fleet included 28,000 sailors on 300 ships, the longest of which were 400 feet. By comparison, Columbus in 1492 had 90 sailors on three ships, the biggest of which was 85 feet long. Zheng He's ships also had advanced design elements that would not be introduced in Europe for another 350 years, including balanced rudders and watertight bulwarks.[3]

However, by 1500 China had turned inward after imperial scholars successfully took over control of the court in a battle of ideology that continued to plague China for many more years. In 1525 the Chinese government ordered the destruction of all ocean-going ships. The greatest navy in history, which a century earlier had 3,500 ships, had been extinguished, and China set a course for itself that would lead to poverty, defeat, and decline.[4]

Intrepid journalist Nicholas Kristof of the *New York Times* was so intrigued by the sunset of China's great empire, he set out to find reasons to explain why Asia's superpower turned inward leading to the takeover of the Asian civilization by the West.

What did the global Asia look like between the 1400s and 1800s?

Was Asia a land of magic, mystery, or mayhem? For much of the 1600–1800 period, Japan was closed to the rest of the world – it sought nothing and did not seek to offer anything to it until Commodore Perry forced it open in 1854.

Prior to China's self-imposed withdrawal from the global economy by the mid 1500s, it would be fairly safe to view Asia as a "globalized" place, one enjoying a fusion of the best the Orient had to offer. Rare silk, pottery, paper, silver, bronzeware, exotic animal parts, tea, nutmeg, clove, pepper, and cinnamon, all these were exchanged in the ports of Malacca (Malaysia), Ujung Pandang (Indonesia), Goa, Calicut, and Cochin (Kerala, India). During much of the fourteenth and fifteenth centuries, Calicut and Cochin were the main entrepots of Asia. Traders from Venice, Constantinopole, Alexandria, Arabia, and Java came to these two cities to trade.

The period between the 1500s and 1800s saw the rise and fall of several empires in the West and the East. The Ottomans emerged as one of the strongest empires in the world, their sphere of influence covered most of the Middle East and the Balkan Peninsula. Large maritime empires were also emerging on the Iberian Peninsula. The Portuguese empire's realm spread to the Indian Ocean with stations in Goa, Malacca, and Macau. The Portuguese also had territories in Brazil and Southern Africa. But by the seventeenth century, Portugal had lost its influence to be overtaken by the Spanish who later lost their grip due to internal struggles during the 1701–1714 period.

In the east, India was conquered by the Mughals, while Russia also developed into a major power under Peter the Great. Meanwhile, China saw the flourishing of the Ming and Qing dynasties, while Japan saw the emergence of a centralized state under a series of shoguns.

In the nineteenth century, parts of Asia came under the control of the East India companies of the British and the Dutch. By the early nineteenth century, the British controlled nearly all of India. It took another few decades or so for parts of Asia such as India, Singapore, Malaysia, and Indonesia to see the emergence of nationalism accompanied by efforts to reorganize their local economies.

Centralization in Europe led to the rise of colonization, including the colonization of many parts of Asia by the Portuguese, the Dutch, the Spanish, and the British.

By the 1800s, the leading world economies, earlier a network of interacting but autonomous urban-centred, agrarian economies, had become a vast global network of commercialized societies dominated by the economic power of western European societies.

Source: The New Context of the 18th Century
http://www.bartleby.com/67/578.html

Kristof sailed to an island off the coast of Kenya, to a place called Pate (pronounced Pah Tay) to look for descendants of Chinese sailors said to be part of Zheng He's mighty fleet. There he found a village elder Bwana Mkuu Al-Bauri, the keeper of oral traditions who told him this story:

"Many, many years ago, there was a ship from China that wrecked on the rocks off the coast near here. The sailors swam ashore near the village of Shanga – my ancestors were there and saw it themselves. The Chinese were visitors, so we helped those Chinese men and gave them food and shelter, and then they married our women. Although they do not live in this village, I believe their descendants still can be found somewhere else on this island."[5]

Kristof wrote: "I almost felt like hugging Bwana Al-Bauri. For months I had been poking around obscure documents and research reports, trying to track down a legend of an ancient Chinese shipwreck that had led to a settlement on the African coast. My interest arose from a fascination with what to me is a central enigma of the millennium: why did the West triumph over the East?"

Indeed, why had the West triumphed over the East? Kristof's conclusion was that Zheng He's great fleet was dismantled as Confucian scholars, who valued stability and order above everything else, were abhorred by the merchant class represented by Zheng He. Indeed, had Zheng He been allowed to continue, and had China sought to raise the level of trade and exploration, the balance of power in the world would have tilted differently, Kristof argues. Had China continued its outward expansion, would the world be using Asian models of HRM? One interesting development we see today is the resurgence of the Chinese merchant class once so abhorred by the Confucian scholars of imperial China. Will the rise of this new merchant class give the world a different management model to work on?

Why did the West triumph over the East? When we say East, which part of the East do we mean? With the exception of a few, why can't Asian companies build global brands? What about Asian managers, are they a different breed compared to their counterparts from the United States or Europe? Can Asians think? These are some questions often asked among business people. Indeed, the search for answers to managing human resources or human capital in Asia cannot be complete without at least trying to understand Asia's past – its blend of Chinese, Japanese, Koreans, Indians, Thais, Vietnamese, Cambodians, and those from the Malay archipelago – and its diverse religious beliefs ranging from Islam, Shintoism, Buddhism, Hinduism, Christianity, Taoism, among others.

REBUILDING ASIA: OF MIRACLES, MIRAGES, AND THE MAKINGS OF A FUTURE

Asia's cultural diversity can be matched by its checkered economic fortunes. In the last few hundred years, the region has gone through a series of development cycles, from poverty, despair, to wealth. For our purpose, the Asia that we will cover is loosely divided into two blocs – the richer, more developed parts comprising Japan, Korea, Singapore, and Taiwan; and the developing worlds of China, India, Malaysia, Thailand, Indonesia, and the Philippines. Asia is home to among the richest nations in the world (Singapore and Japan), as well as among the poorest (India).

Asia is set to remain the fastest growing region in the world despite a series of setbacks seen during the financial meltdown of 1997 and the destabilizing impact of regional and global geopolitics. For most of the 1980s and early 1990s, massive capital investments in technology and education served as locomotives of growth for the Asian economies of Japan, Korea, Singapore, Taiwan, Indonesia, Malaysia, and the Philippines. Asia's remarkable rise to economic wealth led to the term "Asian miracle." It was followed by fierce debate among academics about which set of "Asian values" helped to underpin Asia's remarkable leap in 20 years into economic stardom.

Following the financial crisis, academics were similarly keen to dissect whether this similar set of Asian values was responsible for some of Asia's economic malaise. Some of "Asia's" ills are now well documented by academics. They include poor governance of Asian organizations, cozy links between entrepreneurs and governments in parts of Asia, lack of transparency, and poor management structures of Asian-owned organizations. Despite the crippling effect of Asia's financial meltdown, there is confidence that Asia will, like a phoenix, rise from the ashes. This is already happening in China, Thailand, and to a limited extend in Singapore, Malaysia, and Korea.

Asia today is a source of labor and logistics, distribution, and it is a service hub for multinationals seeking more efficient supply chain models. As the world's fastest growing region, it is also an attractive marketplace for multinationals seeking more consumer dollars. If the current population growth trend continues, Asia will make up 60 percent of the world's population in 2050.[6]

What will Asia's future be? It will be dotted by mega-cities, but be home to a largely "gray" population. By 2020, the proportion of people in Asia living in the urban areas will rise to 50 percent from about 38 percent today, according to the Asian Development Bank (ADB). There will be at least 153 cities in Asia with populations of over one million. Eighteen of the world's 27 mega-cities (cities with over 10 million people) will be in Asia.[7] The phenomenal rise of Asian cities will pose challenges for urban planners and resource management.

By 2022, according to Asian Demographics Ltd, a large part of Asia will be populated by elderly people. None of the 13 countries in Asia surveyed will have 50 percent of their population under the age of 25. This will have implications on the structure of the labor force in Asia. Youth will become a relatively scarce commodity with implications for demand of goods and services.[8]

Because Asia is not a one-dimensional place for doing business, organizations often face multiple challenges while operating in Asia, whether they are using local or global resources. Questions that multinationals often ask center around defining the business values in Asia – as if Asia is a homogenous place. If there were a set of behaviors, values, or goals close to Asians' hearts, what would they be?

UNRAVELING THE ASIAN MIND

In their study *Managerial Work Related Priorities in a Changing Asian Business Arena: An Empirical Assessment in Seven Asian Nations*, Cecil Pearson of Murdoch University, Australia, and Samir Chatterjee of Curtin University of Technology in Australia found that Asian employees placed different degrees of importance to their work goals.[9] However, the study also found a convergence in how much importance Asian managers place on what is labeled "opportunity to learn." Managers in China, India, Japan, Singapore, Malaysia, Thailand, and Mongolia rank it as the most important work goal for them. While salary remains a central focus of HRM, its priority differed across Asia. Salary was ranked at the higher end of the scale (fourth and fifth) in China, Malaysia, and Singapore; and at the lower end (eighth and ninth) by those in India, Thailand, and Japan. Interestingly, most managers in Asia ranked "interesting" work as an important work goal. In Asia, "autonomy" is ranked at the lower end of the scale (sixth, seventh, eighth and ninth) by those managers surveyed. Asian managers also picked "convenience" and "conditions" as a lowly ranked work goal, according to the study. The survey paints a picture of an Asia where managers are beginning to express certain similar attitudes toward work, but there isn't any overwhelming evidence of vast similarities on anything else.

> " When I am recruiting senior staff in Asia, why do they keep asking about who they will report to and what their title will be? So why aren't they grabbing the chance? "
>
> A MERCER CLIENT

In a study seeking to find what drives performance in Asia, strategy consulting firm McKinsey found that Asian companies relied strongly on promoting "values" as a motivation factor for employees. The McKinsey survey of 27 leading Asian companies found that while Asian enterprises were strong in using operational approaches to control business performance, they tended to motivate people using "values" such as "being the industry leader" or "loyalty to the company."[10]

"Despite the difficulty of instilling such values, most of the Asian executives we surveyed rated their companies very highly on doing so. Values are inculcated in many ways: photographs of the company founder and of national leaders in company halls (India and Thailand); references to company values in daily meetings (China and India); statement of values on bookmarks, desk calendars, posters, and – in gold letters – on the entrance to corporate offices (China and many other countries); and singing the company song before meetings (in Indonesia)," the research said.

UNRAVELING THE BAMBOO NETWORKS IN ASIA: HRM NIGHTMARE?

One feature regularly associated with Asia is the importance of networks – a complicated web of social and business ties that bind the fabric of business in Asia. The most prominent is the overseas Chinese network that can be felt across China, Taiwan, Malaysia, Indonesia, Hong Kong, Thailand, and Singapore. The overseas Chinese influence is wide-ranging and the styles of management permeate through the Asian landscape outside of Japan, Korea, and India. In Indonesia, the overseas Chinese make up less than 3 percent of the population but control over 30 percent of the wealth. In Thailand, the overseas Chinese make up about 14 percent of the population but corner a 45 percent share of the economy. In the Philippines, overseas Chinese make up 1.5 percent of the population, while their share of the economy is about 40 percent. In Malaysia, the overseas Chinese make up 30 percent of the population but control 60 percent of the economy.[11]

These overseas Chinese-owned companies control vast tracts of assets ranging from plantations to prime properties and have extensive trade in commodities in the region. These companies are described as being highly diversified; having good relationships with the public sectors of their domicile countries and hosts; having strong familial and informal networks; and their managers tend to use subjective information as inputs into decision-making.[12]

It is common to find these overseas Chinese-owned enterprises run by senior people who are involved in all aspects of their firms' activities and remain so till they retire. These senior people also seem to be able to transfer and apply their skills across highly diversified and often unrelated businesses.

Asians tend to process their information internally. Although their decision-making may be highly articulated, they rarely present their findings in the written or analytical form. They also tend to rely more on qualitative information supplied by people they trust.

In his study, George T. Haley from De Paul University argues that most senior executives of these Asian organizations make decisions quickly, often based on information gleaned from their network of friends, clients, and public-sector contacts. The crux of the argument is that this strategy cannot serve these organizations outside their own markets. Until these network firms, such as the Japanese or Korean firms, rely less on the informal structures to support their business decision-making, they will fail outside their home environment.

While the study serves to highlight how Asians view work, and how Asian managers tend to operate, they also serve to highlight the differences that can present complex challenges when the HRM community tries to roll out programs to Asia "as a region." Here's a teaser: if in-depth knowledge of local markets is a key to cracking the diverse Asian playing field, will a HRM strategy of, say, rotating people every few years contribute to or disrupt the business?

ASIAN STEREOTYPES: LOOKING FOR DIRECTION

Perhaps the most frequent stereotypical picture painted of Asian students in the West is that they are good at mathematics and work a lot harder than anybody else. Similarly, Asian workers are perceived to be non-confrontational and not willing to share their knowledge or views.

Michael Ascot, who runs a headhunting company based in Thailand, paints a candid picture of the typical stereotypes associated with the different people of Asia and from around the world. In a paper, presented at Mercer Human Resource Consulting's Asia Roundtable Conference in November 2003, he noted these stereotypes are necessary starting points to help management come to terms with dealing with Asia honestly. These stereotypes are not intended to be offensive to any particular nationality, but serve mostly to remind top management of the need to have effective solutions to deal with the national and cultural differences at play in Asia.

Country biases are prevalent, whether we make a public view of it or not. In Asia, Singaporeans are viewed as having a superiority complex despite the nation state's small population and geographical minuteness. There is a certain amount of difficulty getting Indian nationals into high IT and finance positions in Thailand, as there is the view of "what does my tailor know about IT or finance mentality?" (Indians have the lion's share of the tailor shops in Bangkok, Thailand.) Koreans are seen as the "hangmen," being able to anything better than everyone else, while the Thais are deemed as being adverse to speaking up in public. The Australians are viewed as a bunch of beer drinkers preferring Bondi Beach to being cooped up in the workplace.

Keeping a family business alive

ABC is an electronics manufacturer that was founded in the late 1960s. The founder went to the United States to study and received a PhD. He was employed in the US university's commercial research lab for six years. Returning to his home country in Asia, he set up a modern facility producing high-quality, low-cost units supplying major PC-makers. Despite his Western-based education, his organization displays the following characteristics:

- Secretive decision-making – Staff often say: "I don't know what's happening."
- Family feuds are rampant – There are many feuds and inconsistencies in the organization.
- Paternalistic – Family members in the company feel: "I'm still treated as if I'm mummy's boy."
- Leadership issues – The company is faced with the "we don't have future stars" problem.
- The company also has no network in the new markets it was trying to penetrate.
- The company doesn't know how to deal with the emerging market in China.
- The company has no measures for performance.
- The company still uses a time-based pay scale.
- The company faces a high labor turnover.
- The company's decision-making process was too slow.
- The company's recruitment system was old-fashioned.
- The company lacked professionals in the support functions.

What we found to be important in addressing this situation was that:

- Progressive rather than radical change should be introduced.
- The company has to set up a clear and effective organizational structure and roles.
- The company needs to recruit new leaders with a proven track record.
- The company needs to explore a new performance-based pay scale.
- The company needs to re-brand its recruitment strategy.
- The company needs to target future stars – that is, what attracts them.

When we talk about Asians, do we think about these adjectives: consensus, submissiveness, the inability to say no, non-confrontational, inscrutable, inflexible, and unable to think innovatively? When we talk about consensus in decision-making, which style of consensus are we referring to? The Japanese consensus, the Korean consensus, or the Thai consensus? Asians in the region display values that are shaped by their country of origin, religion, social and cultural heritage, and economic environment. According to Ascot, because some multinationals are truly global, they often don't think about these differences in decision-making processes.

Cultural mayhem

This MNC struggled with finding the right candidate to head one of its local operations in Asia. The local staff grappled with the cultural idiosyncracies of the different nationalities of country managers who came and went. This MNC had three country managers – a Brit, a German and an Italian - in a span of five years. The staff observed that the Brit seemed nice - he didn't ever raise his voice. Nobody could understand the "wild" Italian character who often came into the office without socks. The German was nice and polite but they say he was not driven. This is a classic case displaying the difficulties the company has looking for suitable candidates to manage a local office. It highlights the disruptions faced by the local staff who were trying to adapt to the differences in managerial styles, the personality differences of these people, and their different countries of origin.

As told by Michael Ascot, Amrop Hever Group,
Mercer Human Resource Consulting's Roundtable, Bangkok, 2002

DEALING WITH "ASIA'S" CORPORATE CULTURE: WHOSE CULTURE?

The stereotypical view of Asian organizations is that they are run by strict patriarchs who rule the company with an iron fist. Inside these corporations, employees have a fair sense of where their place is, and do not challenge authority. Chinese-owned enterprises in Thailand, Malaysia, Singapore, and Indonesia may be deemed as being ruled by a corporate culture showing deference to authority, especially if authority is represented by the founding family members. But the same could not be said of organizations in Korea or the Philippines, where their employees have less fear of authority and unions are particularly active.

Among multinationals, when one speaks of corporate culture, often there isn't a clear sense of whose corporate culture we are referring to. Is there such as thing as a US, European, or Japanese corporate culture, or a local Asian corporate culture? How distinct would Sony's or Toyota's corporate culture be, as opposed to Singapore Airlines'?

A world view seen through managerial cultures

- Teutonic German (my way – the only way)
- Autocratic French (my business school way)
- Colonial Brit (the British way of course)
- Flamboyant Italian (my way but you cannot see my way)
- Cool Egalitarian Scandinavian (our way – all together now)
- Hard-fisted North American (my way – this week)
- Warm-hearted South American (let's see if there is a way)
- Poor Asian Managers!

Source: "The China Syndrome & Other Tales of Tectonic Shift in Asia Pacific Talent Management" by Michael Ascot, The Amrop Hever Group, Bangkok, presented at Mercer's 12th Asia HR Roundtable, 2003.

IN SEARCH OF WHAT MAKES ASIA TICK

The colonization of Asia by different Western powers has left indelible marks on the psyche of the people in the region. The "East meets West" debate has graced many scholarly texts. One interesting debate centers around the theme of whether Asians can think. Kishore Mahbubani, a Singapore diplomat, raised this touchy debate in his book *Can Asians Think?* This debate stems from the fact that in the past few centuries the Europeans, and more recently the Americans, have contributed to the advancement of human civilization while Asia turned inward. He argued: "As we stand on the eve of the twenty-first century, five hundred years after the arrival of the first Portuguese colonists in Asia, only one – I repeat – one Asian society has reached, in a comprehensive sense, the level of development that prevails generally in Europe and America today. The Japanese mind was the first to be awakened in Asia, beginning with the Meiji Restoration in the 1860s … If Asian minds can think, why is there today only one Asian society able to catch up with the West?"[13]

Mahbubani also suggests that the most painful thing that happened to Asia was not the physical but mental colonization by the West. "Many Asians began to believe that Asians were inferior to the Europeans … If I am allowed to make a controversial point here, I would add that this mental colonisation has not been completely eradicated, and many Asian societies are still struggling to break free."[14]

The argument goes that Asia's newfound economic prowess, and the level of education that many Asians have had at the best of American or European universities, have given rise to a new sense of confidence among Asians – be they from China, Japan, India, Indonesia, Malaysia, or Korea. Indeed, Mahbubani is of the view that educational excellence is a prerequisite for cultural confidence. Many Asians now realize their minds are not inferior. But most people from the West cannot appreciate this shift in mindset because they have never directly felt the sense of inferiority an Asian feels.[15]

Mahbubani argues that Asians have now too developed confidence and alternative views, so that they are challenging the aspirations and ideals of the West. An Asian renaissance is under way. Asians now realize they too have a rich social, cultural, and philosophical legacy to draw from.[16] He adds that Asians are also beginning to reject the concept of wholesale adoption of models that have served the Western world.

We shall not dwell on opening the Pandora's Box of the great Asian debate, but this topic is useful in helping us to find a practical and meaningful way to deal with nationalistic and cultural differences in Asia. Because of Asia's cultural and national diversity, managing people in Asia has its share of pitfalls. A common pattern we have seen across the region is the prevalence of a one-size-fits-all HRM solution for Asian offices without much attention being paid to localization. Whether MNCs are rolling out flexible benefits, diversity programs, or performance management systems, the overpowering influence of Western models for HRM in Asia can be a double-edged sword. Proven models in the United States or Europe have often been derailed midway in parts of Asia. This could be due, in part, to the different levels of "Westernization" Asia has been exposed to. On one side of the scale, places such as Singapore and Hong Kong may be more open to internalization of ideas compared to, say, a place such as Korea or Japan, where local culture is still the dominant way of life. Understanding where your HRM test beds are can make or break your HRM programs.

> " The chief executive officer of a leading Thai conglomerate, for instance, said that he had tried for five years to institute a feedback mechanism and failed. "
>
> ASIA'S PERFORMANCE CHALLENGE, MCKINSEY QUARTERLY, 2001 NUMBER 3.

Here is another teaser. When you introduce performance management systems, say in a place such as Thailand, how successful can the system be when you operate in an environment where people do not typically relish giving a critique of themselves or others, and where the Buddhist philosophy of helping everyone to obtain good karma can deter critical appraisals of colleagues or bosses?

In a place such as Japan, where group effort and group output are deeply embedded in the work environment, how easy is it to shift the workers' mindset to a value system based on individual performance? In Korea, where unions hold widespread influence, what are the challenges of moving to a pay-for-performance system? In Indonesia, where indigenous cultures are in themselves so diverse, what price would global companies pay if they miss out on acclimatizing HRM managers to these differences? In a place like China, where unions are formed to help workers get over difficulties, less so to fight for workers' rights, trying to stamp out union activities might not be relevant. In India, where overnight a generation of workers has moved from not having any telephone lines to having mobile phones, what values will go down well in the current generation of workers? These are some of the real challenges for HRM in Asia.

The force of globalization has been a great equalizer. The new generation of Nokia phones hit Shanghai and Beijing as quickly as they flood Singapore, Bangkok, and Tokyo. Starbucks dot the landscape across Asia, so too do the latest Hollywood movies. Will the attitudes toward pay, performance, and work–life issues meet in Asia?

This is the paradox: Although fed by a global culture, Asia is bound by the timelessness of how its people behave when faced with the winds of change. Multinationals and Asian-origin companies will have to deal with the changes brought about by globalization in a manner acceptable to players in the different organizations. This requires global HRM to be mindful of bulldozing through the Asian region with models that have worked well in America or Europe. We have seen successful HRM programs being introduced in a place such as Korea, but not before extensive education initiatives have been rolled out prior to the HRM initiatives.

> **We spent US$1 million rolling out our new business planning and systems development model. The Indians tore it to shreds; the Chinese got bored with it. What is actually happening?**
>
> **A MERCER CLIENT SITUATION**

NEW ASIA WELL UNDER WAY

Will global forces change how Asian organizations are run or how multinationals run their Asian offices? Will there be a confluence or a convergence of management styles or work cultures? Social historian Francis Fukuyama seems to think so. He said:

"In all three areas, however – economic, political, and social – there are good reasons for thinking that the distinctive institutions and practices fostered by Asia's cultural systems will converge over time with the patterns seen in the West. That is, economic life will be more open and subject to market forces; governance will be increasingly democratic; and social structures (as well as social problems) will come to resemble that of post-industrial Western societies. Far from reinforcing Asian exceptionalism, the current economic crisis will

> " We have operations in 11 Asian countries – 80 percent staffed by locals, 15 percent are intra-Asian staff, and 5 percent are Western expatriates. Staff don't cooperate and our western managers can't seem to build effective teams. "
>

accelerate homogenizing trends in all three areas."[17]

Whether Fukuyama's prediction will be true remains to be seen. In Asia, there is already a distinct shift in attitudes toward work and life in that workers desire decent work hours and an equitable salary. In the areas of management, the second generation of Asian owners may be less confined by the rules of propriety or hierarchy that their elders hold dear. How Hong Kong billionaire Li Ka Shing's son Richard Li runs his business may be distinct from how his father runs things. Similarly, Malaysian billionaire Robert Kuok or the Thai Lamsam family's new generation of leaders have been shaped by a worldview that fuses what is pragmatic, convenient, and acceptable to them. The tightly knit structure of a *chaebol* or *keiretsu* in Japan may be unraveling as these networks struggle to find relevance in a world that thrives on seeking the most efficient suppliers, rather than falling back on cumbersome ancient ties. Successful Korean companies, such as Samsung, boast a new generation of innovative and creative managers with entrepreneurial flare. The traditional business models of asset accumulation and trading empires sit alongside the new economy businesses that thrive on leveraging technology to reach customers in the quickest possible manner. The old "Mandarins" of Asia are being replaced by others who have tasted the manna of innovation and creativity. Their wealth of information comes in bytes and is delivered over the World Wide Web, not behind the shroud of secrecy under the guise of *guanxi* (Chinese term denoting relationships or networks). The new economy titans of Asia – Narayan Murthy, founder of India's most successful IT company Infosys Technologies; Sabeer Bhatia (sold off hotmail to Microsoft) and Masayoshi Son, CEO of Japan's Softbank – have businesses that thrive on technology. They demonstrate the convergence of the old and new ways of doing business. In a borderless world, best management practices and human capital are the true business advantage – the new generation of Asian owners and managers know it and will not be coy about adopting these practices.

WILL THE REAL ASIAN HRM MANAGER STAND UP?

Now we come to the question of the Asian HRM manager. How we define an Asian HRM manager is dictated by who owns the company the HRM manager works for. He or she could be an Asian – say from Indonesia, Thailand, or India – working for the regional HQ based in either Thailand, Singapore, or China. He or she could be an expatriate – say, of German, British, or American origin – working in an MNC based in any Asian city, or an Asian working for an Asian MNC in Asia, or a Western manager working for an Asian MNC.

Will it make a difference to a company's performance whether an Asian-origin HRM person or a Western expatriate HRM person manages human resources? There is no empirical evidence that is widely available on the subject. History tells us that successful companies are well run and rely on the competencies of its people to succeed. We would argue that because national cultural differences interact with personalities and the organization's culture to produce the outcome, the sensible approach to introducing HRM programs in Asia would be to adopt features of best practices without sacrificing locally acceptable norms.

HRM's task is to understand three key links:
- What drives the success of the business.
- What culture the organization thrives on; that is, is the local outfit distinct from or equivalent to the global company/American or European owners?
- The internal dynamics of the workforce that is employed within the organization.

In one of the Korean companies we worked with, the company has successfully introduced a performance management program in a difficult environment. HRM and the chief executive worked extensively to build confidence among the workers so that the system would be fair and help the company succeed.

Sometimes East is East and West is West

Here is a client example of how – either because of personality clashes or cultural clashes – the Western managers in this organization did not function well in Asia, neither did the offices in Asia.

A Mercer case study

Client Situation

This company has its regional headquarters in a country in Southeast Asia. The company's operations in ASEAN span Singapore, Thailand, Malaysia, Indonesia, and Vietnam. This company has a very strong market share in Japan and Asia. Its management team in Southeast Asia consists of members from vastly differing backgrounds in terms of their language and culture. There is a distinct gap between the Japanese and the non-Japanese in the organization in terms of how they view the organization's culture and business goals, according to Mercer consultants.

As this organization wants to move toward a high-performance organization structure, there needs to be clarity between the Japan and ASEAN offices. ASEAN's direction needs to be aligned with the headquarter's goals as well as goals to meet the local market. In this project, we helped this company's managers develop a mission statement and vision for the organization.

Our Experience

It was a challenge trying to align a diverse management team, as there were many differing opinions and agendas, expressed through two diverse languages and cultures. The process was painful and slow. To overcome the language issue we created new processes to cater for the culture and language barriers. We realized we had to get around the complex task of managing group dynamics. Mercer consultants had to proceed slowly in setting the scene for communication. We also had to lay strict ground rules at these meetings, including:

- Stopping the session to give people time to cross-reference meanings of words.
- Flashing red cards when managers involved in the focus group felt threatened, or when they felt they were personally attacked (a few red cards were flashed).
- Engineering the sitting and group arrangements throughout the sessions to ensure a good mix.
- Assigning an Asian consultant in the sessions to bridge the cultural gap.
- Focusing on encouraging open communication, and "open-minded" listening.
- Discouraging "silo" mindsets among the different cultural groups.
- To get around the language barriers, we facilitated activities that required less sentence structures than we would normally do.

It is still too early to assess the full outcome of this project. An immediate impact from this exercise was that the various leadership teams from different countries were able to come to terms with the company's shared values and mission. This was a major step forward in helping the region office align with the direction of the head office.

As Michael Ascot from Amrop Hever candidly puts it, if Asia matters so much, there is a great need for multinationals to greatly increase their flexibility to accommodate Asia's diversity. This implies that there may be a need for corporations to disregard some of the models used in the West, or at least to balance them with local needs. This may mean a compromise on the execution or the delivery methods, but not the standards. This may also mean that multinationals seeking to introduce HRM systems may need to adopt a more gradual approach when introducing new HRM concepts in the region.

MANAGING THE GLOBAL, LOCAL TALENT POOL

How can a multinational with operating bases in China, Thailand, Indonesia, and other parts of Asia manage diversity in Asia? Another question we ought to ask is how can a multinational manage a mobile Asian workforce? No longer is an IT expert from India confined to Bangalore. He can easily hop from Bangalore to Silicon Valley and reverse back to Asia, depending on where the best job markets are. Mandarin-speaking professionals can choose to be based in China, Singapore, Taiwan, or Hong Kong, depending on where the exciting jobs can be found. It is no wonder then that when times are good, retention issues are common among organizations in Asia.

Here is a general profile of what the new millennium workers look like. They are:

- loyal unto themselves;
- smart, informed, and demanding;
- multi-career comfortable; and
- more discerning where they apply their skills (they will choose you).

When multinationals move workers around Asia and around the globe, what key challenges will they face in finding an equitable system to reward employees? Is the balance sheet approach to expatriate pay outmoded? What will go down well in Asia to make people move? How do you globalize an Asian workforce? We will return to this at a later chapter on globalization and its impact on managing HRM.

Heard in Asia...

MNC boss: "You are doing a great job. Your next posting is Philadelphia."

Asian worker: "I am doing great. I want to be the boss, locally."

MNC boss: "You must travel to learn."

Asian worker: "I want to work here, I know all about my country."

► BUSINESS TIP

No matter what background your organization comes from, there is a need for organizations to focus on a few key issues to meet business imperatives. They include:
- getting a performance-oriented culture going in the workplace;
- providing a workplace that is stimulating and personally rewarding;
- identifying, attracting, and retaining the key talent needed to drive business success;
- grooming a generation of capable leaders and coaching top management; and
- having an equitable compensation system for your workforce.

What works best in keeping talent in-house:[18]
- Inspiring leadership
- Fun work culture
- Challenging work
- Availability of a feedback system
- Career growth
- Fair pay

And what repels talent:[19]
- Bad bosses
- No career prospects
- No feedback and support
- Broken promises
- No customization for "my" needs
- Wrong people in the wrong jobs
- Too much red tape
- "My" voice is not heard
- No work–life balance
- Poor pay

▶▶ CONCLUSION

How do Asian and multinational organizations manage a diverse region? In this era of globalization, it is easy to forget that Asia has the most sophisticated and richest population, but also the world's poorest. Whether it is fast-growing China or India – which are developing at breakneck speed – or maturing economies such as Japan, Korea, and Singapore – cultural and social economic differences run deep in these locations.

Our view is that these cultural differences contribute to the complexity of implementing HRM programs. This reality has contributed to many failures in HRM programs across the region. Dealing with Asia as a region requires global HRM to realize that it is working in a region:
- still in a time warp of cultural mayhem;
- wrapped in complex business networks; and
- that has broken the shackles of colonization and now wants to put its own stamp on the future.

Asia is also a region bonded by a sort of virtual mindset labeled "Asian," but expresses itself in distinct locations, in unique values, behaviors, and etiquettes. Understanding these differences is a necessity for global HRM.

What makes one HRM program fail in one location, and succeed in another has to do with a complex set of dynamics operating within Asia – including understanding the workforce's needs and preferences, the local organization's culture, and the personalities of people driving the organization. Where we see HRM programs working best is where local employees play an active part in contributing to global initiatives. Some organizations in Asia may need more time to assimilate or absorb best HRM practices. It may not be immediately apparent to them why these best practices are necessary. Getting employees' buy-in is a fundamental part of the program. We have seen successful programs such as pay-for-performance or incentive-based packages being rolled in markets where such programs were deemed destined for failure. Similarly, we have seen poor understanding of local culture derailing the best of HRM intentions in the most sophisticated HRM users of the region. In an era where global talent will be a scarce resource, effective development of the human capital in Asia will be a distinct advantage for organizations.

We return then to the conventional wisdom about Asia – nothing you say about Asia applies to the whole of Asia. But the velocity of globalization is forcing Asian organizations to deal with competitive forces that are changing the way these organizations operate. The shrouds of secrecy behind complex business networks are slowly unraveling as Asian business people join global companies in seeking more efficient locations and supply chains. There is also a kind of "renaissance" in thinking among Asians that not all which is from the West is necessarily applicable. The key takeaway is that mimicry will give way to adaptation – this will spread to the HRM arena. Global organizations have to accept this as the way forward to succeed in Asia.

[1] History Today website http://www.historytoday.com/index.cfm?Articleid+3002

[2] National Gallery of Australia website http//:www.nga.gov.au/federation/Detail.cfm?WorkID=65617

[3] Nicholas D. Kristof, "1999: The Prequel – The Third of Six Special Millennium Issues," in the New York Times Magazine, http://www.nytimes.com/library/magazine/millennium/m3/kristof.html

[4] Nicholas D. Kristof, "1999: The Prequel – The Third of Six Special Millennium Issues," in the New York Times Magazine, http://www.nytimes.com/library/magazine/millennium/m3/kristof.html

[5] Nicholas D. Kristof, "1999: The Prequel – The Third of Six Special Millennium Issues," in the New York Times Magazine, http://www.nytimes.com/library/magazine/millennium/m3/kristof.html

[6] *Fundamentals of Population Growth and Distribution – Population Growth Q&A* http://www.prb.org/Content/NavigationMenu/PRB/Educators/Human_Population/Population_ Growth/Population_Growth_Q_and_A1.htm

[7] Asian Development Bank's website, "Strategy to Meet Challenges of Asia's Megacities," May 9, 2002, http://www.adb.org/Documents/News/2002/nr2002075.asp

[8] Asian Demographics Ltd website, "The Declining Importance of the Youth Population in Asia: 2002–2022," http://www.asiandemographics.com/DI090803.htm

[9] *Managerial Work Related Priorities in a Changing Asian Business Arena: An Empirical Assessment in Seven Asian Nations*, Cecil A.L.Pearson, Murdoch University, Australia, and Samir R.Chatterjee, Curtin University of Technology, Australia.

[10] *Asia's Performance Challenge*, McKinsey Quarterly 2001, Ruby Chen, C.Scott López-Gelormino and Stephen M. Shaw.

[11] *A Strategic Perspective on Overseas Chinese Network's Decision Making*, George T.Haley, DePaul University, US. Haley attributed this figures to two sources: "Overseas Chinese Networks: Understanding the Enigma," *Long Range Planning*, Vol. 28, No. 1. 1995, pp. 61–9 by G Redding, and *The Return of the Merchant Mandarins*, Asia Inc. March 1996 by J Kohut and AT Cheng.

[12] *A Strategic Perspective on Overseas Chinese Network's Decision Making* by George T.Haley, 1997, DePaul University, US.

[13] *Can Asians Think?* Kishore Mahbubani, 2002, Times Book International, p. 23.

[14] Mahbubani 2002, p. 23.

[15] Mahbubani 2002, p. 24.

16 Mahbubani 2002, p. 26.

17 The ICAS Lectures – Asian Values and Civilisation – Asia's Challenges Ahead, Francis Fukuyama. Delivered at the University of Pennsylvania, September 29, 1998.

18 Mercer Private Survey, 2000 – "What are the talent magnets that bind?"

19 Mercer Private Survey, 2000 – "What are the talent magnets that bind?"

3

Globalization: Talent Roulette in Asia

Richard Payne

*T*he great expatriate posting as we know it has come to a gentle end. Globalization has brought sweeping changes to structures in the old economy. Beyond the movement of goods, there is an increasingly fluid market for talent and labor. Expatriates who move out to international postings do so for years, while suitable local talent is groomed to take over. Packages often associated with these great international postings have also drifted to more down-to-earth levels as companies seek to maximize resource allocation and minimize cost. The definition of an expatriate has also changed, largely due to a convergence of various factors, including globalization and the regionalization of goods and services. There is also the advent of the "Asian" expatriate whose skill set matches those of his Western compatriot, and moves easily across the region, or the globe. There is increased mobility in people and jobs. Companies have shifted operations and people halfway around the globe to maximize use of their resources. Six major trends in globalization have forced changes in the talent market and the movement of people around the world. Companies that want to successfully harness a global talent pool or retain top talent have to observe some ground rules or lose out in the war for talent sweeping Asia.

THE GREAT DEMISE OF THE WESTERN EXPAT

In the past, when you recruited where did you look? You probably looked in your own city first and then nationwide, if you could not find anyone locally. As a last resort, you might have looked outside your own country, but only for jobs with unusual or specialized requirements. Most of the time, you would have settled for what you could get locally.

Talent markets were mostly local. Jobs and people were hard to move. Since competition was often local as well, most often you did not need to broaden the search beyond local boundaries. There was no easy way to find jobs or people far away. Trying to recruit at long distances was frustrating and sometimes impossible.

Expatriates (mostly from the parent company's home base) would fill top management and specialist positions, if the right candidate was not available locally. The company's talent search might occasionally extend beyond the local and parent company locations in unusual circumstances, but this was infrequent. "Globalization" of talent meant the transfer of a Western expatriate to a top management position in Asia, usually for a short-term assignment of three-to-five years.

THE RISE OF THE NEW ASIAN EXPAT

Talent markets, along with economic markets, have become truly global. The Internet has made a global external search far easier. For external searches, sometimes hundreds or even thousands apply for a single job. Applications may come in from a highly diverse set of applicants representing many different nationalities and employee profiles. Sifting through the applications for a job widely posted can sometimes seem like "talent roulette." If you get lucky, there's a match! The qualifications, experience, and competencies are just what you are looking for. But, more often than not, you lose. Even with all of those applications, none seem to quite fit and you have wasted a lot of time and money playing a losing game.

Internally, many companies post jobs globally every day. (Every time a job is listed on a website it becomes a global offering.) More and more companies view their employee population as a single global talent pool. Cross-border transfers are encouraged among all nationalities. In recent surveys by Mercer and others, participants report that the number of expatriates of Asian nationality in Asia now outstrips the number of their Western counterparts. An "expatriate" can be from anywhere and located anywhere.

The advent of global and pan-Asian talent markets has had a profound impact on both Asian employers and employees. Employers searching throughout Asia have to specify and vet qualifications and competencies more rigorously in

> " **More and more companies view their employee population as a single global talent pool. Cross-border transfers are encouraged among all nationalities.** "

order to secure the candidates that are right for the job. At the same time, companies have to provide highly attractive employment packages, not only in terms of compensation, but also training, development, and career opportunities to capture the best talent on a regional or global basis.

The employee faces a similar dilemma. Opportunities available to some candidates have widened beyond their wildest expectations due to the global talent market. But there are tradeoffs. Aspiring executives often need to be mobile to secure the best jobs even if they have the ideal match in terms of experience, qualifications, and competencies. For good positions, job seekers often cannot avoid global competition by only looking locally: they often compete against candidates from halfway around the world for those local jobs.

People and jobs have become more mobile. Employers may move a job to where the people are or, alternatively, move people to where the jobs are. Companies have shifted entire call centers that service the US market to India, Malaysia, or the Philippines. At the same time, US high schools in Ohio and software companies in Silicon Valley hire teachers and engineers from these same countries and move them halfway around the world. All of this adds up to a much more complex environment than was the case only a few short years ago.

SIX KEY GLOBAL ORGANIZATION TRENDS

In addition to creating a global job market, the trend toward globalization has other indirect effects that are equally important to HRM. These attributes of globalization are primarily focused on business management; nevertheless, they must be considered when designing a winning human resource strategy.

Six trends in organization management have forced companies to look for a rather different set of competencies in their high-potential executives. The six trends are:

1. Global product line organization.
2. Flatter organization structures.
3. Increased pace of mergers and acquisitions.
4. Greater network and less hierarchical relationships among units of an international company.
5. Emergence of global virtual teams as a common method of management.
6. Less reliance on parent-company nationals to manage international operations.

Global product line organization

Companies are organizing their operations along global product and service lines. Interestingly, globalization does not mean centralization. Instead, worldwide responsibilities for different aspects of a business are dispersed across a region and around the world. Centers of excellence emerge based on competencies or the competitive advantage that a particular group may have.

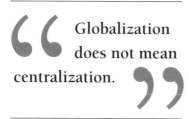

Globalization does not mean centralization.

Responsibility for global product lines puts increased pressure on those units to set a high standard and perform at a level of global excellence. For example, one client that Mercer has worked with (a semiconductor manufacturer) has given global production responsibility to its operations in Singapore. All other operations turn to the unit in Singapore for advice and guidance in complying with global standards.

Consequently, the Singapore unit must ensure it has the highest caliber of manufacturing engineers. As a result, they are recruited not only from Singapore but throughout Asia and Europe. The criteria for selection and advancement are quite strict in order to ensure that the unit can meet its heavy commitment to excellence.

Companies in electronics, chemicals, and automotive components industries, for example, have adopted such models throughout their operations in East and Southeast Asia. In each case, while a unit may feel a great deal of pride with being given global responsibility for a function or product, these units have been forced to raise their standards for recruitment, performance, and promotion.

> **The dis-appearance of middle managers and the transformation of regional headquarters have resulted in a need for greater self-reliance as well as leadership at lower levels of the organization.**

Flatter organization structure

Over the past decade, hierarchies have flattened and layers of management have disappeared from companies around the world, including in Asia. The flatter organization structures also have led to a change in the role of the regional headquarters (RHQ). In the past, the Asia RHQ most often had direct management control over all of the units in Asia. Regional staff had direct operational responsibility for profit and loss for all of the Asian operations. Many companies have changed this model. In some cases the regional headquarters has been disbanded; in other instances, regional executives primarily provide advice and guidance without exerting direct management control.

The disappearance of middle managers and the transformation of regional headquarters have resulted in a need for greater self-reliance as well as leadership at lower levels of the organization. This "empowered" style of management is in direct contrast to the traditional, directive approach to management so common in many Asian organizations as little as 10 years ago.

Mergers and acquisitions

Asian subsidiaries of US-based multinational companies were the first to feel the effects of the worldwide trend toward mergers and consolidation. Now the trend has grown to encompass a large proportion of European and Asian-based firms. With each merger, acquisition, divestment, and consolidation comes a corresponding change in the organization structure of the operations in Asia as well as the rest of the world. The increased frequency of such actions means that many organizations are in a constant state of change. Under these conditions an organization structure cannot be expected to last more than one or two years at most.

The rapid changes occurring in organizations continuously going through mergers or acquisitions or other corporate ownership changes have simply accentuated the need for empowered employees. The fluidity of organization structures in response to continuous change often means that executives must make decisions on their own without clear directions from top management, who are often preoccupied with non-operational issues.

Network relationships

Organizations are increasingly relying on coordination and cooperation among units rather than "command and control" structures to efficiently manage business processes. Top management may set the overall direction but implementation is frequently in the hands of executives that act as peers with little guidance from above. The framework for doing business among sibling companies may be set; however, the actual terms and conditions must be negotiated and agreed upon.

This management style often leads to faster and more efficient decision-making on operational issues among executives with first-hand knowledge of the issues that need to be addressed. At the same time, it requires an entirely different set of managerial skills than are necessary in a command-and-control structure.

Global virtual teams

The advent of globalization as well as the introduction of new telecommunications capabilities has led to the increased use of "virtual teams." A virtual team is a group of executives who work actively together but rarely (if ever) meet face to face. They will work together, often on a daily basis, to achieve a common project goal. Global virtual teams are formed and disbanded as the need arises. As communications tools continue to improve and the need to respond quickly to global developments rises, the increased use of global virtual teams has become a certainty.

> *A virtual team is a group of executives who work actively together but rarely (if ever) meet face-to-face. They will work together, often on a daily basis, to achieve a common project goal. Global virtual teams are formed and disbanded as the need arises.*

Working successfully in virtual teams requires excellent language and communication skills, cultural sensitivity, and teamwork. Asian executives, especially those who speak English as a second language, may at times find working in virtual teams quite challenging. For example, understanding the English spoken by a diverse group of non-native English speakers over the telephone is difficult enough for native English speakers. It can be next to impossible for people with limited experience communicating in English with people from other regions of the world.

Management of international operations

Traditionally, the expatriate executive was the same nationality of the parent company. The command-and-control structure meant that the multinational company primarily was managed by the nationals of the parent company who were sent out for a short-term assignment to oversee and control the foreign operations. The few executives who did not fit this mold even had their own unique name – "third-country nationals" (TCNs). TCN seemed to imply they were neither here (nationals of the host country) nor there (national of the parent company's country). They just did not fit the mold.

Globalization has changed all of this. A labor pool comprised of diverse nationalities has replaced the single-country pool. In recent surveys by several consulting companies, participants reported a sharp rise in the number of nationalities constituting their expatriate workforce. The number of expatriates from Europe and North America in Asia is declining at the same time the number of cross-border postings within Asia is increasing. The reasons most often cited for this trend are:

- Cost – transfers within Asia are less expensive than from other regions into Asia.
- Market awareness – Asia nationals are likely to have a much higher awareness of and sensitivity to Asian cultures and markets then their counterparts from outside the region.
- Availability – the pool of qualified and experienced Asian talent has risen sharply in the past 10 years. Many companies find it no longer necessary to search outside Asia for senior executives.
- Professional development – more and more companies recognize the need to provide executives with exposure to operations outside their home country. The increased integration of operations in the region means that senior executives have to have a broader perspective and knowledge of business throughout Asia.

Talent search in Asia: Six major trends

Each of these global trends in organization management has direct consequences on the profile of the high-potential, most desirable executive. The attributes of a "rising-star" that companies are searching for due to the impact of globalization include:

Self-motivation – Flatter organization structures, global product lines and networking relationships mean that an executive's boss now is quite frequently in a different office, which is often in a different country or region.

Furthermore, reporting relationships are now far more complex with many people having at least two different reporting lines. Due to increased reporting lines and geographic distance between boss and subordinate, a successful executive must be a self starter who has the motivation and initiative to start and complete tasks and projects with minimal or no supervision.

Leadership – Linked to self-motivation is the need for greater leadership lower down in the organization.

International mobility – The executive who is willing to move has become far more attractive. Organizations need the flexibility to move talented people quickly to take on positions where they are needed. Mobility is particularly important in the smaller countries of Southeast Asia, where the small size of single operations limit both career opportunities and the available talent pool. Treating all operations within the region as a single executive resource pool creates economies of scale and opportunities for advancement.

International experience – While multinational companies need employees to be internationally mobile, they also require executives who already have international experience. Experience outside one's home country is often viewed as essential since it provides a broader perspective and understanding of diverse cultures. Overseas experience often helps smooth relationships across borders, a major plus when working as part of a virtual team.

Communication skills – The advent of virtual cross-border teams means that excellent English-language communication skills have taken on an added importance. A person might have excellent technical skills; however, they may be restricted to only operating in their own home country without English-language capabilities. As organizations become more global, this is a major impediment to career advancement.

Global trends are also influencing other areas of talent management in Asia. The most obvious impact is on competition for top talent. With the advent of the global competition for talent, companies must revisit their recruitment, compensation, and career development strategies.

Recruitment strategies must change to reflect the need not only to target those with the necessary global competencies and experience, but also to get these sought-after candidates to accept a job offer. As companies pursue a global strategy for talent acquisition, Asia has become a top source for highly qualified and experienced engineers and managers. The information technology industry

> " For many companies, the location where a top executive happens to live is gradually becoming less relevant in determining their net pay package. Globalization has created a situation where a job can be done from many locations. "

has led the way in aggressively recruiting in Asia for positions in Europe and North America. Even with the global slowdown in the IT industry, software engineers and other IT specialists are finding jobs far from their homes in India and parts of Southeast Asia. Companies that want to hire top talent must show why the best should join their organization. Companies with local operations throughout the region are finding they frequently lose out to organizations that do not even do business locally. Recruitment strategies must consider the global nature of the job market even for positions that are locally based.

Compensation has been equally affected by global trends since the market is set not just by companies hiring locally, but also by companies recruiting for positions abroad. Companies recruiting software engineers in India now routinely set competitive compensation levels by looking at both the prevailing pay levels in India and the pay packages offered by foreign-based IT companies recruiting in India. This trend is not limited to the IT sector. For example, nurses' salary levels in Malaysia have for many years been affected by demand in the Middle East. Trying to set competitive pay levels for high-demand jobs will become increasingly complex as the "market" will be less well defined and more borderless.

Trends in globalization have not only influenced the level of compensation but also the methods of compensating executives. The change is most evident among top executives and expatriates. For many companies, the location where a top executive happens to live is gradually becoming less relevant in determining their net pay package. Globalization has created a situation where a job can be done from many locations. Executives with a regional position may be able to live in their home countries and perform their jobs effectively by frequent teleconferencing and traveling extensively overseas. Their peers may all be either expatriates or living in other countries in the region. Location-based compensation seems a bit archaic under these circumstances.

Career development, promotion, and succession planning all will undergo significant transformation in Asia due to globalization of talent markets. More and more jobs will require prior experience working overseas or at least in-depth exposure to international operations. To ensure an adequate supply of executives with international experience, companies will need to incorporate short- and long-term postings into their career development planning.

A rising diversity of postings will accompany the increased numbers of transfers. Frequently, assignments within Asia may be preferred over transfers to headquarters. Intra-regional transfers have the advantage of helping build a network for an executive as well as exposing him or her to operations of a similar nature. On the other hand, occasionally, transfers to operations in the parent company's country or to centers of excellence in other countries both inside and outside Asia may help disseminate best practices and the latest thinking to operations throughout the region.

On the flip side of international assignments is the sad fact that a large proportion of such transfers end up costing a company a lot, without providing tangible benefits. Studies[1] have shown that nearly one half of all expatriates transferred back to their home country leave the company within two years. Plus, a study sponsored by CIGNA indicates that the cost of maintaining an expatriate in an overseas posting is as much as US$1 million per year. Thus, while companies may want the benefits that accrue from international experience, generally they have been less than efficient in providing executives with the opportunity to acquire that experience.

HOW TO AVOID TALENT ROULETTE IN ASIA

Talent roulette is a game of high risk and long odds. Even the boldest firm should stay away from playing such a losing game. Companies can shorten their odds or even avoid playing talent roulette all together by using the trend toward globalization to their advantage to help improve human resources strategies and practices.

▶▶ BUSINESS TIP

How do you have an efficient talent strategy in Asia? Observe a few of these simple rules:

- Work on an efficient recruitment strategy. This involves drawing on integrated databases or online databases to get the best match between people and the jobs available.
- Going international or regional? Don't be fixated on the balance sheet approach to compensation. Do not be afraid to explore regional pay structures, project-based compensation, local pay plus housing, and local pay plus adjustments.
- Have a coherent strategy for managing your highly mobile employees or you will lose them once the big jobs run out.
- Explore alternatives to allow employees to have international experience without the need for relocation. It may take planning but the results could be worthwhile.

RECRUITMENT TACTICS

Recruitment is an area of human resources management that has benefited the most from globalization. New tools and techniques have emerged that were not even possible five years ago.

The development and deployment of integrated global and regional employee databases have greatly enhanced the internal selection process. Integrated databases enable recruiters to search the company's talent pool for candidates with narrowly defined competencies and experience. Organizations query their employees on their willingness to move, language abilities, international experience outside the organization, and other desirable factors that may influence selection. Some companies have found that this approach unearths some surprising finds. For example, a global search might reveal an engineer in an entirely domestic job in San Jose, California, who is willing to relocate and has the technical and language capabilities necessary for a job in China.

Searching for the "Holy Grail" of an integrated global employee database is certainly not without its hurdles. Legal restrictions designed to preserve privacy, detailed planning both locally and globally, differing needs and requirements among diverse operations are only a sample of the issues that face an organization trying to put together a global employee database that can be tapped for selection. Nevertheless, even incomplete or modest efforts can reap impressive rewards as the game moves from talent roulette to target shooting.

> " Even in a sluggish employment market, investigating what the most desirable applicants really want in an employer can help in designing the most appropriate package, as well as presenting the organization to best advantage. "

The impact of globalization has had an equal impact on the external job market. Online recruitment services such as JobStreet.com and Monster.com have had a positive impact on opening up the recruitment market. For example, JobStreet, which was started in Malaysia but has expanded throughout Asia and to the United States, receives as many as 15,000 job listings in the United States and Asia Pacific every month.[2] Online recruiting sites are mushrooming throughout the region. Plus, they are developing impressive online tools to enable recruiters to sift through applicants and select candidates that closely match their profile. Finding a "needle in a haystack" has become much easier than ever before.

The only problem is that many others can find the same "needle." Thus, companies must develop an aggressive marketing strategy to accompany their search for top talent. In a globally competitive talent market, a company needs to know and to promote its competitive advantage when trying to recruit the best people. Knowing one's own competitive advantage is linked to what potential recruits are seeking. Even in a sluggish employment market, investigating what the most desirable applicants really want in an employer can help in designing the most appropriate package, as well as presenting the organization to best advantage.

COMPENSATION METHODS

Innovative approaches to compensation are emerging due to the pressure of globalization. The classic expatriate balance sheet is giving way to regional pay structures, project-based compensation plans, and host-country based pay plans. Expatriate compensation used to be based on the assumption that most transferees would be those who went on two- to three-year assignments from the parent company's home country in Europe or North America to a location in Asia. At the end of the assignment most would return home. In fact, this model has become the exception, rather than the rule, for a majority of companies.

A recent study by Mercer Human Resource Consulting of expatriate practices in Asia[3] showed that the nationalities of expatriates in Asia have taken a turn toward Asian nationals. The most commonly cited nationality of expatriates was Singaporean, with more than half of respondents indicating that they employ Singaporeans in overseas postings. A third of survey participants reported posting Hong Kong SAR passport-holders abroad. US citizens and citizens of European countries were the second and fourth most commonly cited expat nationalities.

Clearly, a model based on a one-time assignment out from the parent company's home country is antiquated. Companies are now developing plans that cope with multiple nationalities in multiple locations. Some companies have decided that they should not even differentiate between local and expatriate executives.

After all, what are expatriates? Are they:
- Any employees (or any executives or only selected executives) transferred by their company to a location in a different country?
- Employees transferred by their company from Europe/North America to a location in Asia?

- People hired in one country in Asia for a job in another country in Asia?
- Non-nationals (Asian, Westerner, or both) hired locally?
- People hired overseas for a position in their home countries (for example, Chinese returnees)?

Each of these permutations of mobile employees frequently has a compensation package that differs from the package dictated by a company's global expatriate policy norm. Consequently, the "modified" expatriate balance sheet has become the norm for these organizations. Modifications of the traditional approach include adjustments to benefits dictated by global expatriate policies for expatriates transferred within Asia. Such adjustments often include different allowances for cost of living, hardship, or location. Some firms specifically exclude all intra-region transfers (regardless of whether the transfers are within Asia, within Europe, or within Latin America) from their global expatriate pay policy.

A REGIONAL PAY SCALE FOR EXPATRIATES

Some companies have adopted a single pay scale for all of their expatriates in Asia regardless of nationality. The regional pay scale may be based on the competitive pay rates of a single country in the region or even a combination of countries.

Local pay plus housing allowance
Local pay plus housing has become increasingly common for non-nationals hired locally (especially in Singapore and Hong Kong). While some firms simply put all employees hired locally on the local pay scale, others provide housing assistance in recognition of the higher cost of housing for non-nationals.

Local pay scale with adjustments
Some companies have adopted a local pay policy for all employees regardless of nationality or employment status. Inevitably, there are "adjustments" to this policy to account for inequities among employee categories. Such inequities are the result of such issues as:

One company's solution

For one company a more relevant determinant than expatriate status is the cost of replacing the executive if he or she fills a critical global or even regional role. This company has built a regional pay structure for its top executives. Under this plan, the company has a single reference salary[5] for each grade, regardless of location. Thus, an executive in Thailand with an equivalent job to a counterpart in Hong Kong receives the same net salary (adjusted for cost of living). The firm uses Singapore as its benchmark for constructing the grade reference salary due to the stability of the currency and its acceptability to most of the company's executives.

Salaries of expatriates in this company are based on the same structure as for executives living in their home country. But, in addition to the salary, executives living abroad receive a package of benefits that brings them to par with their local counterparts (for example, education and housing assistance). While the cost of such a plan is higher than a local-based compensation structure, the company finds that the increased benefits of greater flexibility and mobility and true market competitiveness for their highly demanded executives justifies the added cost.

This and other new methods of compensation are increasingly relevant for highly mobile and demanding executive talent in Asia. Flexible compensation policies and practices that address the specific requirements of targeted executive groups will be far more attractive and will differentiate an employer from the crowd.

- coverage of statutory retirement benefits (for example, Singapore's Central Provident Fund);
- variance in the quality and coverage of local health care;
- access to local schooling for children of non-national employees; and
- cost and access of housing for non-nationals relative to their local counterparts.

Companies can no longer rely on a single global policy to cover all of their non-national employees worldwide. Increasingly, global expatriate policies will only apply to the small minority of internationally mobile employees that fall into the narrow category of executives transferred from their home country to a country in another region for a short-term assignment of two to three years. The exceptions (that is, everyone that does not fit in this category) will become the rule. The potential for inequity and confusion will rise correspondingly unless companies properly analyze and prepare for the impending change.

CAREER PLANNING AND DEVELOPMENT

As discussed above, globalization has a major impact on issues related to leadership skills, the desired capabilities of key executives, and the experience required before someone can take a senior management position. Many companies have taken strong action to address these issues and to prepare their executives and their organization for the changes necessary due to globalization. Outlined below are some of the steps that companies are taking to manage the impact of globalization.

Encourage executives to take overseas assignments early in their career. International experience will continue to grow in importance in providing the foundation for a successful senior executive. Many companies already recognize this and the nature of overseas assignments has been changing rapidly in the past five years. According to a Mercer survey on international mobility in Asia,[4] companies are sending their Western managers home and replacing them with Asian counterparts. At the same time, the number of cross-border postings is increasing within Asia.

Several factors have contributed to this trend. Until the mid-1990s, there was a shortage of Asian executives who had the experience to take on local top management roles. Western expatriates were filling the shortfall. This shortage has dissipated, along with a greater willingness of many companies to staff their top posts with local nationals. Western expatriates are not being used as frequently as costly "quick fixes" to fill management gaps.

The profile of the Asian executives transferred overseas is different to those of their Western predecessors. They are more likely to be younger, in professional or middle manager positions, and some are on personal development assignments. Getting international experience early on in a person's career can help build the broader perspective and cultural understanding necessary for the global executive. Plus, early assignments help avoid the problems encountered by mid-level executives in taking up a foreign posting. The problems of children's education, loss of spousal income, and family/financial obligations are not as severe for younger executives.

Develop a strategy to capitalize on international experience. Expatriates returning home after an overseas assignment often have some common complaints: "My overseas experience is not recognized." "There seems to be no job for which I am suited … they just don't know what to do with me." "My colleagues who stayed home have advanced, while I am stuck in the same job I had when I left." The lack of attention devoted to retaining returning executives is remarkable considering the expense and effort that went into sending them abroad in the first place. Nevertheless, high attrition of returnees is a fact of life for a large proportion of companies.

Companies need to plan ahead in order to take best advantage of a transferee's overseas experience. In some cases, this may not entail a return home – the executive's experience might be better used elsewhere. If a person does return home, then the company needs to look at the way these people can best capitalize on their foreign exposure. Larger jobs may not be possible for many (especially if the transferee's home country has only a small corporate operation). However, the expertise gained may be valuable in the increasing number of assignments that emphasize network relationships throughout the region, a good understanding of business practices outside one's home country, or frequent interaction regionally or globally. The main aim is to consider the consequences of a return home and look at ways to ensure the investment in overseas development has not been wasted.

Look at non-traditional ways to get international experience. According to the Mercer survey cited previously, assignment duration has become shorter. Companies are reporting fewer long-term assignments (more than five years) at the same time that the average overseas posting term has declined

> " The main aim is to consider the consequences of a return home and look at ways to ensure that the investment in overseas development has not been wasted. "

to two to three years. One company reported that all assignments have been cut short and that assignment terms were always from one to three years.

Some companies are looking at ways to secure international experience without the need for an overseas posting. One company participating in the survey responded to a question regarding trends in expatriate numbers by saying, "Employees need not always have to be transferred to another country – they can work from [their own] base country and yet be part of a regional or global organization. Under such circumstances, the expat population may be expected to decrease, but this will happen over time and not immediately."

Short-term assignments of one to three months, as well as participation in regional or global projects, have also become more common. These have the benefit of lower cost and less potential disruption to an executive's career while at the same time giving him (or her) the experience necessary to take on broader responsibilities.

Create a single executive talent pool for Asia. Some organizations have begun taking action to consider Asia as a single talent pool, rather than one comprised of each country in which they operate. Furthermore, they have even taken the view that expatriates should not be a separate category of staff. "Non-nationals" may have some benefits or terms of conditions that are exceptional due to their unique requirements, but whenever possible, the same terms apply to employment status regardless of whether the person is "expatriate" or "local." This type of approach creates greater flexibility and breaks down barriers in thinking. Plus, there is less need to do so. Performance planning and management often should be done at a regional level to ensure consistency as well as identification of top talent across the region. Decisions on selection have to be made based on the best person for the job regardless of category. In addition, executives can obtain international experience through many routes of which a long-term assignment is only one. Shifting the mindset toward thinking of a single executive talent pool for Asia will increase the opportunities available for top talent and reduce the barriers for the best people to secure the best jobs.

▶▶ CONCLUSION

Globalization means that the competition for talent is worldwide, even in developing Asian countries that have been previously protected from external competition for talent. The consequence for employees is that those who have an international perspective and experience, a proven track record, and a willingness to move will have significant and varied opportunities presented to them. Those without these attributes will find many opportunities closed to them. For employers, it means they cannot afford to recruit and retain "second best." They need to be highly focused and targeted in recruiting, training, and developing their key employees, regardless of whether the job is purely local or more international in scope.

Globalization means that an international perspective and strong leadership skills are required much further down in the organization than in the past. Traditional "command-and-control" structures that have been successful in the past in Asia will no longer work. They must be replaced by cooperative, teamwork relationships that depend only on limited guidance from supervisors, many of whom are either remote or dispersed.

Finally, globalization means that compensation will undergo a transformation in Asia. Companies will give more attention to the competitiveness of compensation on a regional and, in some cases, a global basis. Pay plans will be designed to differentiate rather than homogenize employees. Furthermore, companies will pay more attention to retaining executives that have the attributes of a truly successful mobile, global employee.

In the future, where will you look for talent? The answer, of course, is everywhere. Globalization has opened up the talent search and widened the market far beyond local resources. In so doing, it has created the game of talent roulette, which is risky to play and easy to lose. But, with careful planning and proactive actions, you need not play talent roulette. In fact, globalization can be a boon rather than a bane of a company's talent strategy for Asia.

---

[1] Statistics are from a study jointly sponsored by CIGNA International Expatriate Benefits, National Foreign Trade Council and WorldatWork.

[2] "Careering ahead," Leonie Karkoviata, *Asian Business*, September 1, 2001

[3] "Survey of International Employee Mobility in Asia, May 2002," Mercer Human Resource Consulting.

[4] "Survey of International Employee Mobility in Asia, May 2002," Mercer Human Resource Consulting.

[5] The reference salary is calculated in Singapore dollars net after tax and adjusted for relative cost of living among locations. The actual salary may vary from the grade reference based on the individual's performance, unique capabilities, and experience.

CHAPTER

4

A Path for the Rich: The Challenge of Value Creation

Hugh Bucknall

A sia is not a homogenous place. To many people outside the area, Asia is often seen as "one place" or a single trading bloc. Even within Asia, there is much ignorance about the diversity of the Asian marketplace. Given the socioeconomic and cultural diversity of Asia, HRM's challenges are multifold. One set of HRM solutions that has worked in one Asian country may not work in another. In the rich part of Asia – specifically Singapore, Hong Kong, Taiwan, Korea, and Japan – the onus is on HRM to create value for organizations with breakthrough approaches and contrarian models that differentiate the business from the competitors'. There is a consistent theme running across the rich part of Asia – the need to manage business transformation. As businesses reconfigure to extract new value to meet increased productivity imperatives, top management will put pressure on HRM managers to take on a more strategic role. HRM professionals will be forced to transform in line with the business transformation taking place. There will be demands placed on the HRM function to provide support to management to predict workforce needs, manage talent, harness ways and means to measure the effectiveness of people programs, and find innovative reward strategies to compete for the best talent in the market.

ASIA: ACROSS FIVE TIME ZONES, 3 BILLION PEOPLE AND 80 LANGUAGES

Asia is a diverse and complex continent. Channel NewsAsia has a promotional video that shows images of Asia along with a voiceover describing it aptly as "A place with 48 countries, five time zones, 3 billion people, 80 languages, 27 religions, 39 systems of government and 37 currencies." The landmass of the United States and Europe combined is smaller than the Peoples' Republic of China.

Yet, only about 6 percent of Asia can be regarded as wealthy by global standards. At least 90 percent of Asia lives in poverty. Here's a contrast – Japan remains the world's second largest economy despite recent turbulent times. Just across the ocean is China, still poor by world standards but with 700 million peasants presenting an enviable source of cheap labor and a huge potential for growth.

Nothing we say about Asia applies to all of Asia. There are different lessons to be learnt from history, depending on where you happen to be and at what stage of economic maturity. The rich and poor countries have different paths to follow and this presents different challenges for HRM across all of Asia.

OF ANCIENT GLOBETROTTERS AND STRAITS MERCHANTS: GLOBALIZATION IS AN OLD EVENT

We tend to think that globalization is a new phenomenon. It is not. Globalization is nothing new to Asia. The original Western multinational corporations arrived many hundreds of years ago in the form of the British, Dutch, French, German, and Portuguese presence. Their trading companies still have a legacy in trading relationships. The flow of talent and mobility of ideas also occurred with the Makassin and Malaccan spice traders; the migration of the Cantonese coolies, miners, and traders; plus the empires of the Ottomans and Majapahit many centuries ago. The Japanese have been major investors and have deployed talent across all of Asia and remain a major source of both capital and talent. The creation of huge new capital reserves in China, Singapore, Taiwan, and South Korea is also having a major impact on economic prosperity at home and across Asia.

Japan, Singapore, Korea, Hong Kong, and Taiwan had become economic dynamos by the early 1990s, attracting large amounts of international capital and human capital. These economic powerhouses had experienced almost a decade of unprecedented growth until the 1997 Asian financial crisis. While economists mull over whether Asia's economic growth was a miracle or mirage, there is no doubt the bloc of newly industrialized countries of Japan, Singapore, Korea, Hong Kong, and Taiwan have experienced a period of incredible wealth creation.

The exuberance of economic growth in the newly industrialized countries and the subsequent slowdown provide useful lessons for HRM. And these are lessons HRM will continue to learn as the pattern of economic development evolves. Broader factors fundamentally affect the way we manage people and create a corporate response to new situations. And these factors are different across Asia, driving different responses from the rich and poor countries.

Cracks in the rice bowl

For Japan, South Korea, Hong Kong, and Singapore the wealth of the nation has grown to the extent that they now hold huge reserves in foreign currencies. But their economies are vulnerable and growth has stalled. While growth in Japan, South Korea, Hong Kong, and Singapore has been driven by capital investments and labor input, these factors are insufficient to lift them up the next economic ladder. Some cracks appear, in that while these economies have shown tremendous growth, their growth has come mainly from capital and labor input while technological and intellectual capital creation has been unspectacular.

There is no secret now. Academics have pondered over and produced interesting empirical results to show that total productivity growth in high-performing East Asian countries such as Japan, Singapore, South Korea, and Taiwan have largely lagged behind countries from the OECD between 1970 and 1990. The results also suggest that the high-performing economies in East Asia did not stand out in terms of levels of improvements in technical efficiency compared to the rest of the world, even though they were achieving great strides in development growth.[1]

It is interesting to note the *IMD World Competitiveness Yearbook 2003* showed that Japan and Korea – two of the Asian region's richest nations with populations of over 20 million people – have business efficiency rankings behind India, Thailand, and Malaysia.[2] The report gauges the extent to which enterprises in those countries are performing in an innovative, profitable, and responsible manner. Both Japan and Korea's rankings have fallen over the last three years, while Taiwan's performance has improved from the levels of a year ago, but dropped from 2001 levels. Singapore's ranking has improved from 2002 but is down from 2001 levels.

Productivity has not matched rewards or wage increases in parts of rich Asia, and the rise of cheaper production sources in China and India have forced the rich part of Asia to seek increased productivity gains. Fundamental changes in how goods and services are delivered around the globe have also forced changes on the rich part of Asia. Individual workers in rich Asia are so well rewarded that these countries do not compete on the price of labor. Productivity, reform, and inventiveness are now the modern mantra to unlock more value in the workforce of the rich countries. While the rich countries may have money and capital, the "poor" in Asia – China, India, and the Philippines – have cheap labor and economic momentum.

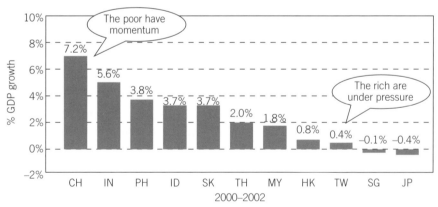

(Left to right) China, India, Philippines, Indonesia, South Korea, Thailand, Malaysia, Hong Kong, Taiwan, Singapore, Japan.

Source: Mercer Asia Monitor Bulletin

Exhibit 4.1 Average Asia GDP growth 2000–02

Rich countries in Asia have moved up the economic chain by first mimicking the best of the world's inventions and designs. They also benefited from making investments in education and the labor market. Next, they moved to designing products to meet the consumers' demands. Take the Japanese cars of the 1950s and the 1960s. They were not regarded as status symbols in the global market in their early days. By unbundling someone else's invention, the Japanese applied superior skill and determination to create products that made heads turn in the world in the 1970s and the 1980s. Now Japanese cars are a challenge to the marques from Germany. The same goes for Korean electronics goods. From producing black and white imitations of the Japanese models, brands such as Samsung and Hyundai are now serving sophisticated products with technological innovation.

Structurally, there is also a need to shift their business models. Take the example of the electronics producers in Taiwan, Singapore, and Korea, who have been major global suppliers to the MNCs. The "commoditization" of electronics goods in Asia has forced a major glut and cutthroat pricing among Asia-based suppliers. Suppliers in Asia now realize the fundamental problem – they have a homogenous range, and versus differentiated products they are prone to surplus and price wars. With a few exceptions, most producers in the region have failed to upgrade into the higher end and rapidly growing market segments for differentiated products that would give them the leeway to command premium pricing.[3]

This brings on valid questions about where the future of Asia's rich countries will need to move to next. There is a convergence of global and regional influences that demands changes in the way rich Asian countries have done things. Singapore is an example. It has thrived as a hub of aviation and shipping and financial services for international and regional businessmen. Not anymore. Bigger and cheaper airports and shipping berths are sprouting in the region, competing directly with Singapore. The same goes for financial services. Its closest competitor is Hong Kong, while in the future, Shanghai could easily pose a threat. The Singapore government has been looking for new sources of income for the future.

A look at the modern expatriate in Asia

The rise of China as a new economic superpower in Asia, coupled with the legacy of high growth seen for a decade in places such as Hong Kong, Singapore, Korea, and Taiwan, have given rise to the modern breed of expatriate. Across Asia, there is a broad trend of talent cross-pollination. It is not uncommon to see a HRM director from India working in an MNC in Singapore, or a Singapore professional heading a key position in Shanghai, Suzhou, or Bangkok.

Quite like their forebears who moved around Southeast Asia in search of a better wage and a better life, modern-day expatriates track the same path – only they are armed with degrees, talent, and are in search of work experience. Instead of putting up with hardship jobs that pay a pittance, the modern-day Asian expatriate leads an enviable lifestyle. Although salaries for regional postings do not match the premiums commanded by expatriates of the old days, the level of compensation is still healthy by today's standards.

These expatriates have different demands, depending on how old they are. This new breed of expatriates presents interesting challenges to HRM. They may not be singularly after pay but job satisfaction, career enhancement, or simply a chance to do different things. In line with the modern breed of workers, these Asian expatriates will possibly want a change every 15–18 months, and autonomy to control where and how they work. Their work and personal life are closely entwined. Managing all these expectations can be tricky for HRM.

Another example can be found in the shipbuilding industry. Traditional giant regional players such as Japan and Korea are now faced with a rising upstart. Based on deadweight tonnes – the weight of cargo a ship can carry – South Korea has 40 percent of the world market, slightly ahead of Japan. China now has about 8 percent.[4] According to the *Far Eastern Economic Review*, China will become the world's leading shipbuilder by between 2015 and 2020 as Beijing invests heavily in new shipyards and support facilities. In fact, China is estimated to be only a decade away from catching up with the quality and standard produced by Korean shipyards.

There is also pressure for big companies originating in Asia to increasingly produce goods that are more innovative and sophisticated. Sony is one. While its founder, the late Akio Morita had a vision that led to a revolution in the portability of music, his company is now fumbling for a new vision – more innovation and better products to meet an increasingly complex market with competing technologies. Sony Corp has 161,000 employees and US$62 billion in sales. When the company created the Walkman in the 1970s, all it took was a couple of people to cook up gadgets during their spare time. These days, it takes about 100 people to work on a single product.[5]

This is the new reality faced by almost all the rich countries in Asia. The market has shifted and so has manufacturing and the supply chain. There is a need not only to stay innovative but to continually produce better and greater results.

There is however one distinct feature about these rich countries – it is their focus on education as a route to wealth creation. Exhibit 4.2 below shows the co-relation between GDP per capita and the number of years of schooling. There is no doubt rich countries will continue to spend on education but the bloc of not so rich, such as China and India, will be keen to pour money into education, too, as a stairway to wealth and prosperity.

Did you know that of the modern expatriates in Asia:
- 60 percent are Asians;
- 20 percent are Americans;
- 10 percent are Europeans;
- 10 percent are Australians/NZ;
- 90 percent are male; and
- 75 percent are married.

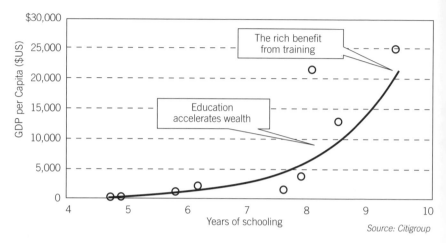

Exhibit 4.2 Education and wealth

Expats are mostly managers or in sales/marketing. Also, they are predominantly in production or are professionals. They are looking for two to three years of:

- skill transfer;
- startups; and
- career development.

IN SEARCH OF ANSWERS FOR HRM CHALLENGES IN "RICH" ASIA?

As the pressure mounts on rich Asian countries to keep their economic growth and performance from sliding, Japanese, Korean, Hong Kong, and Singaporean organizations are coming to terms with dealing with some of the changes taking place in the business operating environment. HRM responses can make or break these organizations.

The HRM challenge is to create value for organizations with breakthrough approaches and to adopt contrarian models that differentiate the business from competitors.

One of Asia's most daunting tasks is attracting, retaining and managing its talent pool. It is no big secret that talent flows to where the best jobs and salaries are. In Asia, the scene used to be that Japan, Korea, Singapore, and Hong Kong were hot spots for mobile talent.

Singapore is heavily reliant on foreign workers to sustain the economy. The government has an active program to retain foreign talent, which makes up about one-quarter of the population. Singapore also faces the challenge of enticing new foreign talent, as well as attracting the cadre of Singaporean graduates who are not shy from picking the best jobs going in the globe, and in the region. In Taiwan, graduates are not hesitant about relocating to China, which is a huge pool for fresh talent these days.

The slew of multinationals setting up base in China is also a source of talent drain from the more matured economies such as Japan, South Korea, Taiwan, Hong Kong, and Singapore. As an indication, salaries in China have already caught up with levels of those in its Southeast Asian neighbors, although China is a latecomer to economic development. One million Taiwanese now live on the mainland of the PRC, bringing money, technology, skills, and family disturbance at home.

Net foreign direct investment

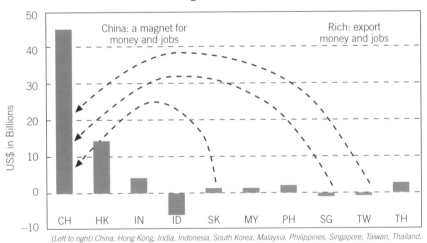

(Left to right) China, Hong Kong, India, Indonesia, South Korea, Malaysia, Philippines, Singapore, Taiwan, Thailand.

Source: HSBC

Exhibit 4.3 China is winning the war for talent!

There are more expatriates in Asia that come from other Asian countries than Westerners. And there is now a general exodus of Western expatriates from the traditional areas of Singapore and Hong Kong. They are leaving for greener pastures in China, or they are returning home because they are too expensive compared to the new cadre of local talent. While Western expatriates remain a significant group, their life has changed. And they now come to Asia for shorter assignments rather than extended colonial postings.

There is growing focus on Shanghai as money, jobs, and mobile talent flows into the vortex of rapid growth. Bangalore in India is now hosting many call centers for European companies, causing industrial action in the West.

There is a new world order. Employees will demand to be treated as customers, not employees, requiring a new set of online HRM tools and customized services that provide them greater choice and flexibility in employment conditions. The HRM function itself will be subject to "do more with less" pressures resulting in tectonic shifts in approaches such as adoption of shared service models.

We list some of the broad trends HRM will be faced with in the rich portion of Asia:

- *Workforce restructuring/downsizing* – Downsizing will remain a feature of HRM in rich countries for some time. As cheaper Asian production locations divert capital from the rich bloc of countries, there will also be forced wage restraints and increasing momentum to right-size or downsize. This implies the need for good exit policies, termination policies, and communication policies among others.

- *Processing reengineering/outsourcing* – There will be an intense focus on processing reengineering. Organizations in rich Asia will be forced to redesign work processes to increase productivity and achieve lower costs. And here, key talent management becomes a mission critical event for the viability of enterprises. Building technical competencies will be a critical focus for any organization needing to change.

- *Managing employee relations/expectations* – In places such as Japan and Korea, managing employee relations will be critical. With an aging workforce and rising life expectancy, Japan and Korea face the task of finding a balance between providing attractive benefits and maintaining a manageable cost structure. Places such as Singapore and Hong Kong will face the same challenges, especially in the issues of healthcare and retirement benefits.

- *Managing rapid technological change* – Capital and labor inputs alone will not be sufficient to drive extra productivity in the rich bloc of Asian countries. Smart organizations in Asia will focus on technology to extract value for enhanced productivity. HRM will be no different, there will be demands to provide better and faster services. Technological savvy will be important in understanding which technologies to adopt for HRM.

BARRIERS AND RESPONSES FOR HRM PROFESSIONALS IN ASIA

For those with business in developed economies and matured sectors, there is a HRM challenge to build capability that creates and captures value. For those in developing economies and growth sectors, the HRM challenge is to build the capacity to capture the value that has made the developed countries rich and famous.

This also means that HRM's role will need to rise in sophistication. A clear global pattern has now emerged. The state of human resource management in some parts of Asia is not sophisticated. This reflects the different pace of economic development experienced by these countries. But such is the rate of change and the momentum of globalization that the HRM function needs to accelerate in order to remain a viable entity contributing value to the business.

In 1998, a Mercer study identified several major goals for HRM professionals.[6] These are:
- increasing workforce productivity;
- lowering labor cost;
- recruiting and retaining a quality workforce;
- setting competitive benefits; and
- developing leaders.

It will be fair to describe the multiple stages of HRM's evolution in the following exhibit. Exhibit 4.4 depicts the progression of HRM from being office manager to personnel department, and lately to the HRM as we know it today. In a recent HRM Transformation Study conducted on 300 organizations across Asia, Mercer found that 84 percent of the participants are involved in some plan to transform HRM.[7] What is more important is that the study confirms that HRM in Asia still spends a considerable time delivering HRM services rather than being a strategic partner to business. The study found that HRM in Asia spends only 11 percent of its time on business partnering activities as opposed to the 20 percent level deemed as best practice by the Centre for Effective Organisation. This implies ample opportunities for HRM to work on in terms of moving up into partnership status with management at the business table.

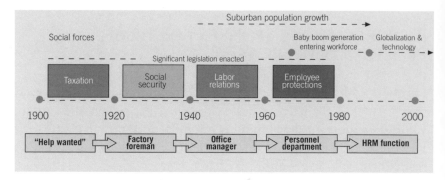

Exhibit 4.4 The evolution of HRM   *Source: Mercer's 11th Annual HR Roundtable Presentation*

Exhibit 4.4 depicts the path traveled by HRM in line with economic forces that have helped shaped organizational transformation. Moving on from the evolution chart above, HRM's future role is in being a change agent and change manager. In the future, HRM requires new skills and new competencies. These new skills include global business savvy, facilitating and managing change on a global scale, and acquiring performance technology.

PLOTTING THE COURSE TO MANAGE HRM CHANGE

The complexities of managing people have forced HRM in Asia and around the world to deliver new and better services. It is no wonder that there have been, and will continue to be, changes in HRM. From basic bread-and-butter functions such as recruitment to payroll administration, the role played by HRM has moved to one that is more complex and multifaceted.

There are three fundamental areas of change in HRM evolution. They are seen in:

1. recruitment;
2. talent management; and
3. measurement of human capital.

CHANGES IN RECRUITMENT

From projecting job openings to targeting the audience and candidates, HRM's role will advance to that of projecting talent and workforce needs. There will also be a major focus on developing global plans to access talent, and a focus on communicating the new requirements to the workforce.

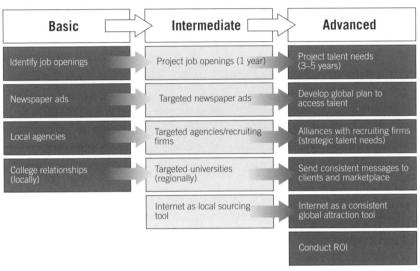

Source: Mercer Human Resource Consulting

Exhibit 4.5 How recruitment has evolved

CHANGES IN TALENT MANAGEMENT

In the future, HRM's function will expand beyond recruitment, managing exit interviews, or employee benefits. HRM will be spending more time on strategic issues such as assessing the organization's performance, building a ready pool of skilled people to run the business, and developing plans to build future leaders.

There will also be a new demand placed on HRM to contribute to broader business goals and outcomes by ensuring the organization can fully meet its talent and capability needs.

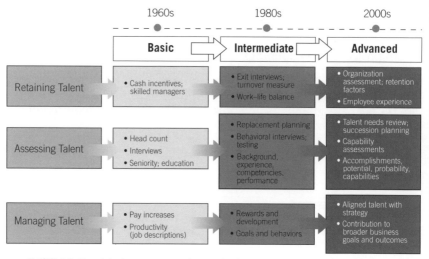

Exhibit 4.6 How talent management has evolved

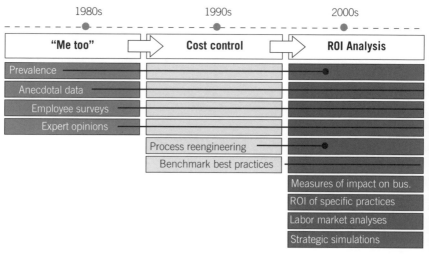

Exhibit 4.7 How human capital measurement has evolved

CHANGES IN HUMAN CAPITAL MEASUREMENT

Under the new operating environment in Asia, there will be heightened pressure on HRM to provide concrete evidence to show the returns on investments made in HRM programs. Old tools that have served HRM such as surveys and expert opinions have played a useful role in the past but more exact measures are now needed. The onus will be on HRM to demonstrate value from investments made. HRM personnel will need to be proficient in assessing the tools, managing their use, and assessing their efficacy.

▶ BUSINESS TIP

How can HRM respond to different types of Asian organizations

Because of the diversity in Asia, the responses from HRM will have to match the right scenarios. This response will be different in a basic manufacturing company operating in Taiwan, as opposed to one running a high-tech manufacturing facility in the same country.

As the rich part of Asia seeks a new role in determining the course for the future, organizations will take on new challenges and reposition themselves. In Singapore, several new directions have already been set. The quest to be the next life science research hub will require organizations to be proficient, not only in business acumen, but in building competencies to support business development. In Korea, the intense focus of some electronics and high-tech manufacturers will place exceeding demand for HRM to set the best practice and policies to support a staff structure high in R&D capability, coupled with effective sales and marketing people.

Here are some scenarios of what can be done to address the different type of organizations we are dealing with.

Scenario 1 Path for the low-cost advantage company
These organizations function as "the factory to the world." Their production involves prescribed work processes and outputs made to order. They depend highly on low cost and productivity to provide a global competitive advantage. Typically, this includes manufacturing companies and call centers – two of the major emerging sectors in China and India. Financial capital and ownership of technology are vital assets to manage for the business.

The HRM response will be:

Production/manufacturing:
Challenges and HRM response

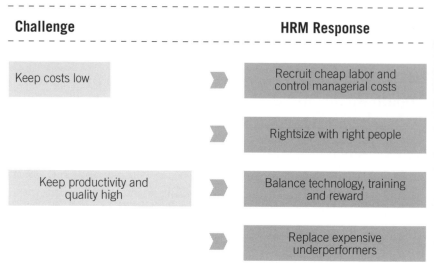

Exhibit 4.8 Production/manufacturing: Challenges and HR response

Scenario 2 Path for the sales- and distribution-oriented company
These organizations have domestic markets as their focus and depend
on sophisticated customer relationships, sales channels, and distribution
networks, plus supply chain management to build markets faster and
better than competitors. The sourcing of product is from business
units or organizations in the first category. This typically includes fast-
moving consumer goods (FMCGs), automobiles, white goods, and
electronics consumables, where first-mover advantage is critical to
success in combination with quality of service. In the case of matured
economies, the fight is for market share, whereas in the emerging
economies, the fight is for market attention ahead of the pack. Client
relationships and supply chains are the vital assets to manage.

The HRM response will be:

Sales & Marketing:
Challenges and HRM response

Challenge	HRM Response
Localize the product	Recruit the right staff
	Train: selling, product knowledge, competitors etc.
Capture market share	Performance management with clear objectives
	The right incentives
Beat the 'copy cats'	Retain best performers
	Give best performers the flexibility to respond

Exhibit 4.9 Sales and marketing: Challenges and HRM response

Scenario 3 Path for the product innovator
These organizations depend on product differentiation, service, and market offering as success factors. Breakthrough technology, new work processes, clever ideas, smarter applications, and value-added functions are examples of the mechanisms that need to be adopted, necessitating an investment in smart people and knowledge systems to create the true value of the business. The inventiveness of the Japanese, Taiwanese, Singaporeans, and South Koreans are essential to ongoing prosperity of those countries and corporations. But it is also the area that the India IT sector is capturing as a global center of excellence as an extension of the low-cost manufacture of IT solutions. People and knowledge are the vital assets to manage.

The HRM response will be:

Challenge	HRM Response
Creating uniqueness	Attract and retain best talent
	Leadership culture
	Learning environment
	Customized rewards
	Striving to be best employer
Market success	Leveraged pay

Exhibit 4.10 Research and development: Challenges and HRM response

No matter which scenario HRM is dealing with there are some fundamentals to observe: having the right people, and paying them the right amount at the right time, and in the right way.

BUILDING AN EFFECTIVE SALES ORGANIZATION IN A VOLATILE BUSINESS ENVIRONMENT

China's meteoric growth has been a source of attraction for investors in recent years. The Chinese market is now viewed as a new geography of strategic importance by anyone wanting a global reach. But aspirants to the Chinese market are fast realizing that this market is harder to crack than before. New entrants are competing head-on with a slew of local companies with strong ambitions to succeed against foreign companies. These entrants are also realizing that most traditional tactics are not suited to a high-growth market such as China.

> " For most Chinese-owned companies who are distinctly handicapped against global competitors when it comes to branding and R&D, an effective salesforce can help drive growth for business success "

For most Chinese-owned companies who have a distinct handicap against global competitors when it comes to brand and R&D expenditures, an effective salesforce is one of the levers they can use to drive profitable growth and succeed in the market. Examples are some Chinese-owned cell phone companies such as TCL, Legend, and Kejian, who have successfully leveraged their salesforce to gain local market share. These days, global companies and Chinese companies alike know that one of the most powerful keys to succeeding in China is optimizing the effectiveness of their salespeople.

WHY TRADITIONAL SALESFORCE FIXES HAVE THEIR LIMITS

Traditional salesforce fixes aren't of very much help because of the dynamism of the sales environment. There are constant changes on both the sales and buyer side. The increasing complexity of the market also requires a more holistic change across the whole salesforce. This means changes in how the salesforce approaches various customer segments; how the organization is structured; what skills need to be developed; and how performance is rewarded (Exhibit 4.11). Take the example of a situation where the salesforce may need to move from a transactional to a consultative approach with customers depending on the evolution of these customers' needs.

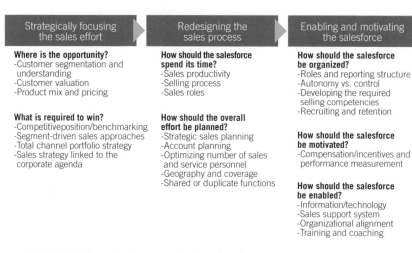

Exhibit 4.11 Elements of a more effective sales effort

Fortunately, there are proven tools and best practices for tuning the sales effort along several dimensions. Based on Mercer's research and extensive experience in the area, we have identified some of the common problems that relate to the management of the salesforce that impede the selling effort. Here are some business tips to guide HRM executives to optimize their salesforce's effectiveness:

- Have an organizational structure and social networks that can integrate both the sales and marketing functions.
- Spend time defining the sales roles and recruiting the right candidates.
- Provide training and development programs to close the capability gap.
- Structure an effective sales compensation scheme.

HAVING THE RIGHT ORGANIZATIONAL STRUCTURE AND SOCIAL NETWORKS

Many companies face the challenge of coordinating and integrating the sales and marketing functions for improved performance. The first step toward solving this problem is having clarity about the roles for both of these functions. In most consumer goods companies the roles of the two different functions are relatively clear: marketing people do the thinking, manage the brand, and provide the support to the salesforce. The salespeople are the executors in the field and sell to the end-users in the market. However, in other industries the roles and responsibilities between marketing and sales are blurred. Even in some consumer goods companies the trend is for sales and marketing to better cooperate for good results.

Designing the right sales organization structure is only the beginning. However, most people expect too much of it. Too often there is the unrealistic expectation that somehow redesigning the sales structure would be the panacea for all internal problems. The truth is that there is no "perfect" structure and there are many tradeoffs to be made during the organizational design. The situation is made more complex by the interplay of social networks within and outside the organizations.

For example, the different roles played by the sales and marketing organizations require different types of people. Such differences often lead people to disregard the importance of the other's function, which may result in an inconsistent strategy and flawed execution. The problem is exacerbated when there is no leader who can bring some equilibrium to the conflicts between two departments.

WHAT DO SUCCESSFUL COMPANIES DO?

Successful companies hire the people who possess both sales and marketing skills, and develop them through rotation programs. At the same time, they nurture the team spirit of the two functions and implement work-together incentive plans to encourage close cooperation.

CASE STUDY

How a pharmaceutical company in Japan took on liberalization

The force of globalization has imposed drastic changes on how companies operate in Asia. This particular medical company in Japan is no exception. Faced with the onslaught of market liberalization, the top management of DDD Japan recognized the impending threats for the medical equipment market caused by changing regulations. DDD Japan, a medical diagnostics company, derived its profit from the sale of medical equipment, as well as diagnostics products. The company was aware that there were major threats to its operations with the government's plan to revamp the medical security system, and the overhaul of the price structure. One of the results of the system's overhaul was the forced review of cost allocation to the health system. Vendors such as DDD Japan may not be able to avoid severe price-cutting from the market as vendors jostle to keep their business.

In assessing their position, DDD's project team (which included all board members) felt it was necessary to change the company's sales structure and personnel cost allocation. The company also felt the need to step up its professionalism. Among the responses it saw necessary were:

1. increasing the flexibility of the sales mechanism for staff when they make client visits;
2. reinforcing the IT infrastructure, enabling easy information access; and
3. renovating the HRM system to support the first two action plans.

Initially, the chairman of the DDD Japan wanted to implement a radical HRM system that would have introduced a reward structure on a person's performance. This would have been completely different from the seniority-based reward structure that the company was used to. A performance-based reward structure was built based on what the chairman wanted, but this caused mutiny and project members were confused and refused to endorse the plan, although the chairman was fully comfortable with the idea.

We had to then rework the initial plan, incorporating a more gradual and flexible approach to the new reward system. The new plan built in the following:

- setting only a portion of the salary based on performance;
- building an element of flexibility in the salary structure;
- providing the comfort element of a fixed base for all employees;
- building a five-year transition plan to get use to the performance-based pay; and
- having a performance review system based on the degree of knowledge contributed.

Based on the HRM interventions, DDD Japan was able to subsequently recruit many high-performing staff from its competitors. These were able to achieve good remuneration based on their performance. A large number of employees left because of the drastic changes, but the renewal was necessary for the company.

The move toward a contemporary reward structure is taking place in many organizations in Japan, with varying degrees of success. But the die has definitely been cast – there is no turning back. Companies now have to work on reward structures that help attract the right talent to produce the best results. A lot of the HRM changes are driven by the need for business transformation.

– A Mercer Case Study 2002

RIGHT JOB PROFILES, RIGHT CANDIDATES

The success of salesforce management starts with clearly defined sales roles. Research has shown that the most important motivation for the salesforce is the nature of the tasks. Although all sales jobs involve the ability to persuade, the requirements for individual jobs differ greatly. Some sales jobs require numerous closes per day, others only have one or two closes in a year, which could produce as much or more income. Similarly, many sales positions require little or no technical background or skills, while others require the salesperson to be a technical expert in a particular product or service.

An interesting way to portray these differences is to position each business and sales effort in a grid that compares the relative prominence of the sales person and the company, and the relative "value" being delivered. Is the customer "buying" what the individual salesperson can provide, or what the "company" as a whole can provide? Are the salespeople merely fulfilling the transaction or delivering value-added consultative service?

When the roles and tasks are in place, the next step is to find the right candidates to occupy these sales positions. Different sales roles require different types of people, especially those with special personality profiles. For example, some salespeople are described as "hunters" who are ego-driven, highly persuasive, and can open new accounts. And others are described as "farmers" who are good at establishing relationships or at severing existing accounts. It is ideal to find someone who has a combination of both profiles, but that's rarely the case.

Successful sales organizations usually acknowledge such realities. They employ advanced tools to identify and distinguish these sales qualities. They strive to keep a balance between a very diverse group of salespeople, some of whom are more persuasive, while the others are more service-oriented. By assigning the talent among the salespeople to the right positions, the company is well on its way toward building a high-performance salesforce.

Another important aspect relating to the recruitment of the best candidates is rooted in whether the company should be acquiring talent from outside or cultivating talent from within.

Many selling organizations such as Procter & Gamble, Unilever, and Coca-Cola hire recent college graduates for their sales positions and put them through thorough training programs. In contrast, other companies may hire only people with sales experience and expect these salespeople to generate quick results.

It's hard to evaluate which practice is better. A lot of factors, both external and internal, affect such decisions. For example, if the labor market is tight, it is normal for companies to seek inexperienced people.

The fundamental issue still lies with how good a job the company does in hiring people with innate sales talent to be good salespeople.

WHAT OF TRAINING AND DEVELOPMENT PROGRAMS?

Sales training programs are aimed at making salespeople successful. High-performing sales organizations provide their salespeople the opportunity to develop their competencies and knowledge to succeed in every selling situation.

These organizations spend plenty of time and money on sales training. But in our experience, many training sessions are sporadically or unenthusiastically attended – for good reasons. The exercises tend to focus on administrative activities and goal-setting, rather than on answering the need to drive quick results. Training needs to add real value.

Here we highlight some best practices relevant to developing a world-class training and development program for sales professionals.

➤ BUSINESS TIP

Best practices for developing a high-performing salesforce

1. Train salespeople to become specialists.
2. Have executives sponsor key global accounts.
3. Incorporate common messages into all training programs to create alignment among salespeople.
4. Offer training that teaches salespeople how to interact with customers in various functions.
5. Develop superior listening and questioning skills to uncover customer needs.

6. Establish mentoring relationships between junior and senior salespeople.
7. Select top salespeople as field-based trainers to share best practices and success stories.
8. Use video scenarios in monthly team meetings to introduce new sale tactics.
9. Offer product training through the intranet.
10. Conduct standardized orientation training to set expectations.
11. Reinforce training on the job through sales managers.
12. Integrate sales coaching into the sales manager's job.

DESIGNING THE EFFECTIVE SALES COMPENSATION SCHEME

The sales compensation scheme, including the sales incentive plan, plays a vital role in salesforce management because the scheme affects the type of the people the company wants to attract, and it influences the activities and behaviors of the salespeople. But too often, an organization's compensation philosophy does not match the overall business objective and the selling environment. Recently, a high-tech company came to Mercer, asking for a review of its sales compensation.

The client operates in one of the most competitive industries in China, selling mobile phones. Customers are becoming more complex and now have enough knowledge to differentiate what phones they want. There seems to be very little value-added service that the firm's salesforce could provide. The market has evolved from being more value driven to being more transaction driven.

Although this company considered itself a high-tech company for its compensation structure, it should in fact be comparing itself to the "consumer" goods industry. The reason is obvious. The peer group for compensation comparison needs to reflect the evolution in the market condition. What's more, if the company wanted to align its sales compensation with the marketplace and for strategic reasons, it should consider other elements of the sales compensation.

➤ CONCLUSION

Asia today is a melting pot of cultures, lifestyles, and diverse economic achievements. The challenges faced by managers in HRM are more profound than ever in an environment governed by shifting rules and playing ground. Who are the players in Asia? The multitude comes in various shapes and sizes: the traditional homegrown company seeking to grow bigger or global; the regional player seeking to grow global; or the global player seeking markets in specific parts of Asia.

Our focus has been based on this tenet: Asia is not a homogenous market. It is a dynamic marketplace with diverse challenges and diverse needs. How an organization chooses its response in Asia has to be rooted in what type of market it is after, and what goods and services it is offering. Japanese organizations are struggling with economic liberalization in the face of restructuring old and archaic rules of business. Our case study shows how a Japanese organization is reinventing itself to meet a liberalized marketplace. Singapore-based organizations face the challenge of finding new markets and businesses to grow the economic pie, while Taiwanese and Korean manufacturers are chasing higher and higher value in the economic chain. We featured the complexity of the marketplace in the study on how sales organizations need to adapt, even in a relatively young market such as China.

In the last 15–20 years, HRM's transformation has been major. Asia's HRM professionals, too, have undergone the metamorphosis, sometimes painful, sometimes haphazard, sometimes organized, and sometimes not. From how payroll is administered, how benefits services are being administered, to how compensation systems have changed, HRM's challenges will only grow in complexity and size.

The challenges for the rich countries in Asia are diverse. But the destination is the same: transforming the business to raise productivity. How this transformation needs to be done has to reflect the social and economic fabric's design. Best practices in HRM can only be a guide at best. Simple HRM solutions can be used in some parts of rich Asia, while sophisticated activities need to be induced in others.

The Asia-based HRM manager needs to know the full spectrum of the HRM system to be effective. He or she needs to be adaptable and flexible in using the range of HRM solutions available. What has worked in the matured markets in the United States and Europe may or may not be easily adapted to the Asian market. The wise HRM manager will understand the organization's people, the business culture, and introduce tools in a manner that is acceptable to the people. There is only one path for the rich countries in Asia, the path of using HRM interventions in a way suited to the local markets.

---

[1] "Productivity, Efficiency and Economic Growth: East Asia and the Rest of the World," Gaofeng Han (University of California), Kaliappa Kalirajan (Foundation for Advanced Studies on International Development) and Nirvikar Singh (University of California): Sourced from: http://econ.ucsc.edu/faculty/boxjenk/frontier1_sept.pdf

[2] *IMD World Competitiveness Yearbook 2003*, sourced from IMD website, http://www01.imd.ch/documents/wcy/content/be.pdf_page_3

[3] Danish Research Unit for Industrial Dynamics, Working Paper No. 99–2, "Responses to the Crisis: Constraints to a Rapid Trade Adjustment in East Asia's Electronics Industry," Dieter Ernst, http://www.druid.dk/wp/pdf_files/99-2.pdf

[4] "The Making of a Juggernaut," David Lague. *Far Eastern Economic Review*, Sept. 18.

[5] "Sony Tries to Stay Cool," Phred Dvorak. *Far Eastern Economic Review*, Sept. 18.

[6] Mercer/Conference Board Study 1998.

[7] Mercer HR Transformation Study (Asia), September 2003.

CHAPTER

5

Japan: In Search of New HRM Dynamics

Reiji Ohtaki and Takao Aihara

*J*apan's HRM transformation is already taking place. The pace for some has been glacial. For others it has been at breakneck speed. Whether Japan's HRM transformation can be termed successful is yet to be known. What is obvious is that Japanese organizations are under immense pressure to continuously innovate, reengineer and reinvent themselves. Massive layoffs in Japan are but one of the side-effects of an economy cluttered with inefficiencies. A dominant trend in Japan is the need to build not only better products that can rival traditional competitors such as the United States and Korea, but new kids on the block such China. Jobs for life, which has become part of Japan's postwar rehabilitation social fabric, is fast becoming extinct. A borderless world has introduced competition to Japan, forcing organizations to extract more value out of the work process and in turn, more out of its workforce. For Japan, the answers are clear. Half-hearted HRM changes will do more damage than good. There is a need for HRM practices that addresses Japan's unique cultural and economic needs. There is also urgency to develop human capital development programs that will help Japanese corporations maintain their competitive streak.

JAPAN: SLASH, BURN, AND REBUILD

Japan is doomed to economic and technical decline unless it changes dramatically – this was the dire prognosis made by former Japanese prime minister Keizo Obuchi.[1] His words are ringing home. Now more than ever. Japan is still trying to gain its feet after the implosion of its stock and property market binges in the 1980s. For most of the last decade, Japan has not been well. It has been called everything from "a sick old man," "arthritic," to being in "comatose."

How, when, and why Japan fell from the stairs of the economic heaven to the pits of an economic hell remains a discourse for current and future historians and economists. Will Japan ever regain its economic might, or will it sink further into economic malaise weighed down by a series of botched banking, corporate, and economic reforms?

Economists have argued with gusto that Japan has yet to bite the hard bullet, that changes made to the economy over the last 10 years have been cosmetic at best. The prelude to growth, according to one school of thought, is the fundamental and profound creative destruction of corporate Japan. This would require a shift in thinking within Japan Inc. – a realization that the old order, based on a centrally planned economy, a lifetime employment, and rigid seniority must fall before a more productive and innovative economy can be formed.[2]

There is an alarming sense of urgency for Japan to get back into shape. Consider this: It has lost a decade fumbling with policies that have gone nowhere. The rise of new economic superstars such as China has raised the ante for Japan and its Asian neighbors to find new ways to keep their economic rice bowls. The Japanese government has spent over 100 trillion yen to kick-start an economy that at its best remains sluggish.

THE ONCE UNSTOPPABLE JAPAN

That the Japanese are an industrious people cannot be doubted. Japanese brands such as Sony, Nissan, and Toyota are household names across the globe. Sony's PlayStations are every child's dream and most modern Asian households' goods such as DVD players are usually a Japanese, if not a Korean brand. The Meiji restoration era in the 1870s and the big industrial push in the 1960s catapulted the nation into a formidable economic powerhouse. As far back as 1976, Japan had already cornered the US market for imported televisions, where some 80 percent of US television imports originated from Japan.[3]

Japan's growth trajectory has been unstoppable since. Economic prosperity reached alarming proportions, so much so that a faction of the world in the 1980s believed Japanese corporations would overtake everyone else. This faction likened Japan's economic prowess to a form of economic imperialism. This was the era where Tokyo land prices were nearly four times the land value of all of America. This was the era where no one believed land or stock prices in Japan would ever falter. This was the era where Japanese tourists flocked to every corner of the world snapping up Gucci, Calvin Klein, and Ralph Lauren Polo luxury goods.

Something snapped along the way. Japan's touchdown from its dizzy economic flight was a hard one, and the effects are still ricocheting.

Fall from grace

The IMD World Competitiveness Survey ranked Japan as the world's most competitive economy through most of 1990s. But by 2000, Japan's ranking had dropped to 21. Today, Japanese corporate bankruptcy rates are at historic highs. Unemployment rates are at record levels and Japan is hurting. During its growth phase in most of the 1960s, 1970s, and 1980s, Japan's inefficiencies were well absorbed. Maverick Japanese banker Masamoto Yashiro of Shinsei Bank is of the view that the low profitability in many Japanese businesses was camouflaged by Japan's former years of high growth. The Japanese economy grew by an average of 12 percent annually throughout the 1960s, 5 percent in the 1970s, and 4 percent in the 1980s. His take is that a Japanese corporation would only need 2 percent return to stay afloat as long as the economy kept growing.[4] This accounts for why few paid heed to the largesse seen in Japanese corporations.

Japanese corporations might have been viewed as success icons with their innovation and clockwork precision at the factories, but the wider system was faulty due to government protection and subsidies for industries. In 2000, a McKinsey Global Institute report noted that Japanese domestic industries' productivity rates were low and there was ample opportunity to improve the rates. The food-processing sector's total factor productivity was at 39 percent of that in the United States, while the overall retail productivity in Japan was 50 percent of that in the United States.[5]

The McKinsey survey found that while Japanese exporters in the auto, steel, machine tools, and consumer electronics were bettering any and all (international) competitors' productivity by 20 percent, domestic industries' productivity trailed competitors. The export sectors mentioned above only employed 10 percent of the Japanese workforce. McKinsey's estimate was that the other 90 percent of the Japanese economy was only half as productive, while sectors such as retail, food processing, home construction, and health care were operating at around 60 percent productivity of similar sectors in the United States.

There is a need for Japanese organizations to retool and reconfigure themselves in ways that would require more than makeshift changes. The future is clear: Japanese corporations have to raise their level of play, look for new ways to produce goods and services for a globalized market, and make a profit at the same time. The challenges come in many shapes and sizes. Where will the next level of efficiency and productivity come from? How can entrepreneurs, chief executives, and managers induce organizational change that will raise Japan's position in the world? HRM system changes that have been adopted by Japanese corporations have done little thus far to extract the most value.

Our view is that the restructuring that has taken place in Japan over the last 10 years should be termed the "lost 10 years." Despite so much pain, the gains have been alarmingly miniscule. There is still a colossal need for Japan Inc. to change the "sub-systems" tied to its HRM revamp – namely, changing the people-side of things. While organizations have implemented system changes, there is still an immense lack of accompanying changes that will provide people with the skills and attitudes needed to survive the new demands placed on them within the new structure. Japan's corporate restructuring is largely incomplete without people changes. It is here that HRM in Japan has the opportunity to give reform a real chance. We will provide some insights into how this can be done.

What were the historical factors that have led to the now untenable situation. Is lifetime employment the reason for the ills? What is the outcome of this nearly half-a-century-old "social contract" between Japanese organizations and their employees? Where will the changes have to take place for Japanese organizations to successfully harness a people strategy that will work for Japan? We will first put the history in context, then provide some basis to help HRM make the next leap in their transformation. This process may involve a lot more than re-turfing of old HRM systems or wholesale adoption of methods from other tested places such as the United States.

LIFETIME EMPLOYMENT

A New York Times article in 1993 by Andrew Pollack was headlined: "For Japan Inc., Company Rosters That Never Die." In this article, the writer features a cemetery, except this is no ordinary cemetery. In Koyasan, among the graves of shogun and samurai, are more than 250 corporate "tombs" built by some of Japan's leading companies to honor their dead employees.[6] These corporate tombs provide companies with a means of enshrining the memories of their valued employees. Nissan's monument features a statue of two workers. The gravestone of electronics company Sharp Corporation resembles a stereo flanked by two speakers, according to Pollack. Japan's humanitarian industrialist Konosuke Matsushita, who founded the company in his name built the first monument in 1938. A monument could cost anywhere between US$500,000 to US$1 million. At the peak of Japan's real estate bubble, a US$3 million monument was built by a real estate company. The company is now bankrupt. These corporate tombs capture the essence of what formed the backbone of industrial relations. This relationship was the cornerstone of Japan's personnel management system. It served a useful model at a time when Japanese organizations needed a constant supply of loyal workers to support business goals.

SENIORITY RULES IN JAPAN INC.

In the period leading up to Japan's bubble economy, Japanese organizations formed this unique employer–employee system to help power its rapid industrialization. This was a system formed under special circumstances. Each year, a massive number of fresh graduates were recruited by large corporations and trained, under a long-term plan, mostly through a system of job rotation. Many were given opportunities to rise to managerial or executive levels over time.

> **"In traditional Japan, employees joined a company rather than got a job."**

Promotions were given, based on an employee's seniority. Annual pay rises were given based on rank and seniority, and the employees' age – not on individual performance. The same went for employee benefits and welfare, including company housing and dormitories. Performance mattered and was measured, but in terms of groups or team outputs, not as individual output.

The personnel recruitment system that existed had the following features: There was no strict screening or selection criteria, and blue-chip companies got the best cuts in getting graduates from prestigious schools. Employees "joined a company" rather than "got a job." Employees secured positions for life as long as they fitted into the organization and made no major mistakes in their assignments.

In compensation, the significance of individual performance among employees was downplayed so no big differences would be reflected in the compensation. Although performance appraisal based on merit existed among enterprises, it was not necessarily applied to gauge individual performance, and it was not linked to compensation. Seniority was the benchmark by which rewards were set.

Compensation came in many forms. Non-cash compensation was more prevalent while the cash portion was capped at a relatively low level. Japanese companies did not share corporate profits directly with employees. Monetary resources were accumulated and used for employee benefits such as housing and company dormitories. It was customary for Japanese companies to support employees and their family members as a whole. Employees felt no compulsion to leave as long as their benefits and welfare outweighed their low cash compensation.

It was a norm for Japanese companies to maintain an egalitarian system where once an employee joined the company, lifetime employment would be guaranteed. There was no need to demonstrate individual capabilities. Salaries and career advancement opportunities were made equal. Employees became "family members" of the company. In turn, employees maintained loyalty in return for the company's support.

HOW DID THE JOB-FOR-LIFE SYSTEM HOLD TOGETHER?

Large Japanese corporations maintained a pyramid-shaped workforce, where each year many graduates were recruited and put through the system. They stayed until the mandatory retirement age of 60 to enjoy the rewards of their long years of service. Over the short-term, an employee did not need to be a star, and his sterling performance counted for little in the larger scheme of things. Tasks and duties were distributed based on groups or functions. During the economic boom years, there were relatively few grudges as employees' pay increases were usually high.

MERITS OF A JOB-FOR-LIFE SYSTEM

Amid this, it is useful to ask whether the Japanese HRM system worked at all, and if it did, why? The seniority-based system had its merits at a time when Japan's industrial push required absolute loyalty and a steady supply of labor. Despite the popular notion that lifetime employment was available to every worker in Japan, it was not. It was largely offered to large corporations or the closely knit . The seniority-based system gave management absolute liberty to relocate, transfer, or job-rotate. Within the relatively rigid universe of a job-for-life company, Japanese companies induced flexibility by frequently reshuffling employees around. Contrast this with the Western industrial system where contractual union agreements often made it impossible to move people or jobs around. In a job-for-life environment, employees secured a place in the company for life, but held little ownership of their career directions. It is no wonder then, that HRM, or the personnel department, was often seen as the apex of power within the organization. Within this limited framework, Japanese organizations were often able to keep attrition rates to the minimal; hence, there was a constant supply of labor at a predictable and manageable cost. Employees, happy to earn a place in a company for life, gave their best to the company. In the absence of short-term performance-based goals placed on the individual, the organization focused on building longer term outcomes and teamwork as a strategy for success. This has been fundamental to the success that made Japan an economic dynamo in the 1960s, 1970s, and part of the 1980s.

This system contributed to the stability of Japanese society as a whole. It was a complete macrocosm, bound by a fabric that was hard to break. Families were supported by the husbands, the husbands were employed by companies, and the businesses of the companies were protected by national regulations. Under the pre-bubble economy of Japan, this system served its purpose and held together as long as the economy kept its growth momentum.

THE LOST 10 YEARS

Several factors, both external and internal, forced dramatic changes upon Japan. A saturated economy, globalization, and an aging society made it hard for Japan to hang onto this seniority-based system. Because of the rapidity of changes, companies were forced to undergo restructuring. The bubble economy had burst, the onslaught of globalization changed the dynamics of operations. From supply chain management, production to marketing, the world demanded that operators be more efficient than ever. Capital went to the best performing investments, companies went to the cheapest locations, and uncompetitive industries died a natural death.

Japan's HRM revolution: Why it had to happen

- The demise of lifetime employment necessitated new ways to distribute resources.
- The maturity of the Japanese economy forced efficient use of resources.
- An aging workforce made it untenable for the system to fund lifetime employment.
- The liquidity in the labor market applied pressures on Japan to change.
- Globalization forced Japan to adopt HRM systems to secure and retain the best talent.

In Japan, the "lifetime employment" contract had to be broken. Companies could no longer offer lifetime employment to their employees; hence, they could not extract loyalty from employees. The cycle was soon broken. Corporate Japan lost one of its engines that fueled its performance and Japanese employees lost their job security forever. By the end of the bubble economy, what had once represented a successful HRM strategy – job security in return for absolute loyalty – became an albatross for management.

QUEST FOR NEW HRM SYSTEMS

Enterprises in Japan went in search of new systems in their quest to adapt to a changing world. Old systems were bulldozed. In their place were new corporate governance rules, new organizational systems, and new HRM administration systems. Japanese workers, long used to not having to pay attention to individual appraisal systems, woke up to appraisal systems that HRM consultants introduced, including pay-for-performance systems or pay-for-position systems. What the seniority-based system stood for, "long-term contributions to the company equate to long-term reward for the labor force," made a dramatic exit. The system that replaced it read: "Quick contributions for the company equates to short-term reward for the labor force."

Performance-based pay also brought with it associated factors such as job sizes and job positions, which Japanese companies were not used to. Since Japan was now competing in a global market for talent, Japanese organizations were forced to reevaluate their age-old promotion and their staff treatment systems. Companies now had to differentiate promotion/treatment of individuals based on performance. External factors have forced Japanese organizations to abandon their equal treatment for all in place of one that will reward differentiation in individual performance. Limited monetary resources also forced Japanese organizations to redistribute their wages and benefits accordingly.

Japan has not adopted the conventional position-based salary system, but a performance-based wage system with a wider categorization. This system has a reward philosophy that takes into account an employee's past contributions. It does not take into account job categorizations. The end result is that a performance-based system in Japan is often quite similar to a seniority-based system.

When Japanese organizations adopted new performance evaluation systems, management by objective was a popular tool used. Companies replaced the indirect knowledge-based or skill-based evaluation methodologies with competency-based assessment.

CRACKS IN HRM REFORMS

While many Japanese corporations have undertaken HRM system redesign, the reform has been half-baked. Focus has thus far been on appraisal and compensation systems – what we will call the "hardware." There is a huge gap in the structural process in place. Sub-systems such as recruitment, selection, placement, training, and career planning, coaching, and leadership development – all these have largely been unexplored.

On the one side, performance management systems focus on outputs of an employee and tailor the rewards based on an agreed set of goals or objectives. On the other side, the assumption is that employees are able to set objectives, focus on areas where they want to acquire skills in, and manage their own career paths, among others. The pity is that most employees are unable to manage their own career paths because they haven't been handheld at all. Organizations that have missed out on providing the tools or systems for employees to handle these essentials have missed out on a fundamental part of the HRM reform process.

Why are these sub-systems such as recruitment, selection, placement, employee training, and career planning so important? Consider this: for almost 30 years, a typical Japanese worker within a large company would go through a system whereby career progression was never an issue. The employee would be put through the mill, passing through a generalist career path whereby his job would be rotated throughout his employment term within the corporation. A generalist employee who could deliver mediocre outcome could meander through the system and enjoy the benefits provided by the company, until retirement.

But corporate Japan has changed. The new economy has exerted new pressures on organizations. Corporate Japan has been forced to attract talent to support its business development. Specialists are the order of the day, not generalists. The demand for new skills and competencies will force the average Japanese worker to acquire specific skill sets. The company will no longer plan his or her career. The worker needs to be a self-starter, independent of the career rotation offered by companies. The worker needs skills that are dictated by the new global economy – the ability to take risks and make new initiatives, the ability to innovate, the ability to communicate and to articulate – skills not requisite in the old order.

TOO MUCH CHANGE, TOO LITTLE GAIN FROM HRM TRANSFORMATION

What we have seen thus far is that the *tsunami* of change forced upon the Japanese workforce has been too rapid. Because these changes have been so drastic, the shock to the system would have been extreme. In many companies, HRM system

> " In many of the wrongdoings reported in Japan, the management has not shown any remorse. Management was only sorry it got caught. "

changes were introduced, often creating chaos and new problems rather than providing solutions. Japan is still at major crossroads in terms of trekking the right path for HRM transformation. The proper path for Japan's HRM transformation may involve more than wholesale import of ideas from other places, with different historical settings.

While businesses have undergone major shifts in Japan over the last 10 years, there have been few success stories. Many companies are still using the trial and error approach in organization change. One of the side-effects from this unfinished reform is the increasing disillusionment of employees with their companies. An outcome of this is the shocking revelation of unethical corporate business standards – quite a few by disgruntled internal employees who don't feel loyal to the company anymore. Internally, the corporate rot unveiled in Japan can be traced to the safety net provided by the tightly knit fabric binding government and the industries, and the industries and their employees. Business owners, protected by the cushy relationship with the government, had low accountability to their shareholders and investors. If management bungled, it wasn't very obvious, nor was it a major issue. In many of the wrongdoings reported in Japan, the management has not shown any remorse. Management was only sorry if it got caught.

Japan is under threat from poor corporate governance, corporate mismanagement, and a lack of leadership at many layers within the organization. Recent reports of major corporate wrongdoings, including Snow Brand Milk Products, Nippon Meat Packers, Inc., and Tokyo Electric Power, are testimonies to these facts. The Global Competitiveness Report in 2002 ranked Japan at the bottom of the heap in terms of the efficacy of its corporate boards.[7] Businesses for decades had poor accountability to shareholders, bearing the knowledge that they would be protected from competition. Boards of directors were often a group of henchmen who never observed their fiduciary duties.

IN SEARCH OF MANAGEMENT SKILLS

Japanese organizations are also suffering from a severe shortage of management skills. It is a situation borne out of the historical paradigm that has shaped Japan's employment structure. The old order values teamwork, loyalty, and perseverance. Competencies were not important. Many of the senior executives were themselves generalists who moved into their jobs as an extension of where they were in the organization not because of the specific skill set they demonstrated.

The lack of management skills should not be confused with operational efficiencies. Japan stands out in terms of operational efficiencies in its export industries. Japan's operational management techniques, such as total quality management and just-in-time manufacturing, so captured the world that countries were scrambling to understand and adopt the system. In fact, Harvard University's Michael Porter in an interview with the Harvard Business School's journal said Japan's total quality management gave an enormous advantage to Japanese companies initially. This operational efficiency, which he also termed "best practice," is what every company should do. However, operational efficiency alone does not equate to strategy, and this is an important element in sustainable competitive advantage.[8]

Will Japan's organizational reforms give its industry the strategic vision it needs? Because employees have been shaped in an environment that rewarded obedience and collective outcomes, what will HRM in Japan have to focus on to develop its human assets in the new economy?

Distrust of new value systems

The organization reforms going on in Japan have created much tension within society. What was once sacrosanct – lifetime employment and absolute loyalty in return – has been shattered. The system that has replaced the old order is as yet unaccepted by many and has not taken root.

It is absolutely necessary, as a step forward to reform, to change human resources management and to develop a new working mechanism. This new system must balance the hard side of HRM with the soft side – putting the HRM measurements in place while providing people the opportunities, skills, and latitude to shape and grow a career.

From ashes to profit: Successful HRM transformation the Nissan way

These days, Carlos Ghosn, the CEO for Nissan is a sort of celebrity in Japan. He stars in a *manga* (Japanese comic book) for businessmen. His fans are keen to know where he got his hair cut and what sunglasses he wears. Some media pundits are predicting that Ghosn's achievements with Nissan will go down in history alongside Commodore Perry's – the American naval officer who forced opened Japan's secluded shores for American interests when he arrived in Edo Bay in huge gunboats back in 1853.

When Ghosn took over the helm at Nissan in 1999, the company had US$5 billion in losses and US$17 billion in debt. His first restructuring plan, the Nissan Revival Plan, focused on a few key things. They were getting Nissan back to profitability within three years; slashing purchasing costs by 20 percent over the same period; halving the number of suppliers to 600; selling stakes in all but a few of its affiliates; closing down five domestic plants; and slashing its workforce by 21,000.

Despite having worked his magic at Renault where his ruthless cost trimmings earned him the name of "le cost killer," Ghosn skeptics gave him a short life span in Japan. Few believed he would succeed, given he was an "outsider" and the internal barriers he would face in an established marketplace such as Japan. His changes were seen as draconian and repugnant in a society long governed by propriety and political correctness.

He quickly took to the scalpel and worked his way through Nissan, which had by this stage accumulated debts totaling US$18 billion and had been losing market share in Japan for 26 consecutive years, and losing global market share for eight straight years.

One of his most notorious feats was slashing the number of *kereitsus* companies tied by cross stock-sharing from 1,400 to four. This removed all but the most competitive of suppliers from Nissan's books. His greatest vindication came when Nissan returned to profitability by March 2002. He has also returned Nissan to a zero debt position within the deadline he set his team.

The latest official company results filed in May 2003 showed that for the financial year 2002 (ended March 31), Nissan's consolidated operating profit rose 51 percent to a record US$6.04 billion. Its operating profit margin on sales was 10.8 percent, a record for the automotive industry.

Nissan's turnaround provides interesting material for any management case study. The lessons cut even deeper from a human resource viewpoint. What did Ghosn do that forced Nissan to change its spots?

What got Nissan into the quicksand it was in?

Nissan was a company beset by communication disaster. The management and employees were not communicating. Employees were greatly demoralized. What was even more glaring was employees' lack of passion for the company's products. Managers couldn't look customers in the eye and tell the customers what great products Nissan made.

When Ghosn stepped into the Nissan universe, he undertook a major exercise and did what no other CEO had done. He personally conducted interviews with 200 management staff. One of the biggest obstacles he faced was getting people to tell him what they thought. He said in an interview to *Trends in Japan* (a Japanese government publication) that the power of hierarchy made it difficult to get communication going. "Here [in Japan] it was important from the beginning to tell people, 'Look, I need to know what you think.' It's very important for the company. And this has taken some time."

The other thing he spent time on was to reconstruct the idea of teamwork within Nissan. While Ghosn felt the Japanese employees were superb team players, the teamwork broke down when he tried to build cross-functional teams. He told *Trends in Japan:* "Engineers work very well together, financial people work very well together, sales people work very well together. But when you start to add an engineer, a marketer, a sales person, and a manufacturer, here all the strengths of Japan in teamwork disappear."

Some of the more critical HRM issues Ghosn dealt with include the following:

- setting the leadership's agenda for change;
- adopting a performance management program;
- setting up clear performance goals;
- building two-way communication channels;
- retaining high performers through an equitable reward structure;
- improving dialogue with the union;
- implementing a new culture, a new way of doing things; and
- drawing on internal sources to power the change agenda.

The old system failed on many parts due to the following factors:

- *Blitz of HRM administration systems introduced* – The focus thus far has been on beefing up HRM administration systems such as performance appraisals and compensation systems. There hasn't been a concerted move to mobilize the sub-systems that we have described as mindset shifts, selection and recruitment techniques, career planning, and talent/performance management tools to build high-performing organizations. Layoffs and wage adjustments have been the focus thus far.
- *A weak HRM reform process* – A flawed HRM reform process can only lead to faulty outcomes. HRM is usually the driver of reform, highlighting to management the need for changes. When the boat is rocked, HRM is in a dilemma as it tries to induce the change while management apathy remains.
- *Chasm between line employees and the HRM department* – When top management drives the change, the HRM department will execute the change process, often sidestepping the line managers during the process. This is where new appraisal and salary management systems are introduced to the detriment of the company. Line managers who do not understand the process will not support the new systems and things revert to the status quo.

The Nissan case illustrates the fact that Japanese-owned companies have come to terms with the need to adapt to the new demands of a global playing field. Renault, the 40 percent shareholder of Nissan is the catalyst for change within the organization, as well as the pace-setter for other auto companies long shackled by the powerful *Kereitsus* and old HRM structures that no longer work. The Nissan "model" of change has given much hope to other Japanese companies to do what they have thought was impossible – breaking tradition. Japanese companies may well be asking "why haven't we done this earlier."

►BUSINESS TIP

Performance management system the Japanese way

Japanese organizations have struggled with the introduction of the performance management system based on the models popularly used in America. It may not be apparent to the rest of the world, but in Japan, historically, companies practiced a one-way evaluation system; that is, the employees were evaluated by the superior. The system functioned like a "Black Box" – without transparency. Line managers in Japan who traditionally conduct these appraisals were not adept at following the open dialogue-based system, which has only been introduced recently. Coaching was done informally, over drinks after work or on the job. This worked well under the lifetime employment practice. Line managers were also often confused about how to set the right performance objectives, which is crucial in the process.

Line managers also often had a problem communicating performance results face to face with their subordinates. In performance appraisal the Japanese way, companies have tended to focus on the qualitative aspect of the person's performance such as the work process, the person's capability, the speed of career advancement, and the person's leadership qualities among others. These factors have been treated with equal importance as the quantitative goals.

After struggling with the concept of performance appraisal for some time, Japanese companies have warmed to the MBO (management by objectives) system. Some have even incorporated a hybrid system combining the MBO with the Balance Score Card approach.

Here are some tips for implementing a performance appraisal system for Japanese employees:

- *All about balance* – The system needs to have a good balance between quantitative and qualitative performance objective-setting measures. A system that is too focused on quantitative results would cause uneasiness among employees as Japanese companies tend to view the work process as importantly as the end results.
- *All about training* – To successfully implement a performance appraisal system, managers have to be trained on first how to set performance objectives; second, how to measure performance results; and third, how to give feedback to subordinates. As many line managers may not have done this before, the training program should contain many role-playing exercises for them to experience open dialogue with their subordinates.

MOVEMENT TOWARDS STRATEGIC HRM IN JAPAN – THE CHANGE HAS STARTED

It may come as a surprise but traditionally the HRM departments of Japanese firms have had much more authority than that of their counterparts in Europe or the United States. HRM in Japan has been primarily responsible for recruiting, deciding salary and benefits, and deciding on job assignments/job rotations among others. HRM-related decision-making was centralized at the HRM department in most companies in Japan. Line management, on the other hand, had little control in HRM decision-making. Line managers could not even decide who to hire. They simply had to accept the candidates being assigned to their workplace by the HRM department. HRM would merely ask line managers to evaluate the performance of the staff for HRM to determine salary increases for employees. In short, the HRM department was run by HRM administrators with super authority.

Despite having such authority, the typical Japanese HRM department was not a strategic partner for the top management simply because it did not have a strategic mindset or sophisticated tools to support the needs of the top management. Japanese companies, therefore, had no HRM strategies to back up the business strategies.

Many Japanese firms are now shifting some of the HRM decision-making authorities to the line management. These include hiring, salary/bonus decisions, and firing. Performance evaluation has traditionally been the domain of line managers. Companies are also outsourcing many HRM administrative functions to third-party vendors, or to the shared service company they created by separating the HRM administration department from the company.

In Japan, there is a trend toward creating small but strategic functions where HRM partners top management in achieving business objectives. This trend is seen in many industries. These functions handle organizational design, organizational development, employee communications, labor planning, workforce distribution, and HRM cost management, among others. These strategic departments also often use third-party consulting firms to do such work, a move that wasn't popular 10 years ago.

NEW THINKING FOR HRM IN JAPAN INC.

To avoid further failures in HRM reform programs, it is essential for companies to take a holistic view, as well as to take a step back in time. This requires that we merge some of the best elements that Japan had in its former employee–employer contracts with pragmatic modern-day tools.

Some questions HRM must ask include: How can we bring back loyalty and commitment with our pay strategies? How can we provide coaching to get top performance? How can we capitalize on employees' penchant for team work by rewarding group effort? What systems do we have in place to develop our next generation of leaders.

HRM programs in Japan cannot be instituted without the following:

- *Involvement of all layers* – from top management and line managers to general staff. It is particularly important in any HRM reform to understand the culture of the organization and the group dynamics. The average Japanese knows of generations of employees who paid the price for an old social contract that was torn to shreds when business pressures mounted. Their immediate concern would be – why trust the management at all.

- *Adapting a change program that is pragmatic* – Although there is the onus to introduce HRM change programs, outright adoption of new HRM administration systems may not be the best path. Consider whether the company is ready for change, and then consider in what quantum the changes need to be introduced.

- *Adapting a system that features short-term rewards as well as long-term goals* – Loyalty is a virtue most organizations need more of. Japan has a lot to teach the world about this. HRM should develop a system that focuses on short-term rewards in compensation with longer term development programs focused on career development and career paths. Restoring the shattered faith in the employer–employee relationship is important in the Japanese context.

- *Creating a new generation of leaders* – Leadership development programs are critical for Japanese organizations. The new economy requires a combination of risk-takers, strategists, and executors. Japanese organizations need to develop a ready pool of executives who can take on risk-taking and strategy development. Talent management and performance management programs will become critical to ensure that organizations have a ready pool of resources able to take on the innovation and strategic position Japanese industries need.

CONCLUSION

Our view is that forcing reforms based on the new dictum – rewards will be based on how one performs – cannot be successful without a complete overhaul of the HRM system. The old dictum of "do and you will be rewarded" is still embedded in the psyches of workers for over half a century.

The old employer–employee contract was insufficient to drive high-performing organizations, leading to Japanese productivity trailing behind other industrialized countries. With structural changes in the world economy shifting production, distribution, and marketing processes, Japanese corporations had no alternative but change. Organization reforms have been mostly done hurriedly and with few success stories. Things have come to a crossroad.

From our point of view, it will be risky to hurry when adopting any new HRM systems, including performance-based criteria. Why? Shifting to this new logic for the Japanese workforce would require that every bit of the old system be removed. The task is colossal. It requires a complete overhaul of the "Japanese mindset." It requires a complete retooling of every part of the Japanese human resources structure as we know it. The backdrop to this is Japan Inc. Our view is that HRM restructuring has not achieved much because the process is flawed. Unless organizations begin to put emphasis on building the sub-systems to support the HRM framework, the success could be limited while the effects could do more harm than good.

Companies operating in Japan or Japanese companies looking at reshaping their human assets have to view new systems in the context of the local business environment, the profile of the workforce, and the management's commitment to change. Once the groundwork is set, top management has to adopt at least a "mid-term vision" of implementing the changes, with a well-articulated communication plan for workers, and an early warning system to tell of failures.

Japan's restructuring cannot wait because of the tide of globalization. Japanese industries that are no longer competitive have no choice but to reconfigure themselves. This involves structural changes that Japan is still grappling with. On one end of the spectrum, there are already highly successful global Japanese organizations such as Sony, Honda, Canon, and Nikon that have consistently led the world in innovation in many ways – in technology, production efficiency and marketing, and distribution innovation. On the other end are weak organizations protected by anti-competitive rules and organizations dominated by a culture that forms barriers to efficiency. Japan's business competitiveness at the micro-level and its business environment ranking are among the lowest in the industrialized world.[9]

So what about lifetime employment in Japan? Is it going or gone for good? Competitiveness guru Michael Porter said in an interview with the Harvard Business School Journal that the notion underlying lifetime employment is a good one, but in Japan, that has been taken to the extreme. "Japan should try to preserve its view of employees as assets to be nurtured and developed. However, this does not mean that the job has to be for life, and that individual employee performance cannot be rewarded. I think it is a matter of a 25-percent correction rather than throwing out the whole idea,"[10] he said.

There is a new Japan in the making. Japanese enterprises are already competing aggressively in the global market. Closer to home, mergers and acquisitions, and the restructuring of the Japanese economy, will cause irreversible shifts in personnel or HRM.

Japanese organizations may have to focus more on cultivating the spirit of diligence it can be so proud of. Japanese organizations have other strong virtues in personnel training philosophies, such as the "Jiko-Keihatu" (which means self-development, self-education, self-actualization, and creative actions), which can equate to individual innovation, or a humanitarian approach to managing people such as that demonstrated by the founder of Matsushita, Konosuke Matsushita.[11]

Adapting the good parts of Japan's personnel management philosophies and making them a pivotal part of today's HRM could be a sensible way forward. Increasingly, the onus will be for HRM to pay close attention to getting a right blend of what has worked for Japan, and what will work for Japan.

There is no turning back on the tide of reforms. Perhaps Japan Inc. today, much like its famous children's cartoon character Nobita Nobi and his magical robot cat Doraemon, can always make the right decisions when it really matters. This is particularly important in shaping tomorrow's HRM.

[1] "Rethinking Asia: Is Japan Doomed?" Michael Alan Hamlin, *Far Eastern Economic Review,* June 3, 1999

[2] "Rethinking Asia: Is Japan Doomed?" Michael Alan Hamlin, *Far Eastern Economic Review,* June 3, 1999

[3] "Tokyo Focuses on Colour Televisions," Tracy Dahlby, *Far Eastern Economic Review,* April 8, 1977

[4] "The Japanese Banker They Love to Hate," Business Column from the Canadian Broadcasting Corporation Website <http://cbc.ca/business/indepth/japan3.html>

[5] McKinsey Global Institute: "Why the Japanese Economy is Not Growing," <http://www.mckinsey.com/knowledge/mgi/Japan/>

[6] "For Japan Inc., Company Rosters that Never Die,", Andrew Pollack, New York Times, 1993., <http://research.yale.edu/wwkelly/restricted/Japan_journalism/NYT_930908.htm>

[7] *IMD World Competitiveness Yearbook 2003,* sourced from IMD website, <http://www.imd.ch/documents/wcy/content/be.pdf/>

[8] Harvard Business School Working Knowledge website article: "Can Japan Compete?" (Part Two), Martha Lagace and Hilah Geer, January 8, 2001. Harvard Business Journal Website: Interview

[9] "Building the Microeconomic Foundations of Prosperity: Findings from the Microeconomic Competitiveness Index," Michael E. Porter, Harvard University. This chapter was sourced from Building the Microeconomic Foundations of Prosperity: Findings from the Microeconomic Competitiveness Index, Michael E. Porter, Harvard University.

[10] Lagace and Geer 2001

[11] Reference to Konosuke Matsushita's philosophy is based on the information found on Matsushita Electric's corporate website: <http://matsushita.co.jp/corp/company/person/en/index.html>, <http://matsushita.co.jp/corp/company/person/en/index.htm>

CHAPTER

6

Paths for Developing Countries: Getting HRM Ready for China

Guo Xin, Lu Qiang, Richard Wen, Cindy Yi and Laurel Qin

---

*S*ome 50 years ago, the world dreamt of China as a market filled with a billion consumers. Today, China has fulfilled part of the world's dream and more. Its great ascent into the rank of economic powerhouses has made it the largest exporter of footwear, textiles, and toys. It is already the world's single largest cellular phone market, with 200 million subscribers. Economists forecast that China will become an economic powerhouse within 10 years from 2001. By 2011 China could contribute almost 2 percent to world growth, most of this due to growing world trade. China's market is bigger than ever. With a population of 1.3 billion, it has a market size almost twice the European Union and the United States combined.[1]

Economists forecast that China will become an economic powerhouse within 10 years from 2001. Whether China can eventually catapult itself into Asia's rich list depends on how well it manages its economic transformation. Part of this transformation involves the remaking of China's human resource management from one that is centrally led, to one dictated by the imperatives of a globalized market. China's demand for talent has accelerated in line with the globalization of Chinese enterprises. This has put pressure on Chinese state-owned enterprises and privately owned enterprises to provide human resource policies that can attract and retain talent from not only China but all over the world.

The economic development in China is accompanied by the need for organizational and HRM transformation. From cottage industries to private enterprises, from a communist-style chain of command to entrepreneurial entities, there are many facets of how human resources need to be managed to get the best results.

We show that given the historical context which China has emerged from, and myriad development stages of China's business entities, there is no one-size-fits-all solution to human resource transformation. HRM, as we see it in China, is a product of the history of the country's market reforms following decades of communist control.

The solutions for HRM in China can thus range from the basic to the complex, depending on which organization we are dealing with. Sophisticated tools and systems can be adopted only at companies that are ready for full-scale metamorphosis. HRM transformation is taking place in China, but on its own terms. Wholesale adoption of systems from outside may be counterproductive in many cases, as our case study illustrates.

FROM ANCIENT MARINER TO ACCELERATED ECONOMIC GROWTH

Ancient China was a land of fables and myths. It was a land of peerless civilization during its time, so much so that when Marco Polo related his travel tales of how magnificent China was, his fellow citizens did not believe him and thought him to be a supreme storyteller. His priest asked Marco Polo at his deathbed if he would admit his stories were false. Instead, Marco Polo replied, "I do not tell half of what I saw because no one would have believed me."[2]

Massive Chinese maritime expeditions powered by 500-foot Chinese junks plied the Indian Oceans, Persian Gulf, Eastern Coast of Africa, and Southeast Asia, led by China's Muslim naval commander Admiral Zheng He. This was the civilization that China was – far ahead of what was available in Europe. China's maritime prowess ended with self-imposed isolation by the early 1500s. A series of historical events would put China through a rollercoaster ride of imperial rule, Chinese Communist Party rule, and the reforms that paved the way for today's industrial prowess.

On the one end, China's superior economic growth trajectory has attracted much foreign direct investments and every multinational wants a piece of the economic action. On the other end, skeptics warn of a China waiting to implode. A large part of China's economic achievements have been made over the last 25 years. China's entry into the World Trade Organization (WTO) in 2001 is seen by the world as a great catalyst for the much-awaited liberalization of the Chinese market. Goldman Sachs expects membership of the WTO to boost Chinese foreign trade by US$800 billion every year to 2005.

Despite China's gain in the economic pie, it remains a "poor" part of Asia indicated by its low per capital gross domestic production. Out of 10 Asian countries, China's GDP per capita is third from the bottom, just ahead of Indonesia and India. Labor productivity, measured by the valued-added per worker, points to Chinese enterprises lagging behind foreign-owned companies. According to a research paper from Université d'Auvergne's Yu Chen and Sylvie Démurger on foreign direct investment and manufacturing productivity in China, labor productivity of foreign-invested enterprises in the consumer, intermediate, and equipment goods industry is between 1.59 and 4.68 times that of township-owned and state-owned enterprises. The authors noted that the foreign-invested enterprise's higher productivity could reveal the major role of foreign managerial practices to encourage employees' at work.[3]

The stakes are high in China. From local Chinese-owned enterprises, to multinationals/joint ventures, and state-owned enterprises, the challenge is to add value for the organization through effective management of its resources. How to move from the US$853 GDP per capita to US$2,000? Is China a talent magnet or will talent drain from it? How can organizations in China effectively manage their human resources or human capital to drive organizational performance?

In this chapter we will look at some of these issues. We will look at the history that enveloped the development of Chinese-owned enterprises. What is the state of HRM in China, and what are some of the successes or failures of several models currently used in joint ventures between local and foreign-owned companies. How can HRM play its role in the economic dynamo that is China today? What are the lessons China must learn, or unlearn to get ahead?

GREAT LEAP FORWARD

China's economy made its great "leap forward" in the beginning of the Chinese Communist Party's open door policies in 1978. The gradual or incremental approach to reform laid the groundwork for institutional reform focused on developing new systems outside the old ones, resulting in the development of dynamic non-state sectors. These non-state sectors consist of community-owned/townships and village enterprises, joint ventures, shareholding companies, private firms, and self-employed businesses. Among these, the private enterprises are performing an increasingly important role in China's economic structure.

PRIVATE-SECTOR DEVELOPMENT: REFORMS IN SMALL STEPS

China moved from a period of a centrally planned economy (1957–1978) to a period of reform without a well-defined strategy or clear blueprint. To borrow a phrase from the chief architect of China's reform, Deng Xiaoping, the reform process was like "crossing the river by groping the stones under the water." Reform happened, first in the late 1970s, with the appearance of a household responsibility system where large collectives were broken up into smaller units, and the emergence of township and village enterprises (TVEs) in the second half of the 1980s.

> **To borrow a phrase from the chief architect of China's reform, Deng Xiaoping, the reform process was like "crossing the river by groping the stones under the water."**

The Chinese leaders did not envision the private sector as the driving force of economic growth. So this sector was relegated to the fringes of the economy and was tolerated in areas where large-scale state enterprises did not exist, such as services, light industries, and agriculture.

In October 1993, in another major ideological shift, the Central Committee of the Chinese Communist Party announced further reforms. It announced that non-state sectors were now able to develop along the state sectors, and it also allowed the sale of state assets. This paved the way for the transformation of non-strategic state-owned enterprises and collectives into private enterprises.

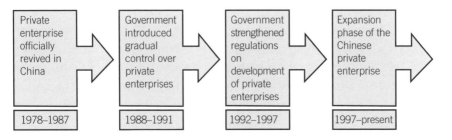

Exhibit 6.1 Birth of the modern Chinese private enterprise

During the early revival phase of the Chinese enterprise, private companies were limited to individual businesses in the transportation, retailing, and crafts sectors. These businesses, called the *getihu*, focused on survival and held weak positions in the political and economic chain. Larger firms grew out of these small ones, out of collectives, and also state-owned enterprises (SOEs). Some private firms had to pay an "administration fee" to the state or collective unit to get registration, earning them the name "red hat firms." But their businesses were manual and relied on simple machinery. Many of these entrepreneurs were farmers, artisans, workers from SOEs, and officials from governments. HRM was a low priority. Employees were usually a trusted set of friends and an extended family.

Between 1988 and 1991, the government focused on the introduction of a series of policies and regulations to control the businesses, hygiene, and product quality. In June 1988, the State Council issued what was called the Tentative Stipulation on Private Enterprises (TSPE) to govern the registration and management of private firms. It was here that the definition of a "for-profit" organization was stipulated. At this stage, private enterprises were constrained by a lack of capital and raw materials.

What followed was a period of expansion. In 1992 Deng Xiaoping paid a visit to the South and made a speech, in which he pointed out that China's reform should be "bold and faster," and that development was the most important indicator. China's economic reform tide soon turned into an avalanche, bringing unstoppable changes to the economy.

By March 1999, private ownership and the rule of the law were incorporated into China's constitution. At the landmark fifteenth Chinese Communist Party congress, president Jiang Zeming pronounced that "the private enterprise is an important component of the socialist market economy."

Despite operating under a period of political, legal, and regulatory uncertainty, the private sector quickly became an economic dynamo. By 1998, the private sector had grown to about a third of China's gross domestic product. In contrast, the SOEs faced a period of stagnation.

Since then, the private enterprise has been experiencing a rapid pace of development. It was during this expansionary phase of China's private enterprise development that the concept of shareholding restructuring and internal management improvements took off.

WHAT SHAPED HUMAN RESOURCE MANAGEMENT IN CHINA'S PRIVATE ENTERPRISES

> " There are only things unimaginable, but nothing is impossible. "
>
> A OLD CHINESE SAYING

Within 20 years, Chinese private entrepreneurs have completed the capital accumulation of billions of dollars from scratch. It was a transformation unimaginable to many. From the rice paddies to tall skyscrapers; from a diet of millet and rice to sushi, steak, Starbucks, and McDonalds – within a decade, China's GDP per capita had risen 168 percent. During this same period, India's GDP per capita grew 32 percent, Indonesia's 20 percent, Thailand's 33 percent, and the Philippines, 7 percent.[4]

The first generation of private entrepreneurs in China focused most of their energies on cultivating closer links with the bureaucracy, and operated under a highly formal environment. Some would say they were not real entrepreneurs or *qiyejia* and can only be called *qiyezhu* – or someone who has successfully utilized the market economy in the transitional economy.

Chinese entrepreneurs can be divided into three segments: one segment comprises farmers and owners of TVEs. The second segment is made up of owners of individual businesses, *getihu*, and the third segment includes those who are well educated and have very successful professional working experiences, such as intellectuals, overseas returnees, and white-collar workers.

The background and personal style of the entrepreneurs dictate human resource management in the private enterprises in China. A Chinese enterprise's corporate and cultural values are very much shaped by the owner. In China's case, family-owned enterprises are often businesses run by family members. The Chinese place a lot of value on the glorification of the family name. In a Confucian society, full trust is reserved for family members. Historically, it is quite usual to find that a company's growth ends when a Chinese entrepreneur runs out of sons or sons-in-law, because the family business could not be transferred to an outsider.

Traits associated with the average Chinese entrepreneur

- depends highly on family members to run the operations
- places high trust on family and clan members
- takes high risks and expects high profits
- exercises full decision-making powers
- values low profile
- relies heavily on business instincts and personal charisma
- places great emphasis on financial goals
- pays little heed to "soft" or "people" issues
- usually operates as a "loner" at the top
- likes to be called "big boss" and sees himself as a "king" or "hero".

FEATURE: THE PROFILE OF A CHINESE ENTREPRENEUR

The conventional picture of a Chinese entrepreneur is his sharp business acumen but slack people touch. Given that most family-owned enterprises have a strong "patriarch" or founder, most initiatives and decisions are made by the founder owner.

Typical traits of an employee in a family-owned business

- the employee is usually someone trusted by the owner
- the employee is often committed to the goals of the enterprise
- a trusted employee has a high chance of running the organization someday
- the employee takes instructions more than makes decisions
- the employee who has little trust of the owner also has a limited chance of moving up
- the employee who has little trust in the owner is a pure pen-pusher

PROFILE OF A TYPICAL EMPLOYEE AT A FAMILY-OWNED ENTERPRISE

Given that employees who work for family-owned enterprises usually have a strong sense of loyalty to the "master" owner, the goal is usually to work the way up the ladder to the inner circle of the trusted people. There is an inherent flaw in this system – it operates much like the court eunuchs, fighting for the emperor's attention and trust. In the end, empires crumble due to the cloak and dagger environment surrounding Chinese dynasties. History repeats itself in a similar manner in modern-day enterprises that have their root in a family dynasty.

Modern management schools have been consistently right about one thing – winning companies succeed because they have leaders not only at the top but also across the organization. Chinese companies have been slow to internalize this point of view. It is not surprising to find that Chinese companies barely make it after the expansionary phase.

However, many Chinese-owned organizations have come to the juncture where they have to make some dramatic shifts in the way they view their management process to cross over from the start-up phase into an expansionary phase. Unless they start crossing the great divide between running a business like an "empire," to one that is professionally managed, there is scant hope the business will survive the competition that is ahead. There is now a demand for leadership and talent management programs within organizations to help businesses meet the onslaught of competition. The ability to succeed will decide whether China can become a global player or a backyard for other global manufacturers to make cheap products.

At the moment, most of the private firms in China are small-sized and produce similar low-grade products. They are competing with each other due to low investments and backward technology being employed. The businesses and industries that private-sector companies are involved in are faced with severe competition, and most of these industries are labor-intensive. Over 60 percent of Chinese private enterprises are involved in these three sectors: manufacturing, retail, and services. Most of these firms lack technology innovation and long-term investment. Their major mode of competition is to cut prices. Professor Peng Jianfeng from the Chinese Renming University pointed out that Chinese private enterprise will soon be squeezed at the low-end of the whole value chain, producing thin profits.[5]

Over the near to medium term, Chinese private enterprises may be under further profit pressure as they continue to cut prices to keep pace with competition. This is not a long-term option. As these organizations strive to move up the value chain, more demands will be made on them to improve profits by making better products using better technology and better market distributions, among others. Major investments will be needed in the human capital arena.

MANAGEMENT STYLES: CONFUCIUS VERSUS JACK WELCH

Social historian Francis Fukuyama (1995) is of the view that Chinese family businesses are unlikely to become global, as Chinese entrepreneurs are deeply rooted in philosophical traditions, making it difficult for the Chinese to enter into a structured and professional management style in a Western sense.

Chinese family-owned companies avoid delegation of duties and tasks whenever they can. This is due, in part, to the weak regulatory enforcement environment where private owners find it difficult to protect intellectual property rights and commercial secrets. Owners of companies often do not entrust employees with technology or commercial secrets for fear these might walk out of the door the minute the employee leaves. Private entrepreneurs also prefer family members to run their business for fear of employees walking out to set up their own business once they have the relative experience and resources. There is a Chinese saying that reflects this aspiration: "I would like to be the head of a cockerel rather than the tail of a phoenix."

There is a tendency for privately run companies to have on board members of their own family in the management structure. As for internal management, the Board of Directors often controls the most important decisions in a firm. In particular, corporations do not delegate more, but less power to managers even in publicly listed firms. Most CEOs are themselves owners, and family members occupy many important management positions. In such organizations, it is often difficult to implement a systematic human resource management system without running into difficulties with the CEOs unless the CEOs are champions of the change process.

As Chinese enterprises grow beyond their start-up phase, they will be faced with a constant need to renew, draw, and retain talent. The average employee in the Chinese-owned enterprise is in his early 20s or 30s, while the average Chinese entrepreneur owner is in his early 40s or 50s. According to a poll done on *Chinese Fortune 100*, the average age of China's most influential and richest entrepreneurs is 45. As startup firms grow in size, their entrepreneurs and investors often find it hard to keep up with the skills needed to manage the firm. The challenge arises as to where to place the old people while bringing new people into the management teams. This is where the struggle takes place between trust and capability in the organization.

There is increasing awareness among Chinese organizations of the need to implement new management processes. But there is also a general view that you can't adopt a ready Western model, but adapt one to suite the local culture and situation. In some organizations, there is a strong commitment to change but the process may be lengthy due to the need to internalize the new process.

HRM CHALLENGES IN THE STARTUP PHASE

In the startup phase of the business, entrepreneurs concentrate their resources on sales, revenue, and profit. Their sole purpose is to make money and survive the startup years. Entrepreneurs are the sole decision-makers concerning business strategy and resource allocation. In such a situation, entrepreneurs are responsible for personnel management, including the selection of employees, simple payroll management, and task allocation. Their main focus is to retain key individuals who either have client resources or technical expertise. Their employees would be mainly family members, relatives, classmates, or former colleagues – hired less for their capabilities than their trustworthiness. For these employees, the most powerful incentive is the prospect of the business and the commitment of the boss. The corporate value is the entrepreneur's personal values, and the organizational model is one based on paternalism or *jiazhangzhi*. There is hardly any training for employees – there are often no resources available. People are usually committed to their work, based on loyalty to the boss and personal commitment to the work. During this phase, the decision-making system is very simple, mostly based on intuition according to the owner's experiences and judgment. There is no formal accounting, finance, or formal HRM structure.

Data shows that the average age of Chinese private companies today is 2.9 years. By the third year, most have gone bust. The first 2.5 years are spent establishing and building the business.[6]

CAPITAL ACCUMULATION PHASE:
A FORM OF HRM IN THE MAKING

At the capital accumulation phase, the private firm would usually have dozens or hundreds of employees. It has now become impossible for the entrepreneur to take care of all the business operations or to allocate tasks. The entrepreneur is now under pressure to establish an organizational structure and to delegate some of the allocation powers. The HRM (or personnel management) function is usually handed over to somebody the entrepreneur trusts, usually a family member or a long-term friend. The personnel function is always combined with another administrative function that translates into what is called a "comprehensive department." Only one or two people would be responsible for recruitment, payroll, and personnel record-keeping. The entrepreneur directly controls the sensitive and key functions such as compensation and personnel adjustments (promotion, demotion, and internal transfer).

These types of HRM departments handle the basic personnel management of the people and maintain simple policies. They play an administrative role and have little business perspective. In many private enterprises, the manager for personnel management does not report to the general manager. In others, there is a vice-president responsible for all administrative work, including HRM.

HRM is at best a record and attendance-keeper in many of these Chinese enterprises. It has no formal communication with the business owner, and is sometimes not involved in the crucial selection or employee-screening process. It is common to find the business departments making selection and recruitment decisions. At the end of the day, HRM is merely there to complete the administrative procedures.

Another feature of HRM during this phase is that many practices are dealt with according to the whims of the person in charge, often with little attention paid to the management framework or relevant regulations. For example, one company has this on the staff notice board: "All employees should attend the meeting at 10 am this Sunday. No one is permitted to ask for a leave. Bonus will be deducted for anyone who is absent." Owners often flout Labor Law regulations by asking employees to do excessive overtime hours or hold meetings over weekends.

The demand for highly skilled employees is forcing changes on HRM among Chinese enterprises. As Chinese companies compete with the multinationals operating in China, there is a heightened sense of awareness that business strategy supported by talent and skills will dictate whether a company survives the competition. Companies are increasingly becoming aware of the need for new knowledge and skills among their employees. One company we know of, DiRui Biology, makes it a requirement for managers to have an MBA to expand their knowledge in management issues.

The demand for talent in China is acute. Entrepreneurs often find it easier to recruit people with hands-on experience to run their operations. Recently, private owners have been prepared to pay very high salaries, in millions of renmenbi, to attract *nengren* or talent. But often, these companies have no effective recruitment or assessment tools to evaluate a candidate's competencies. This practice is consistent with the owners' eagerness for quick success and instant benefits. It is not difficult to see why this can be problematic because of the mismatch between the skills demanded and the jobs people are being slotted into. And once inside the company, there are no internal systems to evaluate the performance for effective compensation. There is also no training system to provide new skills for employees.

EXPANSION PHASE: COMPETING FOR BRAINPOWER

A few big players and many small survivors dot the Chinese private enterprise landscape after the capital accumulation stage and after the so-called "first carve out" stage. In the second stage, these survivors face new intensity in market competition, decreased product margins and capital acquisition challenges. Entrepreneurs, eager to fund their business from public listing on the stock exchanges, are forced to look at internal management issues that they have neglected in the first two stages of their business lifecycle. A part of the internal management review process is to improve their human resource management.

As the businesses grow more diverse, the complexity of the organizational structure increases, accompanied by new demands for more skilled resources to sustain the company. This places the onus on management to beef up recruitment, assessment, compensation, and retention tools for employees.

We have come across many companies which have focused on new HRM systems as part of the organizational metamorphosis. Among them are high-tech companies such as Huawei, UFSOFT, and Legend – companies that have carved leadership roles in their businesses. High-tech companies have been keen users of incentive schemes to retain their key employees. Legend and Stone announced their employee stockholding plans in 1999, all with preference for their core personnel. Legend focused its plan on solving the ownership issue as well as laying the "golden step" – the exit strategy for the entrepreneurs. For these high-tech companies, the focus on retention schemes has been crucial to retaining their core personnel.

When HRM becomes the bottleneck

HRM becomes pivotal to an organization's success during the expansion phase. During the startup phase, private firms are usually desperate for capital and new markets. Often, in high-tech companies, top management comes from R&D and marketing; hence, there is an unconscious prejudice in value orientation leading to "advantageous" departments such as marketing and R&D, and "disadvantageous" departments such as HRM. It is not uncommon that many private firms, even those successful ones, have weak HRM, causing disparity in the organizational development and a bottleneck in the firm's operations. Furthermore, these organizations need to transit from being governed by "person" to one governed by "rules" and "culture." Once organizations pass their startup and expansionary phase, the entrepreneur's vision needs to be accompanied by a set of behavioral codes governing the corporation's business conduct. The company's shared values and missions will become critical, and so is the communication of this to employees. It is in this area where HRM plays a fundamental role in setting the groundwork, implementing the system, and monitoring the outcomes.

BATTLE BETWEEN CHINESE ENTERPRISES AND MULTINATIONALS

The avalanche of multinationals flooding the Chinese market in search of a cheaper means to produce goods and services has exerted pressure on Chinese companies to compete in ways they have never had to. On one end of the production chain, the competition is to be the one who can produce the cheapest goods in the shortest time. China is being used as a factory for cheap production. On the high end, it is the multinationals and Chinese companies competing for an increasingly sophisticated Chinese consumer market. The tussle for market dominance has impacted on HRM practices in both sets of companies. At the multinational level, the wholesale introduction of HRM practices and systems can have a disastrous impact on the business. At the lower end of the chain, companies have to set the system in place to continue getting the most dollars out of their investment in machinery. Some Chinese enterprises have already had a certain degree of success lifting their game to compete in foreign and global markets. A good example is the Haier Group, which makes more than 80 products ranging from white goods to cell phones and televisions. It sells into 160 countries and has 13 factories outside China. It can develop and bring a product to market in a span of five or six months. The same goes for one of China's largest mobile phone producers, TCL International Holdings. TCL uses chipsets designed by France's Wavecom. According to the *Far Eastern Economic Review*, companies such as TCL are able to bring products to market quickly, in as little as six months, by leaving the heavy engineering to other companies and working chiefly on the look and feel of a phone (such as user-friendly screen displays and menu content). Compare that, say, to Nokia, which takes a year or two to design a new model from basic circuitry up. China's rise to economic stardom may not necessarily be traveling the same trajectory as Japan – imitate, rebundle, and later reengineer – but the time cycles are much more compressed and the learning curve much sharper and more intense. This is the global scene China has to compete in.

There is no doubt that these Chinese enterprises with global ambitions will be fast adopters of contemporary and practical HRM best practices. There is a sense of urgency and companies looking for HRM systems tend to want it in a hurry.

The following case study shows how MNCs operating in China often wrongly assume that what works in the West can be adopted wholesale in China. This illustrates why it pays for MNCs to view their China operations as a marketplace with unique local characteristics and that changes need to be made with care.

A MNC in a hurry for profits in China

In 1995 I was a human resource manager in a beverage company in Guangzhou, China, which was a Sino–US joint venture. Its parent company is one of the largest fast-moving consumer goods companies in the world.

Before 1995, the Chinese partner managed the company. It was very profitable but it was managed in the traditional Chinese way – heavy in administrative staff; the Chinese Communist Party played an important role in the operation; and party officials' relatives ran the place while the general manager made all the decisions.

The mistake the US partner made was that it cared about profits more than building a lasting business. In its hurry to ensure it could return profits to the shareholders, the US partner guaranteed the Chinese partner a certain amount of profit and took over the entire operation.

The new general manager (GM) arrived, the new function heads arrived, a team of sales managers and sales men arrived, all from United States, Hong Kong, and Southeast Asia. They wanted to make the Guangzhou operation a model plant and a model market in China. One of the first things the new GM did was to try and remove the unions, thinking the union would stir trouble. Little did he understand that unions in China perform a different role from those seen in other countries. In China, unions organize recreational activities for employees, and from time to time, provide help to those who may run into difficulties that could affect their work life. Unions in China try to maximize the benefits for employees, but tend not to organize strikes or activities against their employers.

The new management soon found out that things would not be as easy as it perceived. Because of the language and cultural differences, management found it hard to communicate with the local staff and the local clients. Even a simple exercise such as the restructuring of salary, based on market practices, was misunderstood by the employees because of language, cultural differences, and poor communication. Because the local market is quite different from the United States and even Southeast Asia, management found selling the "American" way to be very difficult in China. It eventually ended up with a loss because of the high relocation cost for staff, among others.

The new management was forced to send the sales team back to United States and Southeast Asia, and recruited replacements from other multinational companies operating in China. It sent back the function heads to their countries of origin. It hired a local assistant general manager and trained him to replace the GM from the United States.

Two years later, all key positions were localized. The locals operated in a way that merged Western and Chinese management values.

Increasingly, multinationals in joint ventures with Chinese partners are localizing their middle and senior management teams. Expatriates are still brought in, although their packages have been trimmed compared to levels they commanded five years ago, and the number of expatriates brought in has been falling. Hardship allowances for these expatriates have also been less popular as China's coastal cities demonstrate a rise in the quality of living. These days, Chinese employees with the right skills are being promoted to regional management roles. Another trend is a rise in the number of Hong Kong and Taiwan expatriates in China – a crop of people who have the advantage of bilingual skills and exposure to the Western world.

Based on conversations with a former employee of this Company

At Chinese enterprises, the eagerness to compete with multinationals in terms of the adoption of modern HRM tools and management systems may not necessarily go down well in the absence of a complete set of tools to manage the entire process – from business strategy to measuring the business outcomes.

Modern management systems may not be easily absorbed by a segment of China that is still grappling with the crossover from codes of behavior based on rural lifestyles to a manufacturing environment. Consider this: a typical private enterprise in China may be staffed by two groups of employees – one comprising local people and one from the rural areas. China has a system of permanent registry which makes it difficult for the internal migrant population to work in other places due to restrictions on social insurance, children's education, and personal credit. Employers of private companies love this category of people because they offer cheap labor. Using this group of workers has its downside as one Beijing company found.

A Beijing telecommunications equipment manufacturing company hired over 100 rural migrants from a village in Hebei province to do the packaging and conveying work. But when the company tried to introduce the 5S management – a workflow process system – to improve the product quality, these rural workers were unable to accept the system and were highly uncomfortable with it, leading to production interruptions and productivity loss.

In some cases, these rural employees join and leave the company as a group. Private enterprises in China are often caught in the tussle between finding the cheapest labor per head, and getting the most out of the labor quality to achieve good products. Among these companies there is already awareness that training and retooling employees with skills are important facets in their management growth. Providing equitable compensation to workers is also becoming more important as companies strive to retain a shifting working population.

Many Chinese organizations that we have come across, in their eagerness to import HRM practices, have made superficial name changes, calling their personnel departments, human resources departments. In fact, the roles and responsibilities of these HRM departments are limited. Often, they are part of, or an extension of the administration function, rather than a strategic part of the business operation.

HUNT FOR TALENT, HUNT FOR HRM SYSTEMS

Talent acquisition and retention is a major issue for Chinese enterprises. But there is a tendency among Chinese companies to consider talent acquisition as the "end" rather than a means to an end. The competition emerging in China now between Chinese enterprises and multinationals is far more complex – one based on two systems of business ownership styles, and two systems of management and multiple cultural backgrounds.

Among the issues Chinese enterprises have to confront include:
- how does a company extract the best of traditional people management practices that advocates loyalty, trust, and focus;
- how to use, not abuse, the charisma of the entrepreneur to the advantage of the organization;
- how to select the right people based on their competencies;
- how to develop leaders;
- how to develop professional managers; and
- how to measure the investments made in human resources.

Successfully managing all these issues will decide whether the Chinese enterprise can cross the chasm from being a local to a global player, and from being a low-end to a high-end producer.

Currently, there is a tendency among many private enterprises to be wild about HRM tools, including job descriptions, job evaluations, talent-testing, and performance appraisal systems. Can these tools solve all the problems and reach the desired targets once they are in place? The target of strategic HRM is to support and realize an organization's business goals. Human resource management itself is a management system with different inter-influencing functions. It is part of a whole management system. When we conduct HRM consulting, our clients from the private sector always ask the question, "How can we build some measurable indicators to evaluate the performance of employees?" But the ironic thing is that most often than not, the CEO has no clear business strategy or cannot articulate a clear business strategy. The CEO also wants the appraisal system to be applied to the ordinary employees but not to him or her, or the top management. Under such situations, even the most advanced HRM tools cannot improve the organization's performance.

One good example is from HuaWei, one of the most distinguished high-tech corporations in China. The company has set up its corporate development strategy based on a policy translated as "Huawei Corporate Fundamental Law." This strategy covers the company's product and technology policy, its organization establishment principle, and HRM and development policy. One of its core values is: "The target of increasing the value of human capital will take precedence over that of improving financial status." In this corporate document, there are many innovative concepts created, including people management concepts, the setting up of an internal talent market, and employee ownership and management's HRM responsibility. HuaWei demonstrates a crop of emerging Chinese companies that are adopting business and HRM in a systematic framework.

There are also those who take a strategic view of their talent development. One such company is a software company in China that we recently did a project for. Its owners realized that to catapult it into the next phase of corporate growth, it needed a talent and competency framework to guide its human resource development.

SOES: SLOUCHING TIGERS, INEFFECTIVE HRM

" Cadres can go up but not down, employees can walk in but cannot get out.

A CHINESE SAYING

SOEs in China hold the lion's share of important sectors in the local economy such as energy, chemical, telecom, water conservancy, transportation, logistics, mining, heavy industries, and large commercial enterprises. Because SOEs have operated for a long time, they managed to attract the top skills during China's pre-reform days. Pressure from competition has forced SOEs to adopt more contemporary management techniques.

The SOEs receive their authority from the government; hence, importance decisions in operational and functional matters are always referred back to the government. Communist Party Secretaries often hold important functions in the SOEs. The Communist Party hunts for "top talent" when they recruit members. Their top talent usually ends up becoming managers and executives. Within the SOEs, there are always two classes of workers – one is reserved for cadres, and the other is the general worker who can be either white- or blue-collar. The Communist Party develops its members from these two categories of workers. However, there is a movement within some SOEs to eliminate this division between cadres and other workers.

FUZZY ROLES

Some SOEs are also beginning to combine the roles of the general manager and Party Secretary, while others have drawn sharper lines to demarcate the areas of responsibilities between the two. One major characteristic of the SOE is that some employees' full-time responsibilities consist of organizing the Party's activities. Since the wave of SOE reforms began, there has been pressure to detach politics from within the SOE's business structure. Attempts to merge the roles of the Communist Party's senior members with the other employees will lead to challenges of how to deal with internal equity issues, including pay and issues related to job responsibilities.

The Communist Party's hierarchical structure is often transposed onto SOEs, whereby party members assume key positions in them. In some SOEs there are departments formed solely to manage the party members who usually hold positions as middle or top managers. Other workers who are not a part of this usually have less opportunity to progress to the top manager level. SOEs often do not have clear or accurate job descriptions, so an employee's pay is often not reflective of the position or size of the job.

> " It is the same whatever and however you have done it. "
>
> A CHINESE EMPLOYEE'S PERCEPTION ABOUT WORK

The salary structures in SOEs are very conservative. Prior to 1979 the whole country's SOE salary structure was unified. The salary scale for all SOEs was set at the same rate. The scale has been unchanged for over two decades. After the 1980s the practice was to increase the salary by a percentage based on similar departments across the SOE universe.

The resulting impact is that older employees often have equal if not more salary than the top managers. When we compare the SOE's salary to market data, we often find that the SOEs have the lowest salaries and slowest pay adjustments.

SOEs have no internal HRM tools to evaluate performance for effective compensation. In the better managed companies, there are business unit objectives but no individual performance evaluation. Year-end bonuses are set based on the positions held by the employees. Employees often refer to this Chinese saying: "It is the same whatever and however you have done it."

NOT THE RIGHT EDUCATION BUT THE RIGHT TROOP

There is no career path for employees. Often, the politics of the Party decides who gets to the top. There is a feeling among employees that the right thing to do for the young men in the company is not to get the right education but to be positioned in the right troop. Within some important SOEs, the management has a relatively limited right to transfer key employees, recruit the right people, or lay off poor performers. For most people, the SOEs are like safe havens. The turnover rate is often too low compared to the other companies in China.

For many SOEs, however, status quo is no longer an option. They are under severe competitive pressures from multinationals. There is also a tremendous amount of pressure from the government to trim losses of SOEs. A critical shortage of talent has left many SOEs unable to compete in the increasingly competitive market place.

Although the CEOs of many SOEs are keen to see their businesses succeed, they face tremendous inertia from the upper middle and lower middle management.

WHAT SHOULD SOEs DO?

Here is an example of what a large SOE experienced in China in terms of the erosion of its competitive position, and the subsequent change program it adopted. It woke up one day to realize its market share, formerly protected by state regulations, is under the severe threat of being gobbled up by the competition.

CASE STUDY

A SOE in need of transformation

This company is located in central China. It used to be one of the largest in its industry and has a 20-year history and some 2,000 employees. Its employee size is far larger than a competing private company in the same industry with a comparable revenue. The company's employee structure is complex. The company has enjoyed monopoly status since its inception; hence, the employees were not under pressure to create value for the company.

Since China's entry to the World Trade Organization, it recognizes the need to have an efficient market to maintain the health of the economy. As a result, the government has adopted policies that encourage some SOEs to compete in the marketplace rather than enjoy state protection.

Company A suddenly found its competitor's position improving while its market share was dwindling. What's worse, because the company has lived without any shakeups, it did not have any ideas about how to deal with the competition.

The company first asked a consultant firm to help it define its core competencies – it needed to know what it needed to do to survive in the marketplace. But after having the strategy and structure drawn up, the company realized it didn't have the right people to make things happen. It was unable to retain the people it wanted, while HRM didn't have a clue about attracting outside talent. Over the last two years, the company has had a turnover rate of above 40 percent.

As a consequence of its bad attraction and retention results, the company adopted a "three no-policy" — for recruitment. This comprised: "No graduates from top universities, no recruits from rich families, and no one with any great past achievement." This didn't work. The company had a disastrous impact leading to productivity and morale loss.

The management then asked Mercer for help. They asked us to design a competitive and an equitable compensation program for its employees. But after having in-depth discussions with the company, we discovered what their problems were.

SOLVING THE HRM PUZZLE

Although the company had an organizational structure, there were no clear reporting lines or job descriptions at the departmental level. Staff in various departments had no defined responsibilities and no one had a clear idea of what his or her responsibilities were. The department heads didn't think this was a big issue as long as they could find someone to handle a particular matter when the situation demanded. As a result, there was no ownership. No one took the initiative to handle important tasks, despite knowing the importance of getting a particular job done.

The company did not have the skills to develop a position-grading system, nor did it have the knowledge to measure or evaluate individual performance of staff. The pay structure was transparent and determined by tenure and educational background. Everyone in the same department had almost the same salary. Employees were not motivated to take on new responsibilities. The internal equity was such that a general manager's pay would at most be up to three times that of a junior staff.

The management was focused on the idea of not rocking the boat, so it couldn't see the internal equity and external competitiveness problems the compensation program was causing.

After analysis and discussions with the management, it dawned on the management that the company needed to change or suffer extinction.

We recommended the following:

- the company instills a set of new values, achieved through a top-down communication plan;
- the company pays for position and performance, rather than tenure or education background;
- the company focuses on clarifying and defining key roles and responsibilities – this would help increase efficiency and effectiveness in its operations;
- the company develops a performance-driven system to maximize results from employees;
- the company focuses on optimizing its investments in its pay program to attract and retain the right talent; and
- the company explores new technologies and methods for HRM to improve its professional skills.

For four months, we worked extensively to help the company reorganize its HRM system. The feedback from the company was positive.

The top management found the communication, training, and change management process highly useful. The management felt that it learnt valuable tools and was confident of applying the tools and methodology we imparted.

The company is also beginning to notice a change in the work culture – morale has improved and employees are now more willing to take on new responsibilities because they understood their roles.

▶BUSINESS TIPS FOR HANDLING SOEs

1. Start with a comprehensive communication plan for the change agenda.
2. Be explicit about what needs to be changed; how the change will impact employees.
3. Never start without the support of senior or top management.
4. Flexibility is the key to adopting HRM practices; the new system needs to be adaptable.
5. Never adopt a new HRM system wholesale, it can be disastrous.

TRANSFORMATION

The reforms at SOEs must be done with full HRM restructuring. It begins with education. For the SOEs, change involves more than mindset changes. It involves swapping decades of "how we have always done things" with "how we need to start doing things." The task is Herculean. The CEOs must also have the courage and will to implement and see through the change. Then these CEOs must be able to get buy-in from the mid-level executives to manage the change process.

On the operations front, the most fundamental change needed at the SOEs is knowledge concerning what HRM tools are available. SOEs need to be equipped with the basic methodologies in job descriptions, position evaluations, and how to implement these basics. There is also a need to remove the egalitarian mindset that permeates within the SOEs – that the individual's contribution can be differentiated from the rest, and once that differentiation is in place, the rewards can follow.

One of the critical components in getting HRM right within SOEs is providing the incentive for senior managers to assume the risks required by changing the system. Some SOEs in China are large and there is little autonomy for the subsidiaries to drive the change. If the "head office" or parent company decides to drive any change process, the executives across the organization feel the threat of uncertainty; hence, there is also a battle between status quo and change. Inertia is entrenched within the SOEs. These managers need the right incentive to change.

Getting the right structure, the right skills to move on

Our client is one of China's largest independent IT companies. It was founded in 1988, and its software has a wide following among mid-sized private companies and government agencies. The company was listed on the stock exchange a few years ago.

This software company has had a meteoric rise in the Chinese market, gaining dominance in market position for its myriad products. Originally, the company focused mainly on financial software and it is widely accepted that the company has a leading share of the financial software market in China. As part of its growth strategy, the company started growing its enterprise software business, moving from lower value to the high end of the software market. The organization has some 3,000 people, about 600 of whom are software developers. This growth trajectory presented some interesting challenges for the company, which has undergone rapid transformation. The management was aware that its quest to grow the enterprise resource planning (ERP) business will be stretched by a shortage of skilled and experienced people. It lacked qualified research and development staff, ERP sales personnel, and ERP consultants. It also faced the challenge of recruiting people who had ERP product experience. We helped the company put together a two-part solution. The first focused on the organizational design of the company needed to support its business transformation. The second portion focused on developing a framework to develop the skills and competencies needed for its workforce.

A Mercer Case Study

CONCLUSIONS

China, despite its economic success, is faced with major hurdles in its next development phase. It is under tremendous pressure to move from being a low-value producer of goods and services to being a high-value producer. This puts pressure on companies to improve management and production. We have provided a close look at the different sets of challenges that the private enterprises, the SOEs, and the multinationals face in the current environment.

Within the Chinese private enterprise, the most potent change agent is the CEO or the owner/entrepreneur. At the SOEs, the will to change must come from the government, supported by a blueprint that involves senior and middle managers, as well as the general employee. Multinationals have useful and practical tools for HRM in China, but these may not be immediately applicable. Transformation in HRM processes may need to be paced out and localized to suit the Chinese environment.

The human resource practice is still in its infancy in many organizations in China. Among the larger corporations who are market leaders in their industries, the groundswell for change has started. There is a hunger and strong desire to discard these old models for new ones.

There is increasing awareness among Chinese organizations that there is a need to implement new management processes. But there is also a general view that you can't adopt a ready Western model, but adapt one to suit the local culture and situation. In many ways, change has been painful for those who have tried it. However, there is a strong will to succeed.

There has been an enormous frog leap made in organizational transformation and management practices over the last 10 years. In some places, the foundation that has been laid is weak. We have seen companies that have had to go back to basics, to relay their foundation. It can start with something as simple as a request to do a job description. But there have been times when the job description request just snowballs, with us digging deeper and deeper into the fundamental flaws in the system, specifically in the areas of competencies and skills needed for the organization. The job descriptions cannot be done without organizations understanding what their business goals are, and what competencies they need to acquire to achieve their business goals.

Understanding the needs of the organization is the first step in setting HRM processes in place. HRM has been for too long relegated to payroll and leave administration. For Chinese organizations, and many in Asia, the focus should be on educating HRM, not only in the area of HRM management, but in the area of business management.

These are the five questions HRM must ask in China:

1. Does HRM understand the business goals of the company?
2. Does HRM have top management support to drive changes needed to support business goals?
3. What part of HRM must change within the organization to support the business?
4. Does HRM know how to implement, manage, and communicate the change process?
5. Does HRM have the tools to measure the success/impact of the change?

Within China, there is a belief that "management systems" are people made; hence, they can be adapted to suit the needs of people. There is a certain amount of discipline needed within the organization to adhere to the change agenda. There is also a strong determination within China to adapt and apply a HRM system that incorporates a Chinese view. How this model will evolve remains to be seen.

When Marco Polo told of his wondrous journey to China, none of his fellow Venetians believed him. Before China took on the reform route, very few people believed it would ever open its doors to reform. Can China make the next big leap from a low per-capita country to a high per-capita country within the next 20 years? History has consistently shown that China has immense capacity to innovate. History has also shown that while China turned inward, the world moved on. Catching up in a world that feeds on cutthroat competition leaves little room for mistakes. HRM in China certainly has a critical part to play at this juncture in history.

[1] "China: An economic super power?" Sourced from BBC News Website, Dec. 13, 2001:
<http://news.bbc.co.uk/2/hi/business/1708454.stm>

[2] Marco Polo, *Travels In China, 1275–1292*: North Park University Website:
<http://campus.northpark.edu/history/WebChron/China/MarcoPolo.html>

[3] "Foreign Direct Investment and Manufacturing Productivity in China,": Université d'Auvergne's Yu Chen and Sylvie Demurger.

[4] "Snapshot of Asia Today: Economic Trends and Challenges," Mercer Global Information Services Asia Pacific.

[5] *Beijing Youth*, July 29 Issue, 2002.

[6] "Leading the Charge in China's Private Sector," article sourced from *Hewitt Asia Pacific Quarterly*, vol. 2, Issue 1. This was found on the company's website:
<http://www.hewittasia.com/hewitt/ap/resource/rptspubs/hewittquart/issue5/page37.htm>

7

Path for the Poor – India the Talent Mecca and its HRM Imperative

Sunit Sinha and Nitin Dheer

*T*his is a brief exposition on the growth of the HRM agenda in India
*since before Independence and its current realities in the early years
of the twenty-first century. Given India's unique socio-cultural
milieu, it is imperative to provide this historical perspective. The central
theme of the analysis is talent – the abundance of it has been and remains
a major competitive advantage for India, but it is only in the last decade
that this has been leveraged. The growth of HRM as a discipline has been
linked to the state of the Indian economy. For a long time it was very
stable and slow growing. However, the recent economic liberalization has
unleashed forces that have transformed HRM and its role in many
fundamental ways. Some statistics and case studies illustrate what these
changes are and how they have impacted on business organizations. The
conclusion is inescapable – India has arrived on the global talent market,
but a lot of work remains, especially as it is a very late entrant and has
to work double in order to catch up with more advanced countries.*

INTRODUCTION

Change. Speed. Technology. Complexity. Globalization. Demographics. These are forces so profound they can wipe out or create new industries overnight. As the new century progresses, many in positions of leadership in business, government, or the not-for-profit sector wonder what this dizzying pace of change means for them. Times have changed and the forces that worked within human organizations regarding people, practices, culture, and leadership have become redundant at an ever-increasing pace.

The change processes are further exacerbated by the daunting war for talent. An explosion in technology and knowledge is creating a huge demand. The play of demography is imposing constraints on its availability. Till the closing decades of the last century, engineering and mechanization had the ability to add value by 30 to 40 percent. Going forward, underlying information, and communication technologies have the ability to add value manifold. New vistas of knowledge are being created at an exponential pace. According to some social researchers, the sum of knowledge added in the last 50 years is greater than all the published works in previous human history. The relationship between people and business in the industrial and knowledge age are fundamentally different. These are reflected in recruitment policies and strategies for retaining talent. Factors that would attract talented persons today and what would motivate them to give their best have changed beyond recognition. In the past, the public standing of a company was the magnet, promotions, and increment – the source of motivation and the fear of financial uncertainty – or the glue that bound an efficient hand to the job. In the knowledge age, excitement of the challenges in a job attracts the talented. It is a powerful magnet. The creative and democratic environment – the source of motivation and the opportunity of continuous growth – is the glue that binds the talent to a company. As for the reward, it is the talent that dictates the terms.

Demography affects the availability of talent. Today, one-fifth of the American population is above the age of 60. In 25 years this number will increase to a quarter of the population. Germany is worse off. Roughly, one-quarter of Germans are now elderly and in 25 years one-third of them will be elderly. The case with Japan is very similar

China is better off with one-tenth of its population now and a fifth of its population in 25 years being elderly. All these countries will see a decline in their workforce and talent. The United States is already facing a shortage of skilled professionals. This will further accentuate. Over the next 10 to 15 years the professional workforce shortage in the United States will peak at 15 million. Europe will see a shortfall of a million professionals in information technology alone. Germany is already facing a shortfall of about 200,000 engineers. China is estimated to need upwards of 1.4 million management graduates. Japan, Australia, Malaysia, Singapore, and New Zealand are forecasting large shortages of professional talent. This shortage will last at least till the middle of this century.

Warning bells of talent famine are ringing loud and clear. Far-sightedness demands that business leaders elevate management of talent to a burning corporate priority. It is not a walk in the park for the talent market. Quality people are no longer available in plenty, easy to replace, or inexpensive. There is a key to creating value through talent management. It has to do with HRM being at the heart of business. In this global context, India can consider itself relatively lucky. Just 7 percent of Indians are above the age of 60. In 25 years time only 12 percent will be above 60. India will continue to be young and will see a swelling workforce of scientific, technical, and professional talent.

It is true that India's young people are an enormous reservoir of talent. But someone has to equip, train, motivate, and provide them with opportunities. This casts a huge responsibility on policymakers, educational institutions, and business leaders. People are something India has plenty of. But ask any business leader what the biggest problem is today and the chances are he or she will say it is finding the right people and getting them to work productively. That may sound paradoxical. But the fact is that due to its late start on the road to development and a strong history of union activity, India has traditionally lagged in the systematic development of high-quality talent. There have been a lot of talented professionals around, but Indian organizations have only in the past few decades engaged in a focused effort to develop their talent pool.

THE EVOLUTION AND GROWTH OF THE HUMAN RESOURCES FUNCTION IN INDIA

An understanding of the evolution and growth of the HRM function in India requires a brief background of its modern industrial development. It also requires an appreciation of the related industrial relations environment. Industries, in the modern sense, were set up in the middle of the nineteenth century, mainly by the British traders. Tea plantations, coffee plantations, cotton and jute mills, coal mining, and railways, all based on capitalistic methods of production, were started in the mid-nineteenth century. The peculiar feature of industrial growth, for a considerable period of time, was that it was slow and localized in some parts of the country, having a concentration of working population in the factories of Mumbai, Kolkata and Chennai, and in the plantations and coal mines. However, there were sporadic incidents of spontaneous strikes of a limited nature as a protest against inhuman behavior at the hands of foreign management. They were short-lived in the absence of organized institutions in the nature of trade unions in the background. They were led for the particular occasion by some philanthropist with a desire to redress the workers' immediate grievance. The origin of the Indian labor movement lay in the deplorable working conditions and the economic exploitation of the children and women in the factories, coupled with the then government's complete indifference to such plights. The doctrine of "laissez-faire" dominated the outlook of the government so much that its main concern seemed to have been to protect the employers from the workers, rather than to protect the workers from the employers.

The organized trade union movement in India dates back to 1890, when the first trade union, the Bombay Millhands' Association, was organized. It was not until 1926 that Indian workers obtained a legal right to organize trade unions under the *Indian Trade Unions Act 1926*. This Act provided for the registration of trade unions in India for the first time.

When India gained independence in 1947, industrial production was restricted because of political and economic uncertainties, non-availability of raw materials, and machinery and transport difficulties. The previous issues of bad working conditions created a backlash that led to the formulation of very employee-friendly legislation. Five-year plans were formed one by one and a mixed economy was encouraged.

Both the public and private sectors were assigned certain areas of operation. Wherever the private sector was unable to provide the resources, the public sector came in. For purposes of rapid industrialization, the government of India evolved an Industrial Policy Resolution in 1948, which was further revised on April 30, 1956. This resolution spelt out in broad terms the lines on which and the areas in which the public sector would expand. The principles for regulated industrial growth with spheres demarcated between the private and public sectors were built into sectoral plans, and over a period of time the public sectors expanded considerably and attained commanding heights in the Indian economy. The number of public-sector enterprises, which was only five at the commencement of the first five-year plan in 1950, rose to more than 250 at the end of the fifth plan in 1975. By the end of 1975, there were about 71,705 factories with a total fixed investment of Rs.140,290 million (about US$3 million) and employing 6.4 million persons. The total employment position in 1976 in the public sector and private sector was estimated to be 13.37 million and 6.8 million, respectively.

The dominance of large public-sector undertakings and the socialistic policies of successive governments in the 1960s and 1970s encouraged a burgeoning trade union movement. By some estimates there were 37,539 registered trade unions in India in the 1980s. According to a study, the rate of unionism in India in the period 1962–63 was around 24 percent in sectors other than agriculture. The degree of unionization varied widely from industry to industry. It was 51 percent in mining and 37 to 39 percent in transport and communications, manufacturing industries, and electricity and gas.

> It was as if the so-called "Hindu rate of growth" that the country had been stuck with for the last several decades was also restricting the development of sophisticated HRM practices and trends.

Industries with a high rate of unionization were coal (61 percent), tobacco manufacture (75 percent), cotton textiles (56 percent), iron and steel (63 percent), banks (51 percent), insurance (33 percent), and plantations (28 percent).

It is believed that the rate of unionism in India had a clear impact on the development of human resources management as a core function in organizations. The focus remained largely on managing unionized workforces and collective bargaining to maintain industrial peace. This was true of both the private sector and the public sector. In fact, a distinct "welfare" and paternalistic form of people management emerged with organizations focusing heavily on lifetime employment, providing additional benefits, such as free housing in industrial townships, public amenities, and social security. The many small industrial towns that mushroomed across India – Bhilai, Jamshedpur, Pune, Bokaro – all had concentrations of such organizations. The HRM function's role remained limited to personnel management or administration. There were limited attempts in certain organizations to play a strategic role through training initiatives aimed at productivity improvements. However, these were the exceptions rather than the rule.

Nevertheless, by the 1980s there was a growing feeling in Indian industry that it had veritably "missed the bus" when compared to Japan or South Korea, or even to much smaller economies such as Singapore, Hong Kong, Malaysia, or Thailand. While it remained true that this position was governed largely by the regulated economy, there was not much emphasis on attempts to enhance employee productivity or create better talent management processes. The few examples that stood out were in some of the more progressive family-owned business houses or Indian subsidiaries of multinational organizations. It was as if the so-called "Hindu rate of growth" that the country had been stuck with for the last several decades was also restricting the development of sophisticated HRM practices and trends.

The reason for the lack of HRM being a key business imperative was also the relatively low employee mobility. A survey done in the 1980s by a prominent weekly magazine showed that the cream of India's talent was still heading west (the much talked about "brain drain" to the United Kingdom, United States, and Canada – the highest for engineers and doctors) or preferring to join the government. The talent pool that was available to the Indian private sector, or the small number of multinationals, was also limited in the choices it had. The information technology revolution had yet to reach Indian shores. Major sectors such as telecommunications, banking, and insurance were still heavily regulated and dominated by public-sector players and the norm was still career stability. The story of the Indian talent market mirrored the story of the Indian economy – the parable of the elephant – slow, steady, and some would say sluggish. Then things changed. The trajectory of the economy went through a qualitative as well as a quantitative boost in the early 1990s. This set the context for the current turmoil in the Indian talent market and the HRM challenges for organizations.

THE CHANGING ECONOMIC CONTEXT

Starting mid-1991, India embarked upon what is called a large-scale socioeconomic reengineering project. Faced with an economic crisis due to a fiscal lack of discipline and negligible foreign exchange reserves, the country started on the path of economic liberalization. Effectively, this meant the end of the tradition of industrial licenses, a lowering of trade barriers, an open invitation to multinational and foreign investors to do business in India, and a gradual opening up of regulated sectors. The New Industrial Policy of 1991 – which suggested changes in the Exim Policy, encouragement to exports and overseas investments, easy access to foreign capital, and a gradual reduction in duties – also made the trade boundaries more permeable. The opportunities opened up by these changes stimulated Indian companies to start aiming at global operations (see the case study "India Goes Global"). For instance, the AV Birla Group started setting up operations or JVs in several countries, ITC focused on distribution channels for increasing exports, and Reliance started global sourcing of raw materials.

The competitive strength of Indian industry came under scrutiny at home. In a marked departure from previous policy, in just one year, 1992, the government approved US$1 billion worth of foreign investments, which was twice as much as the total foreign investment approvals granted between 1975 and 1991. In the very next year, the approved amount jumped to almost US$2 billion. The openness of the Indian government was matched by the actual inflow of foreign capital, products, and brands. After all, even at that time, the middle income group or middle class in India was estimated at 200 million – a market that was larger than the total population of many countries, or even of some of the trade blocks such as MERCOSUR (a grouping of South American countries) and OPEC (an organization grouping oil producers). The size of the Indian market was also comparable to two of the largest in the developed world, North American Free Trade Agreement (368 million) and the European Economic Cooperation (342 million). What made India even more attractive for foreign investment was an abundance of natural resources, low-cost labor, the world's third-largest technically qualified population, and a large, but not the most productive of industrial infrastructure.

India goes global

The liberalization of the Indian economy had a stimulating effect on Indian business. The increased participation of India in the global economy can be discerned by the following facts:

- Indian exports growth rate increased from 3.6 percent in 1992–93 to 22.2 percent in 1993–94. In fact, between 1990–91 and 1995–96, Indian exports increased more than threefold.

- The number of proposals approved for overseas investments increased from 107 in 1992 to 230 in 1994.

- By the end of 1994, Indian companies had more than 500 joint ventures spread across 69 countries and 300 wholly owned subsidiaries in the United States, United Kingdom, Germany, and Singapore.

While we can keep arguing as to how monumental the paradigm shift was for the Indian economy, based on what the statistics said, the message was clear – the rules of doing business in India were changing. And they were changing in ways that they had never before. In a nutshell, if one was to draw the major themes in the Indian economy in the decade of the 1990s, they would be:

Market and brand visibility expansion – The most visible aspect of liberalization was that the market for consumers suddenly expanded in terms of range and choices available. Most of the world's top brands found a presence in the Indian market – Coca Cola, McDonald's, IBM, or Sony. This was coupled with the entry of multinationals at an ever-increasing pace.

Industry shakeouts – The arrival of new entrants into traditional bastions created a domino effect in the economy. Examples abound – in 1993, at the start of the liberalization era, the refrigerator market, for instance, was dominated by three brands: Godrej, Kelvinator, and Voltas. By the closing years of the 1990s new players such as Whirlpool, LG, and Samsung had left most far behind. Even in a sector such as steel, where the public sector-owned SAIL (Steel Authority of India Limited) and Tata Steel had dominated for years, newcomers such as Essar, Jindal, and Nippon Denro were making deep inroads.

Deregulation – Perhaps this was the most far-reaching consequence. Starting with capital markets and financial services, the traditionally guarded sectors of telecommunications, insurance, and now even power, oil, and gas have been systematically deregulated. The monopolies of the public-sector enterprises have been eroded as either multinationals or Indian organizations have made entries into these sectors, leading to more choices for the consumer, competitive pricing, and enhanced customer service.

The services boom – One of the key differences in India's economic growth pre- and post-1991 is the lead taken by the services sector over manufacturing and agriculture. While the five-year plan era had ensured heavy industrialization, it was only in the last decade that a large services sector emerged in India. This encompasses banking and financial services, insurance, telecom, software, outsourcing, and hospitality. The double-digit growth attained by services had to a large extent driven job creation and salary pressures in the talent market. If one just takes the BPO (Business Process Outsourcing) segment of the services economy, it grew by an astounding 60 percent in 2002–03, as per figures given by industry bodies such as NASSCOM. India has started emerging as the "back office of the world" as some experts put it.

The reverse brain drain – From the 1960s to the 1980s a common complaint was that of a "brain drain" to the more developed economies in the West. This was particularly true of engineers, doctors, and other professionals. While this may have caused significant talent loss in those years, the returns of having such a highly skilled and successful talent "diaspora" became evident post-1991. A substantial contribution to the creation of a distinct "India Inc." brand image, as opposed to that of the land of snake charmers and the Taj Mahal, goes to this segment of Indian professionals. They have also added value through their investments in the software and IT-enabled services sector, and by using their positions in top global organizations to focus efforts toward developing India as a market.

The result of all this has transformed many facets of the Indian socioeconomic reality over the last 10 years. In the early twenty-first century, India stands with one of the most promising potentials for growth. The large talent base, proficiency with the English language, expertise in software, a stable financial and regulatory environment, and a noisy but active democracy are just some of the factors that are cited as a part of India's portfolio of advantages. And the gains on the ground have been tangible. If one was to look at just the talent pool and the dynamics that are operating today, there has been a change that cannot be called less than tumultuous.

Employee mobility – Gone are the days of lifetime employment and stable careers. While in certain sectors such as heavy manufacturing or in public-sector organizations this still may not be a reality, it has fast caught up with the others. New emerging sectors have opened opportunities for people willing to use their skills. Consequently, compensation levels and the focus of organizations on retaining talent have increased manifold.

Diminishing employee loyalty – The increasing employee mobility and proliferation of job opportunities caused the first casualty in the form of eroding employee loyalty. The somewhat paternalistic style of people management had created an aura about being stable with one job or organization. The 1990s saw a total reversal with job changes, and even career changes, becoming acceptable. This was particularly true of employees in sectors such as software, banking, telecom, and IT-enabled services. The longevity of employees started being counted in a few years or even months, as opposed to decades.

The global Indian manager – While there has been a strong population of Indian professionals who have established themselves in the West, a new trend that has emerged is the use of India as a sourcing ground for global talent. In the years 2000 and 2001, the first 20–30 students at the premier Indian Institutes of Management at Ahmedabad, Bangalore, and Calcutta were not heading for jobs in Mumbai, New Delhi, or Bangalore, but to New York, Singapore, Hong Kong, and London. Topping the list of organizations seeking Indian talent were global consulting majors and investment banks. This trend also validated what had already been witnessed in software and information technology: the premium value attached to Indian talent.

Furthermore, many organizations started to use India as a sourcing ground for senior management positions in the Asia Pacific and even beyond. The presence of many Indian CEOs at the head of some leading organizations such as McKinsey & Co. and Standard Chartered Bank only strengthened this perception of the emergence of a global Indian manager.

Crossing the Rubicon – Given the strong welfare focus and the employee-centric labor legislation in India, job security had been a thing taken for granted. However, many organizations, including some from the public sector, crossed this Rubicon in the decade following the start of economic liberalization. The words "VRS" (Voluntary Retirement Scheme) have entered common management language as organizations both in the public and private sector have gone in for a systematic process of restructuring and downsizing of their workforces – blue-collar and white-collar as well in some cases. The ascent on employee productivity and becoming lean has been a fundamental mindset shift among Indian managers.

However, this is just one side of the story. While the statistics are very impressive when compared with the past, it is also a reality that India still has the maximum number of poor people – people who do not have access to the means of expanding their human potential. In terms of social indices as measured by the UNDP Human Development Index, India still ranks above 100, even though it may have one of the fastest growing economies in the world and be among the ten largest economies in terms of scale. In fact, even when compared to the other large emerging economy in the world, China, India is found wanting. A decade ago, India and China had roughly the same GDP per capita. But at US$440, India's current GDP per capita is only half of China's, and India's GDP is growing at a rate of only 5 to 6 percent a year, while China has consistently maintained double-digit growth for over a decade. The 6 percent growth is no mean feat, but could India grow faster? This would require it to leapfrog the slow pace of "trickle-down" economics and leverage modern technology to bring about a transformation in the economy as a whole. Otherwise, this economic miracle may remain restricted to a few havens such as Mumbai, Bangalore, or Hyderabad.

A well-publicized research initiative undertaken by the McKinsey Global Institute on the barriers to enhanced economic growth in India revealed some interesting insights into what was holding back India. One of the factors highlighted was the government ownership of business and the slow growth in labor productivity (see Exhibit 7.1).

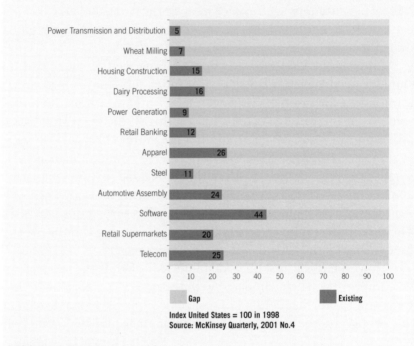

Index United States = 100 in 1998
Source: McKinsey Quarterly, 2001 No.4

Exhibit 7.1. India's labor productivity

The study went on to forecast that India could easily touch or even surpass 10 percent growth on an annual basis if these barriers were removed. The issue of labor or employee productivity is further accentuated if one looks at other research. In 2002 the World Bank funded a global research project that focused on the differentiating factor of a skilled workforce in socioeconomic development. The study looked at data from 112 countries over almost half a century. Some of the findings that came out in a report entitled, "Constructing Knowledge Societies: New Challenges for Tertiary Education 2002"[1] were obvious. The study shows a strong linkage between education spending and its resulting impact on the female literacy rate and the quality of certification and education.

The other findings were not so obvious. For example, growth of value-added for the 1986–94 period was 3 percent for knowledge industries versus 2.3 percent for the business sector as a whole. Between 1985 and 2000, the share of knowledge-based industries in total value-added rose from 51 to 59 percent in Germany, from 45 to 51 percent in the United Kingdom, and from 34 to 42 percent in Finland, according to OECD figures cited by the report.[2] The process of globalization is accelerating this trend because knowledge is increasingly at the core of a country's competitive advantage. Comparative advantages among nations come less and less from abundant natural resources or cheap labor, and increasingly from technical innovations and the competitive use of knowledge – or from a combination of the two. The proportion of goods in international trade with a medium-high or high level of technology content rose from 33 percent in 1976 to 64 percent in 2001.

> **India has the world's third-largest technically qualified workforce but, the quality of this workforce is inconsistent. The challenge for organizations in India is to raise the median level of talent.**

Today, economic growth is as much a process of knowledge accumulation as of capital accumulation. In OECD countries, investment in the intangibles that make up the knowledge base – research and development (R&D), education, and computer software – is equaling or even exceeding investment in physical equipment. Firms devote at least one-third of their investment to knowledge-based intangibles such as training, R&D, patents, licensing, design, and marketing.

In this context, economies of scope, derived from the ability to design and offer different products and services while using the same technology, are becoming a powerful factor in expansion. In high-technology industries such as electronics and telecommunications, economies of scope can be more of a driving force than traditional economies of scale.

A new type of enterprise – the producer services company, which provides specialized knowledge, information, and data to support existing manufacturing firms – has begun to prosper. Experts see such companies as the principal source of created comparative advantage and significant value-added in highly industrialized economies. In the knowledge economy, advances in microelectronics, multimedia, and telecommunications give rise to important productivity gains in many sectors and are also the key components of a multitude of new products in a wide range of industrial and service activities. At the same time, the rapid acceleration in the rhythm of creation and dissemination of knowledge means that the life span of technologies and products becomes progressively shorter and that obsolescence sets in more quickly.

Developing and transition economies are affected by these transformations, but are not yet reaping all the potential benefits. Indeed, the capacity to generate and harness knowledge in the pursuit of sustainable development and improved living standards is not shared equally among nations. In the International Bank for reconstruction and Development/World Bank 2002 report, reference was made to an OECD study which estimated that in 2002, OECD member countries accounted for 85 percent of total investment in R&D; China, India, Brazil, and the newly industrialized countries of East Asia for 11 percent; and the rest of the world for only 4 percent.[3] Among the reasons for the divergence is that the industrialized economies possess the critical combination of infrastructure, expertise, and organizational and incentive structures that allows these investments to be productive.

The conclusions to be drawn from the above are stark. The differentiator for economic growth and competitive advantage for economies and (business organizations) is going to be investment in intellectual capital/knowledge-creation to enhance the quality of the talent pool available. In order to do this the economy needs a sustainable supply of quality, skilled human resources that are world class. This "talent pool" cannot be created just by attracting migrant workforces – an indigenous framework needs to exist for creating it. While India has the impressive standing of having the third-largest technically qualified workforce in the world, the quality of the training or education that comes through is consistent. The challenge for organizations in India is to raise the median level of talent – we have already discussed at length the emergence of Indian managerial talent or in limited sectors such as software, pharmaceuticals, and life sciences. This needs to have a spillover effect in other sectors as well. What is a major issue for the economy at a macro level impacts on business organization at various levels. How the economic upswing and its concomitant implications on talent markets is shaping the role of HRM is what we turn our attention to next.

THE TRENDS FOR THE FUTURE

The scenario of how organizations in India will cope with the present and projected challenges in the talent market is also impacted on by the current debates regarding the role of the HRM function. In the past few decades, one question has repeatedly found a place in research articles, textbook, and business forums, "What is the value of the HRM function?" Maybe we ought to be addressing a different question altogether: "How can HRM create value and deliver results?" More importantly, "Can we measure this value?"

To address these questions, one will have to asses the evolving role of HRM in the context of the dynamic and complex interplay of economic, technological, and regulatory factors that have come to characterize the business environment. First, let us look at some of these forces that are impacting on the role of HRM.

Globalization dominates the business landscape. Despite the recent instability due to the threat of international terrorism and war, this trend will continue. This puts pressure on HRM processes to be adaptive, agile, and competitive across geographical boundaries. And today increasingly it is not just US, European, or Japanese firms that are globalizing. There are a whole host of globalizing Asian corporations that are heading out and setting up operations. Petronas from Malaysia; the large South Korean conglomerates and closer home companies such as Infosys, TCS, and Ranbaxy come immediately to mind.

Focus on cost and growth – Profit is a given in business. Profitability will continue to be a business issue, but the accepted path to profitability will change. Increasingly, organizations will be required to innovate and improve efficiency at the same time. HRM, too, will have to focus on both cost and value. And this challenge of achieving growth while reducing costs will push HRM professionals to deal with their function's inherent paradox – to create value they have to spend more. This leads to greater costs.

Capability focus – Organization capabilities are like the DNA of competitiveness. They are the weapons an organization has in its arsenal in the battle for markets and profit. Similarly, in order to provide a differentiating level of service and value, HRM will have to frame what it does in terms of capabilities. For a long time, HRM functional expertise and "people sensitivity" have been considered a winning proposition – this is not likely to be the case any longer.

Turnaround is not transformation – In the last two decades of the twentieth century, many organizations focused their efforts on turnaround through downsizing, reengineering, an enterprise resource planning system (ERPS), and the like. All this helped make the businesses sleeker, swifter, and maybe more streamlined. However, organizations are now finding out that turnaround is not the same as transformation. As organizations try to change their fundamental business models, HRM will be stretched to continuously keep pace and evolve with the business. As these changes make more and more demands on organizations, HRM professionals will have to increasingly define quantitative and business-linked metrics to assess the effectiveness of their contribution to the business. Moreover, the ability to assess redundancies and overlaps, and find cost-effective business solutions to their problems has become a key skill and will remain so. In essence, without losing the "softer" human subjectivity aspect of HRM, the trend toward hard data driven decisions will intensify. This issue gets further intensified in the case of an emerging economy such as India. There is already a race to "catch up" and these trends just add further pressure. In the context of the new economic realities, we can focus on five broad themes that typify the nature of the HRM challenges in India.

No longer a recruiters' market

As mentioned at the outset, the nature of the talent market in India has changed fundamentally. Up to a few years ago, organizations could consider themselves in a dominant position when it came to recruitment. Brand image, compensation, social status attached to working in a particular organization, and the paucity of job opportunities ensured that this was the case. While these factors remain important, individuals scouring for job opportunities in the market have many more choices today. Statistics from business school campuses tell a story. The average number of job offers per student till five to six years ago never exceeded 1.5 or 2. In recent years on some campuses this has been as high as 3 or even 4. The changed dynamics in the recruitment market impacts on the retention strategies within organizations as well – the usual tactics of paying above the market or high-impact roles may not work anymore. The case of what an organization had to go through to redefine its talent attraction strategy illustrates many of these trends (see the case study, "The talent equation").

The focus on efficiency

One of the key business-linked challenges for HRM has been the emergence of a cost and efficiency focus. Recent trends have shown an increasing tendency to restructure workforces, downsize, outsource, and automate. And this has not just been restricted to the multinationals or the private sector. Some of the largest assignments for downsizing and designing of voluntary retirement schemes as an exit option have been in the large public-sector enterprises. This has happened with the enhanced use of outsourcing and technology solutions to transform the transactional nature of the HRM function. These technology solutions could be ERPS platforms, customized HRM systems, or intranets. Outsourcing has led to cost efficiencies, as well as saving time for more strategic and developmental work. Though the focus of the HRM function in India for many decades was on industrial relations and administration, there always existed a strong cadre of professionally trained HRM managers and specialists. In today's changing context, these professionals are being challenged to show results and deliver tangible value (see the case study, "HRM as a business partner").

Traditionally, the effectiveness of the HRM function was measured by its accuracy and administrative efficiency. To meet these criteria, HRM developed consistency through precision, routines, and reliable procedures. Today, new capabilities should be added to the existing ones.

▶▶ BUSINESS TIP

Here is a checklist of capabilities required of HRM as its job complexity grows.

- Speed – How quickly can HRM work be done without sacrificing quality?
- Implementation – How well can new ideas be turned into actions with visible results in terms of employee behavior or benefits?
- Innovation – How well can your HRM staff think creatively about finding solutions to problems they have not previously considered?
- Integration – How well does HRM work to integrate with strategic plans, customer goals, and external business challenges?

More important than all this is the need for the HRM professional to be a business manager first and then a HRM specialist. In most forums and surveys, when senior executives are quizzed on what they considered were the most important competencies for HRM professionals the results are startling. Only a minority felt that HRM functional knowledge was the most important skill cluster. Many spoke of general management and change-enabling skills and business knowledge (including financial and technological capability) at the top. Therefore, the HRM function needs a much more diverse set of individuals and a wider skill range in order to cope with the increasing demand for the HRM function to be more efficient. All this would of course rest on a foundation of personal credibility that HRM professionals will have to build. Some of the behaviors that will be required for enhanced credibility within the organization include:

- consistency – being predictable;
- keeping commitments – doing what was promised within time and budget;
- confronting in an appropriate manner – being willing to disagree and challenge business managers;
- thinking outside the box – offering alternate perspectives; and
- confidentiality and ethics.

The new employee relations environment

In its report, the second National Commission on Labour in India has analyzed the present industrial relations scenario and delineated the broad trends that are observable. It is increasingly noted that trade unions do not normally give a call for strike because they are afraid that a strike may lead to the closure of the unit. Service sector workers feel they have become outsiders and are becoming increasingly disinterested in trade union activities. There is a trend to resolve major disputes through negotiations at a bipartite level. The nature of disputes or demands is changing. Instead of demanding higher wages, allowances, or facilities, trade unions now demand job security and some are even willing to accept wage cuts or wage freezes in return for job protection. Disputes relating to non-payment of wages or separation benefits are on the rise. The attitude of the government, especially of the central government, towards workers and employers seems to have undergone a change. Now, permissions for closure or retrenchment are more easily granted.

The unions have been putting up stiff resistance to the new economic policies, as well as the demands of the employer lobby to bring the labor laws in tune with the new economic policies. It is clear, however, that the new economic policies have come to stay. To become more flexible in their dealings with the employees, particularly in the backdrop of certain rigid provisions of labor laws, and to become more competitive, the Indian employers have been resorting to various strategies and practices. Some such practices are:

- shifting operations from highly unionized regions to less militant regions, or to export processing zones;
- employing more scientific and objective techniques for recruiting employees, and also for evaluating performance and rewarding, training, and developing them with the dual objective of individual growth of the employee and achieving a greater organizational efficiency;
- training managers to understand and sympathize with the workers and to develop their skills to communicate more effectively with subordinate employees;
- transferring jobs from bargainable/unionized to non-bargainable/non-unionized categories;

The talent equation

Company ABC, a multinational, had started its operations in India in the early 1980s. The nature of its business required the recruitment of bright, high-achieving graduates who could be trained in the global standards and processes the company followed. This worked well for a number of years, but by the mid-1990s, all was not well. New recruiters were promising faster career paths, independence, work–life balance, and more responsibility early on. Moreover, the MBA boom was drawing the best students away. The conversion ratio or hit rate of the company, which showed the number of offers accepted to the number of offers made, dropped from 90 to 50 percent. Something had to be done and done fast.

A multi-pronged approach was adopted. One of the key themes was to catch students early – an intensive campus contact program was initiated; the recruitment process was revamped to make it an experience that any prospective student would be impressed with; and alumni networks were tapped into. This was followed by a rigorous summer internship process with an accent of giving final job offers to the promising candidates. These efforts bore some fruit but in many ways the battle was lost. The company had to accept that the old times would never come back.

HRM as a business partner

XYZ SoftCo., an emerging technology solutions organization, has a unique structure for managing people. The company found that one of its major reasons for the failure or limited success of HRM initiatives was the lack of ownership among the line managers. If they did not take responsibility for their own people, who would? The challenge was to make every manager into a "performance manager" and to create a HRM function that operated on a BOT (build, operate, transfer) model. Consequently, the HRM function was "unbundled" into three distinct organizations, each of which was headed by people who are from the line functions. As a formal process, high-potential managers have to do compulsory deputations or take on HRM projects as a part of their career development. This has turned the traditional notions about HRM's role and the structure of a HRM function on its head, but with some great successes in achieving a high level of integration with the business.

- outsourcing jobs to workers' cooperatives and employing the dependants of permanent employees;
- setting up parallel production centers – this serves as a backup in case of unionization threats to production;
- ensuring transfer clauses in the terms of employment and using this to transfer undesirable employees – this is in light of the fact that retrenchment is a difficult process;
- outsourcing non-essentials – utilizing contract labor in various areas like canteens, transport, cleaning, loading/unloading, security, housekeeping, maintenance, and so on;
- linking productivity with wages in long-term wage agreements;
- changing work – norms, reducing jobs, introducing technological changes;
- demanding an increase in working hours, reduction in holidays and leave, longer settlement periods, and closure of non-viable departments;
- mentioning in wage agreements that technological changes are the management's sole prerogative;
- reducing labor level by not filling up wastage vacancies;
- ensuring that adequate workers are involved in the organization through the creation of communities/committees responsible for productivity/environment and so on;
- ensuring strong processes for regular management–worker communication and grievance resolution;
- influencing spatial diversity – not recruiting everyone from the same residential areas; and
- not hiring any relatives of existing employees.

The net result of all these changes is that the mindset of industrial relations in India has changed. Gone are the days of collective bargaining and the confrontational nature of worker–management relations. Today the emphasis is more on taking decisions that make business sense, as there is the realization that only those will benefit employees in the long run. This is also reflected in many of the changes the government has been contemplating at a policy level and which are being debated at various industry forums (see the feature article "The change agenda for labor").

The change agenda for labor

- Lifting the restrictions on the employment of contract labor for about a dozen activities and 100 percent export-oriented units, and units in special economic zones.
- Amending the law on contract labor by shifting the responsibility for labor welfare from the principal employer (user enterprise) to the contractor.
- Lifting the ban on women working night shifts in factories by amending the Factories Act, 1948. The employer would, however, be duty bound to ensure adequate safeguards with respect to occupational safety and health; equal opportunity; adequate protection of their dignity, honor, and safety; and transportation to the nearest point of their residence.
- Workers' representation on the Board of companies may become mandatory. The government proposes to introduce the amended Participation of Workers in the Management Bill that intends to reserve 25 percent of the Board's strength for workers.

Global Indian companies

This could be one of the most significant new areas that will emerge in the early decades of this century. The liberalization process that we discussed at length in the previous section not only opened India to the globe, but also allowed leading Indian organizations to arrive on the global stage. This trend of globalizing Indian organizations is not just restricted to the software industry. While Infosys, Wipro, and TCS are prominent names and have a significant presence in markets as diverse as the United States, Singapore, China, and the United Kingdom, there are others as well. Large multi-business houses include Reliance, Tata Sons, and the AV Birla Group. Strong domestic players such as Asian Paints, ITC, and a number of organizations in the emerging pharmaceutical sector – Ranbaxy and Dr Reddy's – are among those. These names are just the tip of the iceberg. The conclusion is inescapable – the growth engine for the future would be global expansion of these companies.

This will be a unique challenge from a talent management perspective. While India itself is a culturally diverse country, the challenge of managing diversity on a global scale will be a new one for Indian business leaders and HRM professionals. Till now no consistent framework for managing this area is discernible, as it seems to be handled on a case-by-case basis. It would be interesting to see if Indian organizations follow a US-based model, or a European or Japanese one. It may emerge that they have to evolve a hybrid or a totally new model *ab initio*. The demand for skills that can effectively integrate cultures, manage diversity, initiate communication mechanisms across time zones, and still maintain a core of consistent organizational values will be of premium. The biggest challenge will be for these Indian organizations to develop a global mindset. In Rhinesmith's, *A Manager's Guide to Globalization*,[4] he describes the global mindset as, "… a predisposition to see the world in a particular way that sets boundaries and provides explanations for why things are the way they are, while at the same time establishing guidelines for ways in which we should behave. It is a way of being rather than a set of skills."

Based on the still nascent level of experience of some of the Indian organizations, the key aspects of building a HRM framework with a global mindset will be:

- resisting a "one-size-fits-all" approach;
- ensuring the mitigation of a "head office" mentality;
- creating unambiguous roles and organizational structures to manage regional and global operating models; and
- building sufficient talent pipelines of local skills wherever available.

The search for new paradigms

One of the major debates in emerging economies such as those of India or in regions such as the Asia Pacific is the relevance of universal models. As a large majority of cutting-edge research and practices in the area of management thinking (including HRM) has been in the West, more specifically in the United States, what is the level of "fit" with the realities of different cultures? The presence of a large number of multinationals in India, and their adoption or customization of global processes, has created a pressure on many domestic companies to look at similar initiatives. These range from restructuring compensation philosophies, to redesigning performance management systems, to creating competency-based HRM systems and leadership models. These local adaptations have been very successful in some case, but not in others. As far as the "fit" of these concepts and frameworks to an Indian context is concerned, the jury is still out.

But the need for practical and relevant local research is still a question that needs to be addressed. One of the key challenges for industry will be to enhance its linkages with academia and generate fresh thinking on talent management issues.

Recently, Mercer initiated a research award for the most innovative and relevant HRM research study in Asia. The initiative generated tremendous response from across the region, showing the potential for further leveraging of the intellectual capital available. India is very uniquely poised to lead such research efforts. It has at least a dozen well-established business schools that have faculties trained to world-class standards, and also a large student population that is keen to do such research. However, businesses will have to show greater enthusiasm for such programs and initiative if any fundamental new management thinking is to emerge.

CONCLUSION

This brief analysis of India's path for developing HRM as a discipline has highlighted the great changes that have been seen in the last few years. In many ways, the growth and evolution of the HRM agenda is reflective of the changed socioeconomic realities in post-liberalization India. It is beyond doubt that in the current emerging competitive environment, India has many opportunities to exploit, but here awaits the challenges as well. While great strides have been taken in enhancing human capital productivity and Indian talent is gaining recognition globally, there are vast gaps to be bridged before we can truly talk of a transformation in the talent market. This veritable race against time to build on existing strengths and cover the major weaknesses will engage business and HRM leaders of India in the foreseeable future.

---

[1] "Constructing Knowledge Societies: New Challenges for Tertiary Education, 2002," The International Bank for Reconstruction and Development/The World Bank. Washington DC, 2002, p. 8.

[2] The International Bank for Reconstruction and Development/The World Bank. Washington DC, 2002, p. 8.

[3] The International Bank for Reconstruction and Development/The World Bank. Washington DC, 2002, p. 9.

[4] A Manager's Guide to Globalization, Richard D. Irwin, Rhinesmith, S. Chicago, 1993, p. 38.

CHAPTER

8

The Economics of
Compensation in Asia
Ilya Bonic

T his chapter aims to provide an overview of compensation dynamics
within Asia. It draws a link between the economic characteristics of
the region and compensation practices to provide a framework for
understanding the different emphasis of such practices in different
markets within the Asian region.

Our view is that the starting point to understanding compensation
analysis within the Asian region is to have a complete grasp of the diverse
cross-country patterns of wealth. The most basic interpretation of the
compensation data is that countries with higher per capita gross domestic
production (GDP) tend to have higher compensation levels. But that is only
one level of interpretation. The task becomes more complex as the compensation
specialist incorporates the economic and labor dynamics of the different
countries across the Asian region into the equation.

Given that the economic maturities of the various Asian countries within
the region provide a reliable backdrop against where industries tend to flock
to, HR can provide appropriate compensation strategies and policies based
on analysis of compensation information that incorporates key economic
indicators in the model. The bottomline is being prepared for the extreme
shifts in labor market demand in Asia. Understanding compensation information
and having a hiring strategy based on this information can be a powerful
lever for any organizations not wanting to be caught out by extreme market
volatility. Our analysis shows that Asia is a market increasingly characterized
by wild swings in economic forecasts and expectations. Being tuned in to these
changes can prevent an organization from being caught in a labor price bubble
situation.

THE FOUNDATION: THE INTERACTION BETWEEN GDP AND COMPENSATION

" The starting point for compensation analysis within the region is understanding the diverse cross-country patterns of wealth. "

The typical multinational company will have businesses spanning many geographies across the region: from Japan and South Korea in the north, Australia and New Zealand in the South, India in the west, and everything in between. The structure of HRM within such organizations is to have roles of regional functional responsibility to develop and drive the consistent implementation of key strategies that aim to provide the organization with a competitive advantage in each of the markets it competes in.

For the Regional Head of Compensation and Benefits, a key challenge in implementing competitive pay strategies is to understand the key compensation practices in each country and the relative differences between each. This understanding allows them to understand what elements of strategy and policy need to be modified to ensure successful implementation.

The starting point for compensation analysis within the region is understanding the diverse cross-country patterns of wealth. In Exhibit 8.1 we present a chart that displays GDP per capita levels by country. The data deliberately presented in descending order from the countries of highest wealth within the region (for example, Japan, Hong Kong, and Singapore), through to those that have greatest scope for development (for example, Indonesia, India, and Vietnam).

GDP per capita is an economic measure that serves as a proxy for wealth. In Asia the best talent from the developing countries in the region has always been lured to those more advanced by the attraction of opportunity for increased wealth. We see in Hong Kong, Singapore, and Malaysia examples of government economic development strategies that have deliberately identified and targeted this wealth differential to attract labor from countries such as India, Indonesia, and the Philippines. The GDP labor magnet has allowed these more wealthy countries to rapidly enhance their talent pools and ensure that the

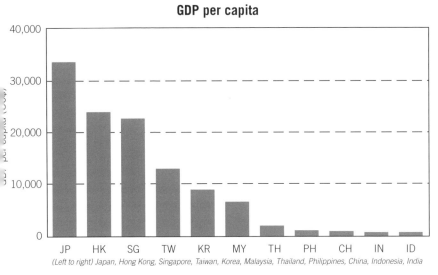

Exhibit 8.1 Diversity in wealth

supply of labor is balanced to take advantage of the available market opportunities.

What does understanding GDP as a magnet for labor allow us to infer about compensation practices in the region? First, at the most basic level, we would expect that there is a strong relationship between GDP levels and actual compensation levels in the different markets across the region. In the more wealthy countries, we would expect higher compensation levels than in the less wealthy countries.

In Exhibit 8.2 we illustrate relative compensation levels across the region. There are two definitions of compensation considered: base salary and guaranteed cash (which equals base salary plus all guaranteed cash allowances). The chart is built from Mercer survey data that has standardized all currencies to US dollars. Salary levels for the same job in every country are then compared to those in Singapore. If a bar within the chart stretches to a value of 1.5, it means

> " Within Asia, Japan and India tend to have a very high proportion of their pay mix focused on guaranteed allowances, typically because they are more tax-effective elements of compensation. "

that compensation in this country is 1.5 times that paid in Singapore for an equivalent job. If the bar stretches to a value of 0.5, it means that compensation in this country is half that paid in Singapore for an equivalent job.

By inspection, we observe that there is a trend for salaries to be higher in the more wealthy countries, and lower in the less wealthy countries. The correlation with GDP per capita, however, is not perfect. Nevertheless, the comparison between salary and GDP per capita provides us with a point of discussion and a useful heuristic framework for those practitioners with regional compensation and benefit responsibilities.

From Exhibit 8.2 we can see:

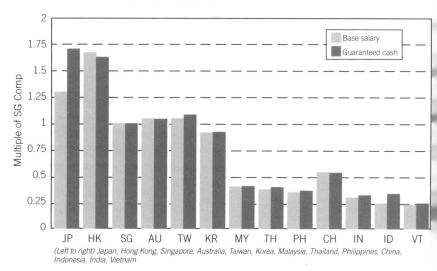

(Left to right) Japan, Hong Kong, Singapore, Australia, Taiwan, Korea, Malaysia, Thailand, Philippines, China, Indonesia, India, Vietnam

Exhibit 8.2 Compensation relativities / spending

- Hong Kong is the most expensive labor market in Asia – Hong Kong's salary levels are higher than Japan's and it is the most expensive labor market within the region. The data presented excludes executive salary data. If executive data were included, we would still see Hong Kong salary levels extend higher.
- There are different cost relativities for base salary versus guaranteed cash – Some countries in the region have a very high proportion of their pay mix focused on guaranteed allowances, typically because they are more tax-effective elements of compensation. This is particularly true for Japan and India. The takeaway here is that for cross-country compensation

comparison purposes, guaranteed cash is a more reliable measure than base salary.

- Compensation levels in China appear higher than we would expect from the GDP per capita exhibit – In addition to absolute wealth levels driving talent flows within the region, year-on-year GDP growth rates also serve as a powerful labor magnet. In recent years, China has stood head and shoulders above all other economies as the market with the greatest GDP growth momentum. This momentum has led to a significant imbalance in the supply and demand of labor with the experience required to take advantage of the growth and investment opportunities. We see compensation levels spiraling accordingly. Note that this outcome does not apply for all types of labor within China. Specifically, in the manufacturing sector there remains access to a production workforce for which the direct compensation costs stay at about 5 percent of the levels seen in the United States.

- A ready reckoner for compensation levels across the region can be inferred – Specifically, Japan and Hong Kong salaries are approximately 150 percent that of the Singapore market. Taiwan, Korea, and Singapore salaries are comparable; Malaysia, Thailand, and Philippines salaries are 35 to 45 percent the level of Singapore; China at about 50 percent; and Indonesia, India, and Vietnam at around 20 to 25 percent that of comparable jobs in Singapore.

COMPENSATION MOVEMENTS AND FORECASTS

One of the core activities for compensation and benefit practitioners is to manage the salary review budgeting and implementation process. The economic and labor market dynamics of Asia conspire to make this base activity a much more complex task than would be appreciated by the casual observer.

It is not uncommon to find HRM practitioners who are new to Asia who view with a certain degree of skepticism that year-on-year movements in compensation can be in the order of 15 percent. This is especially so when one finds within the same region that one country may have these large market movements, while the country just next door has zero or negative year-on-year movements in salary levels.

Such is the case that has been observed in recent years where neighbors such as Indonesia and Singapore, and Hong Kong and China display these dynamics.

Exhibit 8.3 provides a guide of typical year-on-year salary increase levels observed in the region. Here we have grouped countries with comparable salary movement levels and also referenced inflation levels that many see as a key driver in market movements. As in the earlier GDP relative analysis, this framework serves to provide readers with a simple tool for remembering the patterns in Asia's compensation.

Three groupings of countries are presented: first, Japan, Hong Kong, Singapore, and Taiwan; second, Malaysia, Thailand, and South Korea; and third, the Philippines, Indonesia, and India. China is included in two of the groupings. This is because its year-on-year market salary movements are comparable to Malaysia, Thailand, and South Korea; while its inflation levels are at the same negligible levels as Japan, Hong Kong, Singapore, and Taiwan. From Exhibit 8.3 we observe that over recent years, salary increase levels have moderated markedly. The horizontal dotted line that crosses the bar chart illustrates the shift that has occurred over the past two years as Asia moved from the high-growth period associated with the emergence from the financial crisis in 1997/98 to the boom period of the late 1990s, to the more moderate levels of economic performance observed today.

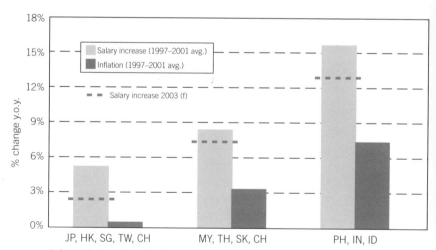

(Left to right) Japan, Hong Kong, Singapore, Taiwan, China, Malaysia, Thailand, South Korea, China, Philippines, Indonesia, India

Exhibit 8.3 Year-on-year salary movements and inflation

While this example serves as a useful categorization of market salary movements, extreme caution needs to be exercised in assessing and forecasting year-on-year movements in the region. Key inputs available in making budgeting decisions for annual salary reviews include salary surveys, and economic statistics such as the inflation rate presented above, and the forecast GDP levels. The assumption is that the higher the GDP and inflation forecasts are, the higher the salary budgets should be.

In Exhibits 8.4a and 8.4b we show the actual relationship between salary movements and the key economic variables of GDP and CPI that feed into the salary review budgeting decision. The exhibits present salary movement data sourced from Mercer salary surveys in 12 countries in Asia in the period 1994 to 2002. They compare salary movements in each country with the actual GDP and CPI statistics for that same year in that same country.

►BUSINESS TIP

For budgeting salary increases in Asia, it is important to factor in multiple data sources; namely, the economic data, salary survey data, and the expectation data drawn from the market.

Knowing how much emphasis is placed on this economic data in building the business case for salary increase budgets, it is surprising that such a poor relationship exists between actual salary movements and these key economic variables.[1]

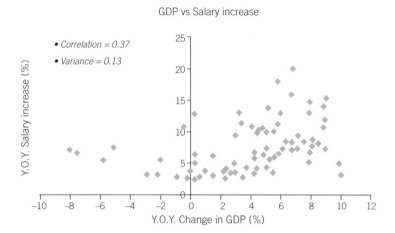

Exhibit 8.4a GDP and salary increase relationship

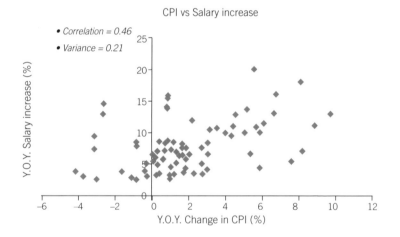

Exhibit 8.4b CPI and salary increase relationship

LABOR MARKET PRICE BUBBLES IN ASIA

The econometric analysis in this segment provides a good introduction into an analysis of the conditions that lead to labor market "price bubbles" in Asia. By the term "price bubble," we mean the conditions where the price for specific skill sets within a market, or the price of labor across an entire market, spirals quickly to cost levels that can catch HRM by surprise and leave them lagging in market opportunity behind their competitor companies, which have already identified, targeted, and actioned a response.

We recall that in making salary increase decisions, compensation and benefit practitioners typically consider such economic variables as GDP growth and inflation. The forecast data for these economic indicators is published on monthly and quarterly basis by economic analysts, forecasters, central banks, and in the business literature. Usually, the changes in these forecasts from period to period are gradual.

In Asia there can be significant economic volatility. A good example of one such year is 2003, which saw significant shifts in forecasts primarily because of one-off events like SARS, and now, with the emergence of an anticipated recovery in business conditions, a correction in previously conservative growth forecast.

Exhibit 8.5 shows data reported by IMA Asia, an economic forecaster, and member of the Economist Network. The exhibit shows a shift in 2004 GDP change forecasts from a snapshot taken in August, and then another taken in October 2003.

By comparing the two GDP forecast columns labeled "2004" in Exhibit 8.5, we see that in the space of only two months there has been a significant positive shift in GDP forecasts for Japan, Taiwan, Thailand, and China (compare the two GDP columns labeled "2004"). The majority of the remaining countries also went into 2004 with forecasts at the top end of economists' expectations. Business sentiment was in a much better shape than originally anticipated. The conclusion drawn from this information is that business sentiment will be much better in 2004. (Note: This analysis is based on data gathered capturing forecasts for the 2003/2004 period.)

	AUG Forecast: GDP Growth (%)			OCT Forecast: GDP Growth (%)			OCT F'cast: Inflation (CPI an. Av.)%		
	2003	2004	y.o.y. change	2003	2004	y.o.y. change	2003	2004	y.o.y. change
JP	1.4	1.2	▼	2.1	2.2	▲	-0.4	0.2	▲
HK	1.5	5.0	▲	1.5	5.0	▲	-2.0	0.5	▲
SG	1.2	4.5	▲	1.2	4.5	▲	0.4	1.2	▲
TW	2.8	3.5	▲	3.0	4.0	▲	0.2	0.8	▲
KR	3.8	6.5	▲	3.8	6.5	▼	2.8	3.5	▲
MY	3.8	5.0	▲	3.8	5.0	▲	1.0	1.5	▲
TH	5.0	4.5	▼	6.0	6.5	▲	1.7	1.5	▼
PH	4.7	5.4	▲	4.0	4.5	▲	3.2	3.4	▲
CH	6.8	7.5	▲	7.8	8.3	▲	0.8	1.8	▲
ID	3.0	4.0	▲	3.0	4.0	▲	6.5	6.0	▼
IN	4.6	6.0	▲	4.6	6.2	▲	3.8	4.5	▲
VT	6.3	6.5	▲	6.2	6.5	▲	3.8	3.3	▼

Legend Top to Bottom: Japan, Hong Kong, Singapore, Taiwan, Korea, Malaysia, Thailand, Philippines, China, Indonesia, India, Vietnam.

Source: IMA Asia; October 2004

Exhibit 8.5 A discontinuous change in GDP forecasts

Usually, the positive outlook will most likely be accompanied by upward revisions in company sales expectations, higher revenue growth forecasts, and a corresponding increase in investment to deliver on the opportunities inherent in an improved market.

In Exhibit 8.6 we illustrate a theoretical relationship between a company's revenue growth and the recruitment required to deliver this revenue growth. In scenario 1 we have continuous gradual increases in cumulative revenue growth expectations over time. Here, the revenue growth is accompanied by a corresponding moderate increase headcount growth to deliver this expected revenue growth.

In scenario 2 we see a discontinuous shift in revenue growth expectations. This shift was most likely in Asia during the fourth quarter of 2003, where economic forecasts for 2004 pushed toward the top end of expectations. The impact for headcount increase is a comparable discontinuous shift relative to scenario 1.

For compensation movements in the Asia region, the impact in scenario 2 may be significant. This shift in revenue growth expectations may cause a spike in labor market prices, as companies simultaneously rush to recruit to take advantage of expected demand before their competitors do (see Exhibit 8.7).

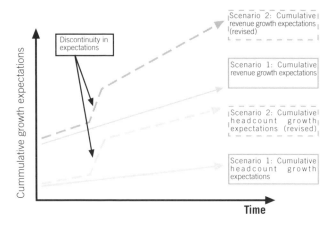

Exhibit 8.6 Scenarios for headcount growth associated with varying economic conditions

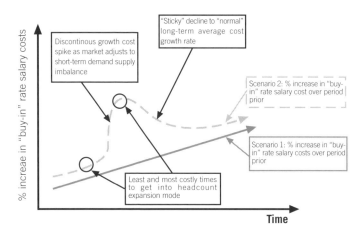

Exhibit 8.7 A potential spike in labor prices looming as demand exceeds supply

WHAT DOES THIS MEAN FOR SALARY FORECASTS AND BUDGETING?

It is critical that HRM remains closely attuned to the economic dynamics of the markets for which HRM professionals have responsibility. In Asia in 2003–04, the markets in which such "price bubbles" are likely to occur are in the India, Thailand, and China markets in particular. Additionally, the strategic reference needs to incorporate the interaction between economic variables, historical salary levels, market expectations of salary movements, and increasingly, an understanding of the demographics of the labor market and business strategy in Asia. As a case in point, we conclude this chapter with a brief look at compensation dynamics in Asia associated with the sales function.

MARKET PREMIUMS: SALES FUNCTION

> " Sales skills and the salesforce would most likely command a premium as companies take advantage of revenue growth opportunities. "

For multinational companies, Asia represents more that just a market in which they can seek to outsource production to lower cost centers. As Asia's wealth grows rapidly, companies are presented with a rapidly expanding consumer market that they can target for sources of new global revenues.

To understand the growth of this market, Exhibit 8.8 illustrates the demographic composition and trends in household wealth growth. The illustration is in two sections. The first contains a focus on the number of households earning greater than US$30,000 per annum. For demographers, this represents the criterion definition of "wealthy households"; namely, those that have enormous spending and consumption capacity. You will note that in Asia there is a significant growth in this category of household.

The second element of Exhibit 8.8 focuses on those households that will cross the threshold of US$6,000 into the lower middle-class category. This category is characterized by a significant acceleration in expenditure as the households now have their basic needs of food, shelter, and clothing met.

The demographic shifts forecast by Asian Demographics in Exhibit 8.8 will rarely be found in any other region in the world. For businesses of all kinds this growth in household wealth provides significant opportunities for new revenues. This level of growth becomes increasingly attractive as growth opportunities in the more mature markets in other regions become far and few between.

The opportunities illustrated above are not known to only a few companies. Rather, insights such as these are common knowledge for business strategists. This means, that with many companies observing the opportunity, there is/will be a growth in investment to quickly capitalize on the opportunities in parts of Asia. This is why we see incredible levels on investment in markets like China and increasingly in India. From the material covered above, we would expect that these business conditions would quickly lend to the occurrence of a labor price bubble or spiral. Sales skills and the salesforce would likely command a premium as companies take advantage of revenue growth opportunities. In Exhibit 8.9 we present evidence to support this hypothesis.

> " For the compensation and practitioner, the takeaway here is that economic dynamics and market opportunities in Asia interact to create significant market premiums that may be extreme but usually logical and predictable. "

The data presented in Exhibit 8.9 is drawn from Mercer's database for the Information Technology and Telecommunications sector. The sample of organizations includes global market leaders such as IBM, Microsoft, HP, Cisco, Nokia, Intel, EDS, and others. They are all are making very large investments in the region. The illustration compares base salary plus on-target variable pay for sales jobs versus non-sales jobs of comparable scope and impact. It also differentially compares jobs with managerial (managerial stream) and non-managerial (individual professsional stream) responsibilities.

The emphasis and priority for companies acquiring sales capability in the region is clearly reflected in Exhibit 8.9. Sales jobs command market premiums of between 1.1 to 1.5 times non-sales jobs across the region. Premiums for sales jobs are higher in the less-developed/higher opportunity markets (for example, Thailand, the Philippines, China, and India) versus the more developed markets. Also, sales roles without managerial responsibilities command a higher premium compared to those with managerial responsibilities.

When a company grows too fast too quickly, the compensation structure can grow out of shape very quickly as this high-tech company soon found out. The company had to pay premiums to recruit non–executive-level staff to run its growing business. At the same time, its compensation for key talent was not satisfactory.

Client Situation/Background

This high-tech company is an amalgamation of several Japanese firms and a state-owned company in Singapore. It was established over a decade ago, employing leading-edge technology to produce high-tech components. The organization's workforce size had within a short period of time grown to approximately 1,000, from a force of around 300 in 1998. There was also a change in job scope of some positions. Competition for talent was tough, largely attributed to the increase in investment and expansion of operations by existing players and entry of new global players in the market. The organization also faced an average of 15 percent staff turnover at the commencement of the project, with the engineers forming the biggest chunk of this figure.

This high-tech company engaged Mercer to help it deal with the challenge of attracting and retaining a workforce that is hotly sought after in the small and competitive high-tech labor market in Singapore.

Approach

Mercer interviewed key line management to understand in detail the challenges facing the business and the management of people. Mercer also worked with HRM to review the current compensation policy and practices as part of the diagnostic process. Next, we reassessed the job sizes of existing benchmark positions and evaluated new benchmark positions, involving key line managers and HRM to produce a relative organization chart showing the relative job sizes and their relative positioning in the organizational hierarchy.

Following this, Mercer identified a group of 'comparator' organizations to whom the company typically loses its talent to and from whom it attracts talent from. Mercer then undertook an external competitive and internal equity analysis to quantify the gap and impact of the high-tech company's current pay structure for its base salary program. Using Mercer's compensation tool, we designed a grade and salary structure that catered to the client's short- to long-term needs.

Recommendations

Analysis of the company's compensation level showed that it sat in the median of a selected market group in terms of base salary and total cash. Mercer also found huge internal equity issues at the non-executive level, confirming the client's suspicions that the company might have been more than generous in its remuneration during the startup phase when there was a need to attract people quickly.

What was also lacking was clarity in the company's management levels and a well-defined career path to help manage internal staff movement. Too many engineers wanted to become part of the management group (thinking that this is the only way to go), and they did not see the technical path as attractive. The engineers perceived their pay to be uncompetitive and their prospects unattractive. Mercer recommended a new grade and salary structure, pegged competitively against its comparator group to ensure attraction of talent for key talent groups (for example, engineers) at various levels.

To ensure internal equity and proper progression and development, Mercer also recommended a set of grade levels and titling that are tied to the organization's generalist and specialist career paths, and facilitated the communication of this structure to employees. In addition, Mercer also provided guidance and advice on how to manage the career and salary progression of its key talent (such as the use of level descriptors and a merit matrix model to guide annual merit pay increase), and manage rewards holistically to better retain talent.

Impact

The client was very satisfied with the rigorous process Mercer conducted in validating the job sizes and relativity across divisions, the detailed analysis and quantification of financial impact of the current and new pay structure, and the transfer of tacit knowledge in reviewing job sizes and pay structure.

A Mercer internal case study: December 2002.

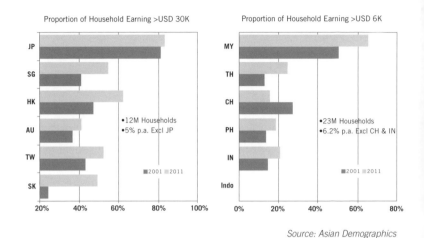

Source: Asian Demographics

Exhibit 8.8 Growth in household wealth

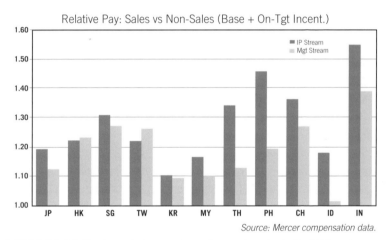

Source: Mercer compensation data.

Exhibit 8.9 Relativities in pay between sales and non-sales roles in the IT&T sector

For the compensation and benefits practitioner, the takeaway here is that the economic dynamics and market opportunities in Asia interact to create significant market premiums that may initially appear extreme, but are predictable and logical. These premiums may be generalized across markets/countries and/or they can be reflected among specific occupational groups. The challenge for the compensation and benefit practitioner is to identify the market pressures and premium before the competition to take advantage of the supply and cost conditions that exist prior to the emergence of a labor price spiral.

CONCLUSION

The diverse nature of the Asian region means that there is a matching diversity in pay practices and compensation levels. A key challenge is to grasp and understand the drivers of this diversity and to use this information as a strategic advantage in managing compensation and benefit programs.

A fundamental driver for pay dynamics in the region is the absolute level of wealth in an economy and the growth momentum in wealth generation. Year-on-year salary increase levels also vary significantly across the region. It is possible to group countries by the historical increase level, which will serve as a useful heuristic for testing recommendations for salary adjustments in different countries.

While many place a strong emphasis on GDP and inflation statistics as the basis for determining salary budgets, the relationship between these variables and actual salary changes is not high. However, it is possible to build detailed econometric models that bring science, objectivity, and predictability into this process.

For compensation and benefit practitioners in Asia to maximize their effectiveness, it is important that they focus not only on HRM variables in managing pay, but that they also remain sensitive to the changes in business conditions, competitor strategy, and the demographics across the region.

---

[1] Note: Mercer has used econometric modeling techniques with a range of economic and HRM data to build predictive models that can explain between 78 and 92 percent of the variance in salary increases depending on the market and industry in Asia.

9

HRM Questions for the CEO

Reiji Ohtaki

What personifies the quintessential Asian chief executive and what importance does he or she place on the HRM function? From family-patriarch-type owners such as Li Ka Shing of the Cheung Kong group in Hong Kong to Stan Shih of Acer in Taiwan, the breed of Asian chief executives reflects the diversity of the business landscape as much as the cultural fabric of Asia. Competing with Asian-origin chief executives are astute and tested chief executives of multinationals. An example is Nissan's Carlos Ghosn. What questions should CEOs in Asia ask of their HRM? The broad questions are related to three business issues: what a business needs to do to stay ahead of the competition; what a business needs to do to continually anticipate the customers' needs; and what a business needs to do to stay relevant into the future. The answers will help CEOs to build a business strategy that can survive the ravages of a digital age. There is also the need to harness a talent pool to power the business strategy. This chapter helps the CEO gain an understanding of the principles and building blocks of building competency models for an effective talent management strategy. More than ever the CEO has to integrate HRM into the company's business planning process. Knowing what HRM questions to ask is part of this imperative.

CURRENT REVIEW: THE CEO AS THE HRM CHAMPION

The call for HRM to get strategic sends an implicit message to the CEO – HRM needs to get to the boardroom and start contributing to strategy rather than merely playing the roll of being a pure administrator. The pressure-cooker environment that most organizations operate in these days leaves little room for error. The CEO's role will also change in line with the changes in HRM. Whether you are a hands-on CEO with 100 staff, or one with 1,000 or 10,000 staff, there is a need to define the vision for the company and mobilize the people to help you translate that vision into action. CEOs we meet often have very similar concerns:

- How do I stay competitive and profitable?
- How do I find the right people to power my business strategy?
- How do I stop my top people from leaving?
- How do I motivate my employees?

Whatever the leadership style, CEOs of large companies tend to leave HRM to do the recruiting, hiring, and firing. This has a practical side, for after all, how can a CEO be hands-on and deal with things HRM, as well as play the role of a visionary and strategist. It assumes that top management and HRM are in sync about where the business is heading. It also requires HRM to be business savvy and to understand the factors driving the organization's success. More often than not, this isn't the case. It is not uncommon for HRM to come into the picture late into the blueprint, and HRM often plays the role of a fire-fighter and intermediary between line managers and employee.

If personnel management was the catch phrase of the 1970s and 1980s, strategic HRM is the mantra for the new millennium. The changing tide of talent flows locally, regionally, and globally; it presents CEOs with the new challenge of getting the best talent to build sustainable businesses. A talent management strategy requires heavy commitment and involvement from a CEO to articulate a vision for the company to be an employer of choice. This demands that the CEO champions the philosophy of the company relating to compensation, performance and talent management, and career development. In Asia, the owners of businesses have yet to come to terms with having a total HRM strategy that can help underpin a business strategy. CEOs in

Asia have yet to fully synthesize business management with HRM management to achieve maximum results.

In the following section, we deal with some of the people issues CEOs tend to focus on. Not all CEOs are precise in their recruitment strategies. Some are more decisive than others in the kinds of personalities they want in the company and what areas of technical or non-technical strengths these people bring with them. Others are less so. These different people goals of the CEO give rise to the corporate cultures in a particular organization.

CEO: WHAT KIND OF PEOPLE DO I NEED TO RUN MY BUSINESS?

- *I want someone who will put the company's interest first, someone who can learn from mistakes.* Liu ChuanZhi, chairman of leading Asian PC-maker, Legend Holdings, strikes a good example of a top executive with a vision of which type of people he wants to run his operations. He applies two criteria when he hires people. "The initial criterion is whether he [the employee] could put the interests of the company first. The second criterion is talent, or ability. What I emphasize in talent is the ability to learn, to do well at different tasks. Can he learn from foreign companies? Can he learn from practical experience? I don't care whether he succeeds or fails at a particular task, what I care about is whether he is able to learn from his failure and what he does afterward."[1] Clearly, this is a leader who holds a very firm philosophy about the profile of the people he needs to run his company – a company manufacturing for the local Chinese market, but competing with global products.
- *I want a community of entrepreneurs, a lot of little John Waynes.* Victor Li, Asia business leader and chairman of multi-billion dollar company Li & Fung in Hong Kong, is a CEO seeking a community of entrepreneurs to run his organization. He strikes a balance between being in command and providing autonomy. His criterion for talent is entrepreneurship. In his interview with PriceWaterhouse Coopers in January 2003, he explained how employees are given the freedom to exercise entrepreneurship. His breed of workers has to be able to exercise

judgement everyday without nanny bosses looking on. "We all know exactly what is going on. But we don't tell our managers what to buy, what price to sell, how to sell it, or whom to sell it to. We like to think of these people as little John Waynes, if you can imagine."[2]

- *I want loyalty, integrity, and discipline.* A contrasting style is that associated with Robert Kuok, one of Asia's richest men and Asia's "sugar king." Kuok is well known for his ability to build relationships across boundaries in Asia, and move seamlessly between the traditional patriarch-run family culture that he comes from and the international scene dominated by savvy businessmen in crisp suites and polished mannerisms. Despite Kuok's international savvy, his family empire is tightly held and the strength of his personality permeates throughout. He rarely gives press interviews and he rarely reveals his thoughts on business strategy or management style. His company's motto is integrity, loyalty, and discipline. Kuok's management style remains nebulous to the outside world simply because he doesn't talk about it. His business empire stands at a crossroad – it is now led by Kuok the founder, but managed by second- and third-generation family members. Will his management style withstand the ravages of the digital age? Will he be considered shy or non-transparent? Only time will tell. But Asia's family-owned enterprises are already feeling the need to loosen the iron hand, to allow more debate, and a more open style of management. Across Asian-owned enterprises, CEOs will start to feel the need for more proactive management of people at the level of key resources.

ASIAN-OWNED BUSINESSES AT CROSSROADS

Many of Asia's family-owned enterprises are at a major crossroad. From the Chung family of Korea, who owns the Hyundai brand, to the Lamsams in Thailand, who own the Karsikorn Bank (formerly Thai Farmer's Bank), these families are tossed between hanging onto age-old traditions – where heads of the clan make all-important decisions and set the pace – or moving ahead with the new dictates of managing a business in a borderless world. The Asian financial crisis that hit the region in 1997 gave many of these family-controlled enterprises a rude awakening – the effect has reverberated across Asia, crippling family empires in Korea, Japan, Malaysia, Thailand, Singapore, Indonesia, and the Philippines. In Thailand, the impact was heavily felt. Bad loans and poor accountability brought the banking system to its knees. Families that have built their fortunes in important sectors of the economy – in particular, banking, finance and securities, agro-industry and telecommunications – have been hit. Some have had to relinquish generations of prized family assets. In Thailand, major families such as the Sophonpanich (Bangkok Bank), the Lamsam (Karsikorn Bank), the Techapaiboon (Sri Nakorn Bank), the Chearavanont (Chareon Phokaphand Conglomerate), and the Chirativat (central department store and hotel chains) are some of the examples of business dynasties that have been forced to revamp their business styles.[3]

In some cases, such as Korea's Hyundai Group, sibling rivalry from two of founder Chung Ju Yung's six children in 2000 scarred the image of the company so much that the founder had to step in and declare his choice of successor. Another Korean conglomerate, the Daesung group, has suffered badly in terms of investor confidence due to the sibling battle for control after the death of the founder Kim Soo Keun. Kim on his deathbed in early 2001 had assigned a role to each of his sons, but within months of his death, his children had begun to feud. The end result is a business weakened after being broken into parts by the rivalry among siblings.

Other Korean-owned chaebols have had less turbulent transitions of power. Samsung founder Lee Byung Chull designated his third son as his heir 15 years before his death, while LG Group chairman Koo Cha Kyung transferred the reins to his eldest son in a formal ceremony.[4]

Other multinational names with Asian origins, such as Toyota, Nissan, Canon, and Samsung, have been meticulous in planning their leadership to transform themselves from local to global companies. The key to their success is developing a strategic business plan accompanied by a plan to harness their people to power their business strategies. Before exploring this theme further, let us take a look at who actually owns the businesses in Asia, outside the multinationals. The profile of Asia's business ownership reinforces our view that succession planning is a critical business issue.

OF FAMILIES AND ASIA'S MAJOR LISTED CORPORATIONS

According to a paper from World Bank researchers and the University of Chicago, in many of the East Asian countries researched, two-thirds of Asian publicly traded companies are controlled by a single shareholder, very often the founder.[5] Japan is the exception where corporate ownership is heavily concentrated in the hands of financial institutions (38.5 percent), while families own 13.1 percent of listed corporations in Japan. Indonesia represents the extreme with some 71.5 percent of its publicly listed companies being held by families (at the time of the research). The researchers in this case use the 20 percent threshold to define ownership control. In Hong Kong, family dynasties control 66.7 percent of listed corporations, while in Thailand it is 61.1 percent, Malaysia 67.2 percent, Taiwan 48 percent, and Singapore 55 percent. In Singapore about 24 percent of its listed companies are held by state-owned companies. The researchers also found that often, there isn't a clear demarcation between management and ownership control. This implies the need for management changes as Asian businesses come to terms with the forces of globalization already sweeping through Asia. As local companies compete with foreign ones, CEOs of family-run concerns will need different models to compete. Younger generations of CEOs from Asian enterprises are already showing signs of moving away from their clan elders' style of management.

THE NEW GENERATION OF ASIAN CEOs

CEOs bring with them various styles of leadership. Their distinctive styles dictate the shape of the organization they run. Asian-owned enterprises range from patriarchal family concerns to companies run by MBA sons of these patriarchs. Increasingly, family-owned concerns in Asia have to grapple with the dilemma of either holding tight onto management or letting outsiders run their companies. We are seeing a new generation of family-owned concerns led by MBA sons schooled in the best universities in the United States or Europe. Singapore's Eu Yan San's health food company is one example. Richard Eu represents the new generation of business leaders in Asia. Schooled in the

University of London, he is just as comfortable with modern jazz and modern management metrics as in things Chinese. The Eu Yan Sang chain was started by his great-grandfather Eu Kong, who left Foshan in southern China for the small mining town of Gopeng in Malaya in 1879. Eu's great-grandfather carved his fortunes in tin mining, rubber, and traditional Chinese medicine.

The younger Eu modernized his family's business when he took over stewardship. He introduced a contemporary feel into age-old Chinese herbal recipes, swapped old shops for modern retail outlets, and brought in trendy packaging. With a little innovation, he provided traditional Chinese herbal remedies and tonic food into a form that the modern-day consumer could relate to. Eu also started collaborating with universities in Hong Kong and China to research new products, and started distributing his existing product lines through supermarket and pharmacy chains in Singapore, Malaysia, and Hong Kong.[6]

"We have had to change from managing a traditional business in a traditional way to redefining what business we are in and how it should be run," Eu says. "This meant reinventing all aspects of the business in order to make it relevant. Seeing the changes in the world around us since the day I started in 1989, if we had not done so, I wonder if the business would have survived."[7]

Other offspring from Asian-owned family dynasties are also coming to their own, often putting aside rigid traditional management structures for flatter ones. In Thailand, the Lamsam family, which owns the Karsikorn Bank (formerly Thai Farmers Bank), had for four generations been under the grip of clan elders running the bank the traditional way and being adverse to risks that could rock the family business. Employees often had to battle layers of bureaucracy to get a small message across to the owners. From the time he could count, Banthoon Lamsam's father had been grooming him to take over the Lamsam family business.[8] The Harvard-trained executive could never get clan elders to listen to his management ideas. When the baht collapsed in 1997, he saw the opportunity to push through the changes he saw necessary. He cleaned up the bank's balance sheet and sold off some of the bank's assets to foreigners. The first thing he attacked was what he called the "very old cronyism and nepotism" prevalent in Thai organizations. "We brought in everybody – McKinsey, Andersen Consulting, Oliver Wyman, Booz Allen, Goldman Sachs, you name it," Banthoon told *Business Week*. "I was accused of being un-Thai," he told the magazine.[9] Although his efforts have helped the bank through one of its most difficult periods, the verdict is not out on whether the bank will propel itself into a high-growth phase, while Thailand's domestic banking system grapples with the indigestion of its excessive lending.

What Asian CEOs have to come to terms with is a changed model of how businesses are shaping and reconfiguring. As the barriers to trade keep getting dismantled, local companies will have to reengineer themselves to achieve productivity never before seen. The competition is not limited to domestic markets, but international ones. The entrance of labor-rich economies such as China and India will unleash competitive pressures never seen before in Asia. The competitors are not only the traditional MNCs, but new MNCs and regional Asian enterprises.

Unless companies have a well-defined business strategy and a robust people plan, they have no hope of succeeding in the future. Only 5 percent of family-owned businesses around the world continue to create shareholder value beyond the third generation, according to McKinsey's research. There is a popular Chinese saying that alludes to this: The first generation starts the business, the second generation grows and expands the business, and the third generation squanders all the wealth created. One of the challenges for family-owned enterprises in Asia has to be dealing with succession issues. Talking about leadership change is still taboo and often the owner keeps very close to his chest who he intends to pick as his successor. This model of power transition may not hold for long. To build a business that can compete in the future, CEOs need to plan for a ready pool of people who can lead and manage the business.

How do I build a business that can sustain the ravages of time and competition? This must be one of the most pressing concerns for CEOs. While building a sustainable economy holds challenges that are quite different to building a sustainable organization, Singapore's Lee Kuan Yew has a pragmatic approach to managing sustainability. The economic transformation Singapore has gone through offers interesting lessons for every CEO.

Singapore has consistently had to transform itself after gaining independence from the British colonial masters. From a dilapidated backwater island, Singapore has been remaking itself since the 1960s. It thrived first as a cheap entrepot, but knew this trade had a limited number of years before direct trade displaced this. The island state has actively courted foreign direct investments for manufacturing industries to provide jobs. Whether it is electronics or pharmaceuticals, or other growth industries, Singapore is unabashed in seeking out new niches for itself. All these have served Singapore well, giving it over 20 years of unprecedented growth. Underpinning this has been a policy of openly courting talent from around the world to help manage and run Singapore. Singapore has about one million foreign workers today and a local population of 4 million.

An avid believer in succession planning and a true talent strategist, Singapore senior minister Lee Kuan Yew has actively nurtured and cultivated the best-in-class people to run Singapore. The island state is now focused on getting Singapore ready to compete with global companies. One of the most radical moves Lee has introduced has been the freeing up of the local banking arena for foreign competitors, so local banks will be forced to innovate or be left to idle by global competitors.

> **We cannot keep the big companies out. The choice is simple. Either we have a first-class airline, a first-class shipping line, and a first-class bank or we will be declining.**
>
> Singapore senior minister Lee Kuan Yew

One of the key challenges for Asian companies will be growing themselves into global organizations from local or regional ones. There are some examples of successful Asian corporations that have built a global presence. These Asian-origin global names grew because of a well-mapped strategy for growth that covered business as well as people strategies. Consider some of the successful Asian brands such as Samsung, Toyota, Sony, or Canon – they have worked and reworked people strategies, focusing on succession and talent planning to accompany their business goals.

BUILDING A SUSTAINABLE BUSINESS

Toyota's example of succession and preparing for the future

Asians typically don't relish talking about death or dying. This explains why succession planning and talent planning issues don't figure on the radar screens of Asian owners. It takes a vision and a lot of foresight for an organization to plan for the future. One global brand that has successfully grappled with the "ghost" of the future is Toyota.

Toyota had its roots in Toyoda Automatic Loom Works, which was founded by Sakichi Toyoda who is popularly known as "King of Inventors." Toyota today produces more than 5.5 million vehicles per year. It enjoys a profit of US$24 billion and employs 1.3 million people. Sakichi set up the company in 1937 and is known for his creativity and inventiveness. Toyota's quality checks instituted through the Jidoka system has its roots in Sakichi's own innovation in the early twentieth century, where he placed a device in his textile looms that would stop operation whenever a thread broke to ensure quality. This system is still widely used in Toyota today where production is stopped once a defect is noted and the worker sets about using problem-solving skills to correct the problem.

Like many Japanese-owned companies, Toyota had to confront the issue of whether or not it should appoint a family member to head the business when in 1995 it struggled with the challenges of declining car sales. In the United States it was faced with crippling sales from the impact of tax on imported luxury cars. Hiroshi Okuda was the first outsider appointed to head the Toyota family business in 40 years. Three former CEOs, Eiji Toyoda (5th president of Toyota) Shoichiro Toyoda (6th) and Tatsuro Toyoda (7th) made the selection. Hiroshi's selection was based on a few factors: his international exposure was seen as critical for the company, which was at the crossroads; his non-conventional way of dealing with problems; and his frankness in viewing his opinions. Toyota's top management was fully aware of the qualities needed for the top job. Companies have to regularly ask themselves what competencies they need, not only for today's business but for the future. Toyota managed this very well.

Toyota's remarkable ascent from a near-bankrupt carmaker to a dominant global player did not succeed by chance. Its success has been grounded in the long-term vision to be the dominant force in the auto market.

Eiji returned from a trip to the United States in 1950 with a vision of large-scale production and sales to the US. He told colleagues he didn't see anything in the United States that was beyond Toyota's capability. He set out with his company's production guru Taiichi Ohno to make many cars in small batches more efficiently than the big car companies. The Kanban system was born – auto parts and supplies were ordered as they were being used rather than having large stockpiles. Every Toyota worker was an inspector and everyone was empowered to stop the production line when there was a defect found – much like the automatic loom system invented by his uncle Sakichi. Success had its pitfall. Failure was part of the process.

> **When I went to Detroit in 1950, we were producing 40 cars a day. Ford was making 8,000 units, a 200-times difference. The gap was enormous.**
>
> EIJI TOYODA AS TOLD TO *TIMES* MAGAZINE

Toyota fell flat on its face on its first crack at the US market with its Crown model. In the 1960s, Toyota had more success with the Corona and then the Corolla models. It took another 20 years, in 1989, before Toyota's luxury Lexus model had its major success. By 1991 the Lexus became the top-selling luxury import in the United States. In 1986, Eiji went on another research mission to America and on his return brought back a new vision for the company. He decided Toyota could no longer thrive on being a copycat. He felt that the path to the future was through innovation.

Toyota's story is a tale of remarkable persistence. It is an epic development of 90 years – starting as a textile company turned copycat manufacture and lately, a leader in innovation and R&D. This endeavor requires not a focus on short-term profits, but a long-haul commitment to build a lasting business. Much of this success is due to Toyota's ability to harness its people – from those who conceptualize ideas to those at the production level at the factory workshop – to dance to the same tune of achieving precision, excellence, and innovation.

When Hiroshi Okuda took over the helm in 1995, he "inherited" a business that was beginning to feel the forces of globalization. Toyota could no longer make cheap vehicles and was forced to look for cheaper ways to make automobiles. It had to enhance its brand and sharpen its distribution channel. Hiroshi was chosen because he was deemed unconventional and had the requisite experience. More importantly, he was chosen because of his outspokenness. The Toyota management took on board someone whom they feel could lift the company into the next phase of its development – a non-conventional Toyota person. Hiroshi worked on penetrating the European market and expanding manufacturing capacities in America. He also made a decision to enter the Formula 1 Grand Prix to demonstrate Toyota's advanced technology, as well as improve the company's corporate image. Hiroshi Okuda's revolution was succeeded by Fujio Cho in 1999, another succession for a top position not of the Toyoda clan. Fujio has improved the company's performance and set tougher goals – to make Toyota a truly global company. He also wants to corner 15 percent of the world car market from the 10 percent it currently has. To achieve his vision, he set up the Toyota Institute, an in-house executive education program aimed at putting in place the human resource foundation necessary for the global workforce that supports Toyota's business goals.

According to a company press release when the Institute was announced: "Toyota has also undertaken a fundamental review – at both the tangible and intangible levels – of its human resource training structures to identify how best to ensure a continuous reservoir of personnel with a shared commitment to the Toyota Way, whose members will play key roles in Toyota's 21st century business development."[10] The organization is headed by Fujio himself, demonstrating his leadership and commitment to the cause. The aim is to train about 180 business leaders per year across the globe and some 300 middle managers.

> " Because people make our automobiles, nothing gets started until we train and educate our people. "
>
> TOYOTA PRESIDENT FUJIO CHO

Fujio and Hiroshi were two non-family members brought in by the Board to continue the development started by foresighted members of the Toyoda family. Toyota has a firm view of the future and has defined how it can be successful and what it needs to do to succeed.

The future for Toyota is clear in its own strategic map – a giant carmaker with a passion for cars, selling everywhere in the world, manufacturing in the most cost-effective locations. In its map of the future, Toyota is also seeking to make cars that run on clean fuel; hence, it is ahead of competitors in producing hybrid vehicles. Toyota cars are designed by the best talent around the Toyota world.

In Asia, CEOs will increasingly have to define business strategies and set on a path to achieve these business goals. HRM will be a central piece to this business strategy, and succession planning will be a key component. CEOs cannot afford not to be intricately tied to HRM decisions. One of the developments to watch at Toyota is whether or not it will continue to have to deal with the issue of having a member of the Toyoda clan at the helm. There is speculation that Akio Toyoda, who is the eldest son of Shoichiro, and currently a senior managing director, will eventually succeed Cho within the next few years for the leadership. Time will tell if Akio will be appointed. It would be hard to see Toyota opting for "nepotism," as it has made a clean break from the tradition of not bowing to the pressure of appointing someone from the Toyoda family, who now only owns 2 percent of the company's shares.

BUSINESS TIP

Here are some HRM questions CEOs must ponder in developing a succession plan:

- Do we have a well-defined plan to prepare the business for the next three, five or 10 years ahead?
- Do we know what competencies we have now, and what we need for the future?
- Do we have a profile of who our future leaders or managers are? Do we have a reliable, tested system to assess our future business leaders?
- Have we matched the profiles of who we have against what we need for the future?
- What contingencies do we have in place for our future business leaders?
- Do we have a system in place for the development of our future leaders?

CEO INTERVIEW

In this interview, we speak to Eddie Koike, the CEO of Cerebos Pacific an Asian-owned food and health supplement enterprise, about business and people issues that keep him awake at night. The interview highlights our views that CEOs need HRM as a strategic partner for a business to be successful.

Q: What keeps you awake at night?

I sometimes find it very difficult to sleep after we have invested a large amount of investors' money in a new business, when I think of the progress we have made in the investment. Competition has been getting tougher so it is not easy to establish a successful new business. In the case of Cerebos, we have been doing very well with a traditional product, Essence of Chicken, but we have not been doing well in the surrounding health supplement market. Because of the success in one product, we felt comfortable and did not realize that there has been an expansion in the health supplement business. The health supplement business has grown over 10 times in the last 10 years. Cerebos made a decision four years ago to enter this business. We are investing SG$30 million a year for branding, marketing, and sales of our new products while this business currently generates only SG$20 million a year at this stage. This is a good example of what keeps me awake at midnight.

Q: When we say HRM, what comes to your mind?

Corporate strategy and HRM strategy form a single piece of a company's strategy. They cannot be divided. Our success depends so much on people nowadays. I believe HRM is a part of the CEO' job. The role of HRM is to support the CEO to do a good job. personally spend approximately 30 percent of my time on HRM issues such as senior managers recruitment, HRM policy development, performance management of direct reports, etc. For example, I have changed 80 percent of the top 30 managers over the last five to six years. I needed the best management team to pursue the strategies of Cerebos. I did all the recruiting. HRM supported me in the course, but it was clearly my job. I plan to get more involvement in the learning and development programs for managers. Again, I will work with HRM on that.

Q: *What are some of the most pressing people issues you face in your organization?*
I face two challenges at Cerebos. The first one is the relatively high turnover rate among non-management staff – especially those within the late twenties to mid-thirties age group. We may be successful in hiring top talent, I am afraid we might not be as successful in training them properly for further growth. I also want to encourage my managers to delegate more to their staff. Developing subordinates is clearly a responsibility of managers. Managers need to know how to empower their staff.

The second challenge is to develop right leadership within Cerebos. My definition of leadership has to do with the management of behavior that leads a person to do and act outside his or her current peripheral. True managers should get out of their silos and achieve results beyond their responsibility area. This means achieving results not only for their department, but also for other departments and for the company at large. Once a manager holds this view, internal politics will be a thing of the past.

Q: *Where do you look for "talent" or to power your organization?*
We do recruit people from outside, particularly our middle managers and the staff level. We do not, however, head hunt people from our direct competitors. Unlike Japanese companies where the management has a large amount of young staff readily available for them to do the job, we at Cerebos must first find the talent before tackling a strategy. It has been a constant challenge for us to identify the right human resources to help us pursue our strategies. In early days, we made many mistakes in assessing candidates. Now we have accumulative experience to help us do the job more effectively. In addition to the usual screening methodology, we are now using new assessment systems such as behavioral event interviews in our selection process.

Q: *In your view, what should HRM be doing for your organization?*
As I mentioned earlier, HRM is clearly a big part of the CEO's job. The HRM function must effectively support the CEO. In that sense, HRM has to be a strategic partner of the CEO. Cerebos is in the process of changing its organizational culture from being product-centric to being customer-centric. We used to think that if we

developed good products, they would automatically sell. We did not pay much attention to customers to understand what they really wanted. We now realize that a change is necessary. HRM promotes such a change through training programs, whereby our employees, including non-sales staff, can interact directly with our customers. We are currently implementing a CRM (Customer Relations Management) process. It is a very important strategic shift for Cerebos. Our HRM calls CRM "Customer Relies on Me" in the training programs for our employees to promote this cultural change. HRM is an important agent for the change process. Up until five years ago, we relied on third-party distributors to sell our products. When we decided to do our own sales, HRM supported me in implementing a customer-oriented and sales-oriented culture. HRM was the catalyst for this process.

Q: What is the greatest motivator for good performance in your organization?
I have heard other CEOs say it is not money. I hold a contrarian view. I do believe money is the most important motivator for good work. We, at Cerebos, have a policy of evaluating the employees' performance properly and paying them fairly. We do not want to use career promotion as a motivator, because positions are limited unless the company has unlimited growth. Our incentive programs are short-term and mid-term (four to five years). I do not believe we need a long-term (say 10 years) incentive, because even CEOs cannot predict what will happen 10 years down the road for the company. The business environment is so dynamic and fast. Having said that, a short-term (one year) program causes a lot of problems, so we have mid-term incentive programs as well. This combination of short-term and mid-term programs seems to work well, and is well accepted by managers and employees.

Q: In your view, how do you build a sustainable and competitive business?
It depends on the quality of our human resources, for sure. When a company tries to establish its new business model, it definitely needs innovative people who can build new products that are non-existent in the market and new distribution channels no one ever thought about. At that stage, having a few "geniuses" is very critical

to the building of this – let's call it "castle," which can be difficult to "attach" to the whole organization. Once the company successfully builds the "castle," it will need many reliable human resources, who can work as a team to operate and maintain the "castle," or the new business model. These new people or human resources need to be working as a team with other existing people. If CEOs can effectively use a combination of these parts of human resources within the organization, they can build a sustainable and competitive business.

DO I HAVE A READY SUPPLY OF TALENT TO RUN THE BUSINESS?

Talent will be a scarce commodity in the future. In Asia, China is already surfacing as the most aggressive place for talent. India is seeing a shortage of skilled IT professionals to support its information service industry. Campus-based recruitment by organizations is happening at a fast and furious pace. The secret is out – the hunt for talent in growing economies such as India and China is happening and CEOs ill-prepared for the race will be faced with the risk of not getting enough talent. They risk paying too much in a tight market, to get the right people for their business. If you are a global company, the challenge is to develop a pool of employees who can fit into a global business. To meet the demands of being a global company means having to educate, train, and develop people who can understand a certain set of values associated with what the organization believes. What does the "Toyota" way or the "Sony" way mean? How do these companies induce employees to adapt their company's DNA or "way of life"?

People development through conventional training programs or through on-the-job training may not yield satisfactory results. Some Asian multinationals such as Samsung, Canon, and Sony have started developing leaders through their own corporate universities. Many of them are using GE – Crotonville, where GE spends US$1 billion annually on training and development programs – as their benchmark. It is well known that their ex-chairman and CEO, Jack Welch, spends a large portion of his own time and energy in the program on the following:

- interacting with his managers;
- making sure all GE staff understand GE's values or DNA; and
- selecting the right individuals for leadership development.

As a Japanese-born multinational, Canon has the aspiration of developing a global oasis of talent to push through with the continued globalization of the company. The company employs 98,000 employees all over the world, with approximately 75 percent of its revenue generated outside Japan. The organization has become just too large and too global for Japanese expatriates to manage. Canon found that it needed to develop a pool of global employees who could understand and act consistently in accordance to its missions and values. Exhibit 9.1 demonstrates the Canon concept of mobilizing a global talent pool to facilitate its globalization strategy.

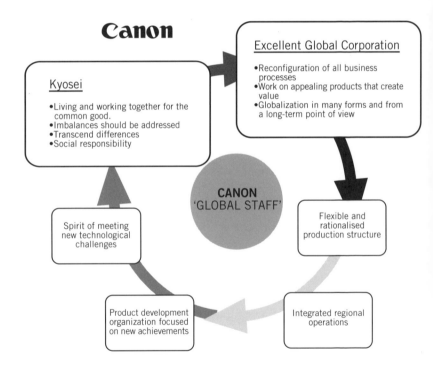

Exhibit 9.1 Corporate Mission and Values

Canon

Steps to establish Corporate University

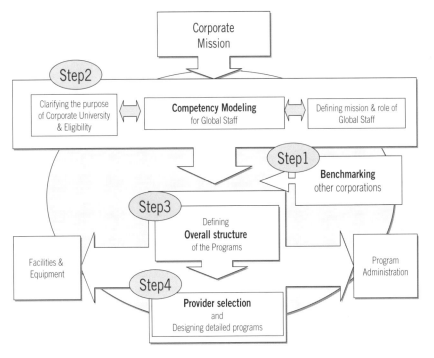

Exhibit 9.2 How Canon built its Corporate University

While many companies just rename their conventional training programs as 'Corporate University', Canon's approach is worth attention. Canon started the process of developing its Corporate University by defining who will make up its 'global staff' and what the requirements are for its "global staff." The second part involves benchmarking its high-performing global senior managers to identify key requirements for this pool of global staff. The focus is not only on job knowledge and hard skills, but also soft skills, including the behavioral skills needed to succeed as a global leader. The third part involves defining the program structure for the Corporate University, and preparing the detailed specifications for each of the learning and development programs. It then issues a request for proposals to source the best providers of learning and development programs to ensure high-quality delivery of its tailor-made programs.

EFFECTIVE LEADERSHIP DEVELOPMENT THROUGH THE COMPETENCY MODEL

The competency model approach is a highly effective way to define select, and develop a ready pool of talent for a company to be able to gain the strategic competencies needed for the company to succeed in its business goals. Competency profiles synthesize skills, knowledge attributes, values, and express the requisite behaviors needed for an employee to consistently achieve high performance.

Mercer's competency model is focused on soft skills or behaviors that lead to a person's high performance. Based on our research, we are convinced that hard skills (job knowledge and technical skills) are not the sole determinants of superior performance. What we deem as more critical success factors are a series of soft skills or behavioral patterns that help an employee succeed in consistently delivering high or superior performance in his or her designated roles.

CASE EXAMPLE OF COMPETENCIES DISPLAYED BY TWO SENIOR MANAGERS

An example is shown in the case study below of two semiconductor researchers working for a Korean electronics manufacturing company. The linkage between one's performance and "soft skills" becomes much stronger for managerial employees and executives. Our case study highlights the different behaviors displayed by two senior managers having the same technical knowledge needed for a job. Our example highlights the point that for senior-level people, "hard skills" are no longer a meaningful determinant for performance.

C A S E   S T U D Y

Research group leaders, Mr Kim and Mr Park, work for a leading Korean electronics manufacturing company.

- Both are 36 years old.
- Both hold a master's degree in electronics engineering from a Korean university.
- The two were promoted to Research Group Leader at Semiconductor Research Lab at the same time.
- Each is a leader of a six-member team undertaking several projects.

How about their performance?

Mr Kim	Mr Park
• He achieves outstanding results. • He files a larger number of patent applications than others. • He has led many projects to the development of commercial products. • The technology of Kim's team is put to use at the production line. • The production line staff say, "If we have a difficult problem, we will seek Mr Kim's help." • Mr Kim is almost idolized by the staff of the marketing division and the production division.	• He shows average or mediocre performance. • He is unusually devoted to the ongoing projects. • He works until after everyone else leaves, and works on some holidays. • He is uncompromising in data taking, and reprimands subordinates who carry out sloppy experiments.

What behavioral characteristics of the two people explain the difference in their performance?

Mr Kim

- He can see things from the other's standpoint. Sometimes from the manager's standpoint, sometimes from the production line's standpoint.
- He can develop products efficiently without wasting time.
- His information-gathering ability is a great asset.
- He is never self-satisfied, but gathers a lot of necessary information in a short time through his personal connections and draws sound conclusions.

- He is of the view that it is possible to develop products efficiently to reflect the needs as well as the seeds.
- His good communication with the production line staff makes it possible for the teams to shift smoothly from development to production.

Results

Outstanding performance

Mr Park

- He is not a good listener.
- He is unable to choose words or use expressions that can be understood easily by others.
- He believes that research and development is a respectable and creative job, but other divisions are solely concerned about making money.
- He believes that he was born to be a researcher.
- He does not know much about the work done at production lines.

- He is seeds-oriented and believes that "all we have to do is to invent good products."
- He does not know much about the work done by the related divisions. Even if a good product is developed, it cannot be shifted smoothly to the production process.

Results

Mediocre or average performance

Neither job knowledge nor academic/career background leads to superior performance, but behavior does.

BUSINESS TIP

Mercer's competency model is a useful framework for those seeking to understand how to define and build similar models to profile the skills or behaviors needed to succeed in certain jobs or functions. Our model has 28 competency factors illustrated in Exhibit 9.3.

		4 types of action			
		Ability to carry out	**Ability to coordinate**	**Ability to consolidate**	**Ability to create**
		Carry out, Pursue, Hold, Maintain	Adapt, Communicate, Cooperate	Develop, Plan, Influence, Coach	Change, Innovate, Create
7 object areas	**Self Management**	Ability to control one's emotion, discipline, under any circumstances	Ability to flexibly adapt oneself to surrounding environment	Ability to expand one's potential corresponding to surrounding environment	Ability to change oneself keeping up with change in environment
	Interpersonal Management	Ability to maintain long-lasting and stable reliance with others by tenaciously interacting	Ability to sensitively support and cooperate to others	Ability to influence and coach others	Ability to affect and change others
	Achievement Management	Ability to persistently try to achieve goals	Ability to organize team to realize the best result as a team	Ability to consolidate available resource under complex circumstances to achieve the best result	Ability to create and challenge objectives in unknown field
	Process Management	Ability to steadily carry out regulated process ant to maintain high quality	Ability to flexibly and accurately adjust plan or schedule of team	Ability to establish process to achieve goals under complex circumstances	Ability to create and proceed with process in unknown field
	Concept Management	Ability to maintain logical way of thinking, speaking and writting to lead to the conclusion	Ability to communicate and share thought or concept with others	Ability to apply logical framework to complex subject	Ability to create and apply logical framework in unknown field
	Information Management	Ability to seek information keeping strong interests in new trend	Abiltiy to effectively arrange and communicate the information	Ability to gather, analize, consolidate and utilize various information	Ability to create value-added information
	Time Management	Ability to pursue speed or efficient usage of time.	Ability to realize team efficiency	Ability to plan and develop systems to improve productivity	Ability to generate innovative idea to advance productivity

Exhibit 9.3 Competency matrix (28 competency factors)

The process involved in building a competency framework need not be complicated. The following lists the steps we follow.

Step 1 – Mercer discusses with top management to determine the organizational units for which the management wants to develop a competency model. At this stage we also identify superior performers in the unit based on the company's performance records.

Step 2 – Mercer analyses the behavioral characteristics of the superior performers by using questionnaires on his or her subordinates, peers, and superiors.

Step 3 – Mercer sets up a hypothetical competency model by using the data obtained in Step 2.

Step 4 – Mercer conducts behavioral event interviews with the superior performers (and sometimes with the average performers).

Step 5 – Details are provided for the competency model. This is where we determine the critical competency factors needed for a position by using the competency matrix.

An important part of the process is to extract key behavioral attributes contributing to these people's high performances. Average performers, who are in the same job group, can then model their behavior based on the key performance drivers for a particular job. The company can also build a gap analysis by benchmarking the average performers' competencies or behavior against the high performers.

Once the competency model is developed, it can be applied to many areas of HRM such as selection, training and development, staffing, performance measurement, career planning, and succession planning (see Exhibit 9.4).

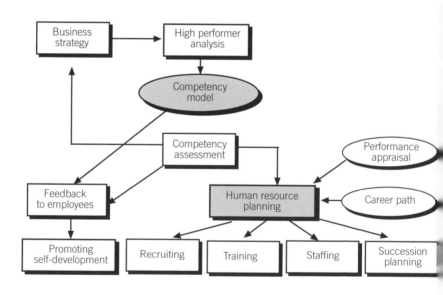

Exhibit 9.4 HRM based on the competency model

Combined with performance management by MBO (management by objective), the competency model approach gives us effective ways to find and develop talent needed by an organization. Many line managers hold a biased view that the competency model is a technicality of the HRM people. This is completely untrue. The competency model is a useful management tool to align people's behavior to the corporate strategies for better performance. Once line managers familiarize themselves with the competency model, their management skills could be greatly enhanced. For example, if managers have a good knowledge of the competency model of sales people who report to them, the managers will know exactly what kind of behaviors would lead to better sales and better customer satisfactions. They can then give effective coaching advice to salespeople on their day-to-day activities.

HOW CAN I CHANGE MY PEOPLE'S BEHAVIOR?

One characteristic of an adaptive corporation is the ability to change, and then to manage the change process to build lasting results. CEOs build visions of the future for their organization, but mobilizing the organization to get to this future destination is a complex exercise. Mercer's experience with clients tells us that over 75 percent of change management efforts flop because the management focused on changing the organizational structure, process, and programs, rather than working on changing mindsets. One often hears this phrase: "We changed our organizational structure to better serve our customers," or "We have just implemented a new CRM (customer relations management) system" as if these superficial changes were complete in themselves to push the organization to a better performance. Changing structures alone is akin to touching the tip of an iceberg. The harder part to reach is the bottom of the iceberg – organizational behavior. How does one define organizational behavior? To put it simply, it is the sum of an organization's everyday behavior. The everyday behavior of an organization will not alter unless there is a distinct effort made to change people's behaviors and mindsets.

Mercer has been successfully helping clients implement change management programs. The following approach can be an effective way of implementing and managing the change process.

1. Top management sends a clear message of its vision for the change, outlining the goals and measures clearly.
2. Top management implements a company-wide communication and promotion plan for the change program. This includes both internal and external communication.
3. Need for personalizing the change – clarifying individual performance goals and measures for each employee in line with the new direction.
4. Need for personalizing the change – identifying competencies and behaviors that each employee needs to develop or improve in line with the new direction, and to create a personal improvement plan.
5. Maintaining the change – developing reward and incentive schemes in line with the new strategy to maintain the changed status.

This five-step program has been a very effective framework to manage a change process. Again, we must reiterate that change management will succeed only if you can successfully change your employees' everyday behavior and mindset.

HOW DO I GET EMPLOYEES TO HAVE SHARED VISION?

CEOs can lead, but will the troops follow? A vision can be specific or broad in its sweep, but every employee needs to be focused on the goals of this vision. Creating a shared vision can be a Herculean task for the CEO, as we have worked with companies that have had various levels of success implementing a shared vision for its various business units operating in multiple locations. The challenge becomes even more complex in a multi-location and multicultural environment. What is the CEO's top priority? It is that of selling his or her vision to the management, to the rank and file employees. Failure to "market" this vision to the employees is akin to having embarked on a journey without a destination.

CASE STUDY

The CEO's role in change management

In Korea, we helped the CEO of a leading financial institution to set the organization on a course to recapture its lost position as a market leader. An employee opinion poll done by the bank showed that 96 percent of those surveyed felt the changes were necessary for the bank. A restructuring of the bank's HRM system was needed as a fundamental step toward getting the organization realigned with its business mission of being a market leader. The financial institution came to us to help it implement a new job evaluation system and a system for appraisal and managing staff performance. This organization had over 4,000 employees in some 300 job functions. The CEO of this institution worked on progressively changing people's attitudes and mindset by constantly communicating the need for the revolutionary changes. In a series of communication exercises completed over a few months, the CEO touched on issues covering the need for change and what the changes were. The CEO also detailed the desired outcomes for these changes. In communicating the rationale for change and the details involved, this CEO was able to steer and manage change in a way that was acceptable to a change-resistant organization.

CASE STUDY

Japan's Asahi Glass Corporation's (AGC) bid for shared vision

How does an organization that has grown global quickly cope with building a shared vision? In Japan's Asahi Glass Corporation's (AGC) case, it was with difficulty and a bit of video technology. The company is a major glass manufacturer in the world, generating US$12 billion in annual revenues. It has 50,000 employees scattered around the globe. The company's strength is in the manufacturing of flat glass for construction and automobile glass. Its acquisition of Glaverbel in Europe and the AFG Industries in America has thrown it into the arms of globalization a lot faster than other Japanese manufacturers. Its CEO and president Shinya Ishizu felt that the pace of the organization's globalization was not fast enough. One of the major changes he instituted was the appointment of two non-Japanese people as presidents of two major divisions. He then proceeded to create a new vision and a set of shared values for Asahi Glass' global employees (see Exhibit 9.5).

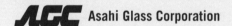

/AGC   **Asahi Glass Corporation**

Vision

We, the AGC Group, *"Look Beyond"*
to make the world a brighter place.

Shared Value

1. Innovation & Operational Excellence
2. Diversity
3. Environment
4. Integrity

Exhibit 9.5 AGC vision

Ishizu believes that one of the most important responsibilities of top management is to be a sort of "missionary" propagating the company's vision to the employees. But a major obstacle he faced was that the vision he created was not well shared by employees, especially those from outside Japan. This was attributed to the differences in culture and language of the offshore operating units compared to the Japanese headquarters. While he continues to champion his vision by speaking to as many employees as possible, he has explored alternative ways of instilling this sense of shared vision among his global employees, one of which is to have them absorb the vision statement by making films about what AGC's vision means. In AGC's leadership development forum for global managers, one of the itineraries is a film-making session. Managers have the task of working with their colleagues to produce a three-minute promotion film about what it means to be an AGC manager. The film has to explain the company's vision and shared values to other AGC employees. This is a novel experience for many of the managers. Managers are given a digital video recorder to work with. The rest is a matter of creativity. This process has been highly effective for the company as it found that managers are forced to interpret and convert the AGC's vision – a conceptual theme – into something visual and easily understandable. The film-making venture presents a nightmare for many of the managers who have to work with people from different language backgrounds to get the film out. But it forces managers to internalize the mission statement. The exercise has also helped build bonds among teams of managers who have worked together to interpret and deliver a message on the company's shared vision. It has been a fun and powerful exercise for the global employees involved.

▶▶ CONCLUSION

How much does a CEO need to get involved in mapping an organization's strategic people initiatives? As much as possible would be a good way forward. CEOs cannot afford to be disengaged from being a champion of people programs. As organizations become increasingly global, CEOs have to build a believable future for the organization, sell this vision everyday, and harness the entire organization into achieving the company's vision.

We have focused on the broad themes of getting the right talent to power business goals and the need for succession, and we have provided a model for business leaders to work on. CEOs will be constantly inundated with critical business issues that force them to focus on profitability. Our argument is that the foundation for good management has its roots in strategic people development. This requires the top management to be partners with HRM in shaping, defining and implementing a talent management strategy.

In Asia, where major companies are still mostly owned by family owned concerns, getting involved in HRM is going to involve changes in mindset. But the forces of globalization are already forcing Asian owned enterprises to look at their organizations with a view to achieving optimal performance. Whether Asian CEOs like it or not, HRM issues will have to be a top business agenda. Without a strategic HRM vision, organizations in Asia cannot effectively compete for a stake in the future.

[1] McKinsey Quarterly 2001, No. 3 – A Computer Legend in the Making.

[2] PriceWaterhouseCoopers CEO Survey – Leadership, Responsibility and Growth in Uncertain Times, 6th Annual Global CEO Survey.

[3] "Corporate Governance in Asia – A Comparative Perspective: The Challenge Facing the Thai Economy," Deunden Nikomborirak and Somkiat Tangkitvanich, presented at an OECD and Korean Development Institute conference in Seoul, March 1999.

[4] "A Battle of Brothers," Todd Crowell and Laxmi Nakarmi, *Asia Week*, April 7, 2000.

[5] "Who Controls East Asian Corporations," Stijn Claessens and Simeon Djankov from the World Bank and Larry H.P. Lang from The University of Chicago. This report was sourced from the World Bank's website: <*www.worldbank.org/html/dec/Publications/Workpapers/wps2000series/wps2054/wps2054.pdf*>

[6] "Medicine for the Masses," Trish Saywell, *Far Eastern Economic Review*, August 7, 2003. Sourced from the *Far Eastern Economic Review*'s online archive.

[7] Saywell 2003.

[8] "Thai Farmers: 'A Good Bank in a Bad Environment,'" Frederik Balfour, *Business Weekonline*, June 10, 2001.

[9] Balfour 2001.

[10] Company Press Release – "TMC to Establish Toyota Institute to Instill the Toyota Way," <*http://www.toyota.co.jp/en/news/01/1221.html*>

10

Business Questions HRM Must Ask

Richard Payne

*T*he boom years of the 1990s did little to prepare HRM professionals to cope with the demands of the twenty-first century. Capitalizing on growth in the 1990s meant that recruitment and staff retention were the highest priority, while cost control, administrative efficiency, and performance management took a back seat. The Asia economic crisis of 1997 changed the basic tenets upon which HRM managers were operating. Staff retrenchments and salary freezes were widely adopted. Training budgets dried up and recruitment was no longer a sought-after expertise. Companies began to value the skills of those HRM professionals that knew how to cut personnel costs and manage layoffs.

Demands from headquarters have compounded the economic pressure being felt by HRM professionals in Asia. Corporate HRM is more carefully reviewing local performance pay plans and payments to ensure they are aligned with corporate goals and results. Furthermore, global HRM policies and procedures are taking precedence over local practices.

At the same time, Asia has become a major source of talent for the rest of the world. Recruiters in Asia must compete, not just with other local employers, but also increasingly with companies in Japan, Europe, and North America. The demographic trends in the developed world clearly will compound the problems of labor shortages in many industries across the Asia region.

Unpredictable crises have hit Asia, and the world at large, with increased frequency. HRM professionals must be prepared for crises no matter when, where, or how they occur. During these crises, HRM professionals must be contingency planners, advisors to management, the coordinators of the response, and the communicators to employees.

A new set of competencies, beyond those needed in the past, are required to meet today's challenges. The HRM manager still needs the skills, knowledge, and experience to efficiently manage the day-to-day activities of the HRM functions. But, the HRM professional in Asia must also have greater understanding of economic and political issues, broader business savvy, and greater communication skills than were required in the past.

Increased uncertainty and turmoil have characterized the environment over the past 10 years. HRM practitioners have had to adapt and respond flexibly to a series of unforeseen events. The Asia economic crisis of 1997, the terrorist attacks of 2002, and the SARS outbreak of 2003 have all presented unique challenges to HRM. Top management has drawn HRM into a central role of corporate decision-making as they increasingly recognize the impact that HRM issues are having on the performance of the organization.

This new role for HRM has led to new responsibilities that require a more analytical, future-oriented approach. HRM needs to become a far more proactive function that must continuously ask two critical business questions:

1. What trends will reshape the HRM function?
2. What does an effective HRM professional need to know?

TRENDS THAT WILL RESHAPE HRM

The critical trends that will impact on HRM practitioners in Asia fall into four categories:
1. economic;
2. business;
3. demographic; and
4. crisis management.

ECONOMIC

The boom years of the 1990s

The economic environment that HRM practitioners must cope with today traces its roots back to the legacy left by the economic growth of the 1990s. For most of that time the United States economy fueled continuous economic expansion throughout the region. While starting the decade in the doldrums, the economies of Europe gained strength and the Euro Zone was achieving a real GDP rate of nearly 3 percent per annum during the closing years of the decade. Europe increasingly became an important market for many Asian companies. Among developed economies, only Japan's economy persistently turned in disappointing results.

Developing Asia effectively capitalized on the strong and consistent growth in the United States and Europe. From 1990 until 1996 the annual real GDP growth of Asian economies (excluding Japan) averaged 6 to 8 percent. This impressive growth was matched by consistency. Thailand, for example, saw its economic growth rate averaging around 10.5 percent between 1986 and 1990; and an average growth of 8.3 percent between 1991 and 1995. The economies of China, Hong Kong, Korea, Singapore, and Malaysia could also be counted on for at least 5 percent annual growth rates from 1986 until 1996.

The positive and predictable economic climate had a direct impact on the management of human resources throughout the region.

Focus on capitalizing on growth

HRM's role during this period often was one of supporting management in its efforts to capitalize on the potential of business expansion. Recruitment and staff retention were the highest priority while cost control, administrative efficiency, and performance management took a back seat. HRM was tasked with filling the jobs created by building new plants or expanding into new markets. Staff turnover was a primary concern since the loss of experienced employees meant increased recruiting, the distraction of basic training for new employees, and the risk of not being able to achieve ambitious expansion plans.

Talent shortages among professionals and managers

Rapid growth created more and more jobs. The jobs created increasingly required technical skills or managerial experience. The growth in the talent pool could not keep up with demand. Inevitably, career paths became telescoped. People often were hired with the minimum of prior experience and promoted to take on more responsibilities after fulfilling the basic requirements of their current roles.

Guaranteed annual salary increases

Employees expected salaries to increase at least at the level of the previous year, regardless of individual or company performance. Job opportunities were plentiful, especially for skilled or experienced workers and professionals. Companies that faced the ever-present risk of employees leaving for better paying jobs elsewhere often paid salary increases across the board based on market increases. On top of the across-the-board pay rise to match the market, many companies offered additional increases to keep their high-performing employees.

High-fixed, low-variable compensation

Companies were reluctant to introduce variable pay plans during such a strong period of growth. The hot market seemed to dictate a fixed-only pay policy. Performance pay was often given lip service with bonuses expected as a "right" of employment.

High-flying HRM professionals across Asia developed a set of skills that focused on market awareness. The best were adept at identifying and recruiting large numbers of workers and attracting experienced professionals and managers. At the same time, they kept their fingers on the pulse of the market and responded with proposals that would ensure their companies' compensation levels remained attractive and their workforce secure.

During this period the best companies devoted attention to broad-based skills training and management development programs. Training concentrated on upgrading the capabilities of the workforce, while management development focused on providing freshly minted managers with exposure to world-class management practices.

THE ASIAN "CORRECTION"

The long period of economic growth and stability did little to prepare HRM practitioners for the wrenching changes brought about by the 1997 Asia Crisis. The economic crisis started in Thailand, quickly spread throughout Southeast Asia, and then went further afield to Hong Kong, South Korea, and Taiwan. In 1998 the developing economies of Asia shrunk by 2.4 percent – the first overall decline in 14 years. Indonesia and Thailand were particularly hard hit (real GDP shrunk by more than 10 percent in 1998), while the Philippines, Hong Kong, Malaysia, and South Korea also experienced negative growth.

The impact of the economic crisis on HRM practitioners was profound and wide-felt. Staff retrenchments and salary freezes suddenly were needed where such action had previously been unheard of. Training budgets dried up and cost control became the corporate mantra. Recruitment was no longer a sought-after expertise. Rather, companies valued the skills of those HRM professionals that knew how to cut personnel costs and manage layoffs.

> " The long period of economic growth and stability did little to prepare HRM practitioners for the wrenching changes brought about by the 1997 Asia Crisis. "

Since 1998 many of the economies of Asia have been on a rollercoaster ride. For example, after eking out 0.3 percent growth in 1998, Singapore's economy rose by 5.9 percent in 1999 and 10.3 percent in 2000. It then shrunk by −2 percent in 2001 before limping back to a positive growth of 2.8 percent in 2002 and 2.5 percent in 2003. The rapid changes in economic fortunes have forced HRM professionals to adapt quickly to changing circumstances. It also means that they need to keep abreast of economic changes and the likely impact on corporate operations.

HRM's economic questions

- What are the key economic indicators (for example, real GDP growth, inflation, US dollar exchange rate) that impact our company's operations?
- Do we monitor economic forecasts and actively use them in our planning?
- How do we interpret and use economic data and analysis?
- What key economic indicators have the greatest relevance to identifying trends in such areas as talent management, training, compensation, recruitment, and retention?
- Do we know what economic factors have the greatest relevance to our company's operations?

BUSINESS

HRM professionals in Asia have been whipsawed by continuously changing expectations on the part of management and employees as a result of the wide swings in the economy. Retrenchments due to the downturn were followed by pressure to hire to capitalize on renewed growth. Demands to keep salaries competitive came on the heels of dictates to freeze salaries.

A proactive approach that strives to identify emerging issues and trends can be highly effective in forestalling undulating pressures thrust upon the HRM professional. The cost of only reacting is clearly displayed in a survey Mercer conducted of business response to the 2001 downturn in Asia. According to the survey, the most common HRM response to the 2001 Asia downturn were:

1. hiring freeze (60 percent of respondents);
2. reducing salary increase (34 percent);
3. retrenchment (28 percent); and
4. wage freezes (24 percent).

When asked what the impact of their responses was, 36 percent said the actions helped. However, 39 percent indicated no change, while 25 percent said the actions taken even hurt their operations. Furthermore, while these short-term solutions may have been necessary to make it through the temporary downturn, they did not prepare the companies for the subsequent upsurge. Nor were they helpful in preparing the companies for future uncertainties in the economic climate.

Being proactive and attentive to local business conditions is not enough. Demands from headquarters put added pressures on local operations within Asia. The markets are putting increased pressure on corporate executives to perform. The average tenure of an American CEO has declined to only three short years. Consequently, the pace of change has accelerated as corporate leadership strives to make an impact in the short time allotted.

The pressures from headquarters have had a direct impact on HRM in Asia. The pendulum that swings between centralization and localization appears to be moving in the direction of the center.

1. Local operations increasingly feel pressure from US and European headquarters to control cost regardless of local economic growth patterns.
2. Corporate HRM carefully reviews local and regional performance pay plans and payments to ensure they are aligned with corporate goals and results.
3. Global HRM policies and procedures increasingly take precedence over local practices. Local operations are tasked with implementing practices that are in line with global policies.
4. Technology often is used to implement greater consistency in HRM practices on a global basis. The advent of PeopleSoft, SAP, and other HRM information systems mean that local practices are much more transparent and open to scrutiny.

To de- or not to de-centralize?

HRM in Asia is often subjected to decisions that come from corporate HQ and these decisions come and go with the change in leadership at the top. In recent years, there has been a marked shift toward centralization of business units and processes, including HRM. We spoke to the HRM director of a fast-moving consumer goods company based in Asia who has been a part of this exercise. This case highlights the merits, pitfalls, and lessons to be learnt from moving toward centralization.

Q: What is the business case for centralization?
A: The case for centralization is fairly simple. It is beneficial if you have global product forms and brands and customers. For instance, if the product forms are the same or at least largely similar, then having common manufacturing processes, raw material suppliers, and common manufacturing equipment makes good economic sense. If you are buying five machines instead of one, you get lower prices, better service, among others, from your supplier.

In a similar vein, if your customers are global (for example, you are selling to the same retailer in 30 countries), then the way in which you go to market with that customer, or all similar customers, is largely the same with a centralized process. This process ought to be transparent at all levels.

In Europe, for instance, MNC retailers are represented in many countries where there are no tariffs or duties; where distribution crosses borders easily every day; where manufacturers provide their products with multinational packaging (often packages with four to eight languages on them) of common brands. In such an instance, it is important that a manufacturer's pricing and promotion policies be transparent and common across all units, or retailers will look across all the countries supplying their stores and buy from the manufacturer's lowest price unit for all their retail units across all countries.

From the corporate view, there is the benefit of standardizing "best practices" across all their units, especially so when market forces are driving the industry to common product forms, brands, packaging, pricing and promotion, among others. All units will benefit from implementing best practices, improving quality, lowering price, and increasing the flexibility of the organization in moving human and financial capital to where they are most needed.

Q: Isn't it the case that business units that are against centralization always say "but we are different?"
A: The more regions are centralized, the more other regions have to ask of themselves: "Why do we need to be different." If there is a business benefit (best practices, lower costs) to standardize, then it should be pursued. A collateral to this argument then is if something can be standardized, then it can be looked at as a candidate for outsourcing. Today all companies have to look at everything they are doing and ask: "Is this process core to our business or do we just need this function done with the highest quality at the lowest transaction cost?" If it is core to our business, maybe this is a process that we should commercialize and sell to others; that is, if we are able to do it better and cheaper than anyone else.

Q: What was your company's experience with centralization? What were your key lessons?
A: The centralization of our business in Asia was carried out over a six-year period – it started with our merger with another company – that carried on into the end of 2002. We looked at the issues I raised above. For instance, having common suppliers of raw materials gave us negotiation power. This gave us the opportunity to raise the quality and service from suppliers and helped drive down our costs. Common product forms and packaging meant that we could consolidate money spent on product development, market research, advertising, and packaging supplies. This gave us improved flexibility to move products in the event of a manufacturing disruption or in the event of a dramatic increase in volume in any market. All these also lead to our looking at how we went to market with common customers across the region to assure that we were conducting fair dealings and not creating problems for ourselves, our consumers, or other customers.
  We started with asking ourselves these questions:
* *how consumers differed from market to market in terms of preference for certain product features and benefits*
* *what messages appealed to them in terms of advertising claims*
* *how our competitors were going to market*
* *what retailers (customers) wanted and needed from our products, brands, business methods, and distribution systems*
* *what represented best practice either from within or outside of our company.*

We used key metrics and started benchmarking from unit to unit. We sent people from the lowest level of metrics to the place that had the highest metrics so that they could talk to their colleagues across the world to find out how they were getting more for less out of their processes. This took a lot of time and trust, and involved a lot of people travelling. However, it paid off.

We started doing this in one line of our business (following the merger, we had become the largest supplier of this particular business in the world). The merged business had between them hundreds of years of experience. We thought, if we can't make the world's best in this product at the lowest cost, who can?

Q: What are the pitfalls to avoid in undertaking such a major move at centralization?

A: *The pitfalls are that everyone (within the organization) thinks that he/she is the one who is the "best," and if someone is doing it faster or cheaper then there is a good reason (for example, lower electricity prices, lower wage rates, less costly distribution, less competition, among others). It took a long time for people to break down their defenses and to say, "Yes, their electricity rates are 18 percent lower than ours, but their overall energy expense per tonne of goods produced is 26 percent lower … there must be more to it than just lower (electric) rates."*

Another thing that we learnt was that when you centralize your operations, you will find too many people doing the same things in each country that the new centralized organization will not need. Similarly, you will also not have enough people in the central HQ to do the new thing you are taking on. It is very important that a company takes inventory of the people who are "out there" in the country units to find out which of them has the capability of handling a centralized role and is willing to relocate.

To achieve successful centralization, you need to have the ability to critically assess the level of talent available – using the criteria of skills, experience, and abilities required for success in the new central role – to make the new organization work.

Centralization means fewer people in each function than in the total decentralized organization, and companies must learn to harvest the headcount and try to find suitable roles for those who had responsibilities in the decentralized organization. The ones who don't match up well will need to be separated from the company or they will fight a guerrilla war behind the new centralized organization to assure that the new organization does not work.

Another critical thing to observe when choosing to "De or Not to De" is to recognize the whole thing as a significant piece of change management. The discussion within the senior leadership team (region or country) has to be focused on "What will we have to do differently to make these common processes work?" The discussion cannot be allowed to get into, "Should we do this?"

Helping teams with change management techniques, employing process-mapping to identify how the existing process will have to change helps enormously in preparing to explain the change and the case for change. Most of these efforts, as we know all too well, fail not because the ideas were flawed – there were many good ideas, but rarely one best suited for all companies or industries – but because of failed execution due to either resistance or lack of understanding on the part of the people who are implementing them.

Q: What do you consider as the key rewards, after all the pain of going through the process?

A: Once you have standardized your processes, you can do a far better job of benchmarking and creating meaningful key performance indicators (KPIs) internally and externally. You can then really gain ground on improvements to quality, costs, improved service, and improved market insights, among others. The key here is that you get everyone to understand that we are in fact always thinking about global competitiveness and not resting on the success of our business in one market, where there may be temporary protection from competitors by tariffs, or due to a lack of competitors, or other factors that mask your true ability to compete in the marketplace.

For us, the big achievement was that after the merger, we found that over the next three years, we were going to be able to remove about US$400 million in costs per year out of our business processes (inventory reductions, improved productivity, lower materials usage, more effective market research, improved advertising, and promotion effectiveness)!

Instead of responding only to the immediate demands of the business or pressures from corporate headquarters, HRM practitioners have a responsibility to plan for future uncertainties and demands. They need to respond to a series of questions that will help devise a HRM strategy that will survive upturns and downturns.

HRM's business questions

- How do we afford and sustain our current level of reward spending?
- How can we bolster growth through the use of our compensation strategy?
- How can we reallocate compensation to achieve better control over spending?
- How do we recognize and reward our highest performers?
- How can we ensure that pay reflects and encourages productivity and results?

DEMOGRAPHIC

The compounded impact of declining fertility rates and increased life expectancy in the developed world have created a unique situation where fewer workers are entering the workforce at a time when people are living much longer after leaving the workforce. Consequently fewer workers need to support more retirees.

Region	Current	Projected 2020
North America	3.05	2.05
Europe	2.35	1.75
Australasia	3.10	2.55
Japan	3.2	1.40

Exhibit 10.1 The ratio of working-aged adults of retirees[1]

The aging of the workforce in developed economies is well documented; however, its impact on the developing economies of Asia is less well known. The numbers above indicate that shortages of workers and professionals are virtually inevitable in the developed world. As the population ages, the economies of these countries will increasingly look outside their own borders to fill vacant positions. At the same time, Asia's talent pool has continued to increase with rapid population growth, rural–urban migration, and increased investment in education. Nevertheless, demand has outstripped supply in many sectors.

Asia has become a major source of talent for jobs in technology and health care. The demand for such people will rise further and spread to other industries. Thus, the demographic trends in the developed world will have a direct impact on the talent pool in Asia. Asian recruiters must compete not just with other local employers, but also increasingly with companies halfway around the world that are willing to offer highly attractive compensation packages in order to lure executives into moving. The career opportunities for talented executives willing to relocate will become increasingly attractive and hard to counter.

The demographic trends in the developed world clearly will compound the problems of labor shortages in many industries across the Asia region. This means that the complexity of talent management will rise further as companies in Asia are forced to compete in a global market. Asian companies must maintain their competitive cost advantage while attracting the best talent and offering challenging career opportunities that match anything offered elsewhere in the world.

HRM's talent management questions

- What is the impact of demographics on our ability to attract and retain talented employees?
- Where will we face shortages in the years to come?
- How do we create career opportunities that match what is available to the best talent in North America and Europe?
- How do we "sell" the advantages of a career solely within a person's home country?
- Do we offer jobs that can lead to careers within the Asian region?
- What are the constraints to regional and global careers within our company and how do we overcome these obstacles?
- How do we become a "learning organization" that grooms our employees to meet the changing needs of the business?

CRISIS MANAGEMENT

The SARs outbreak in the first half of 2003 hit many parts of Asia hard. Travel ground to a halt, business demand fell, and supply chains were disrupted. HRM practitioners found themselves in a critical role as companies tried to cope with both the concerns of employees and the needs of the business. The quick actions of many HRM professionals were a positive contributing factor to limiting the damaging effects of the crisis and facilitating the resurgence that occurred as the spread of the disease waned. After the crisis died a feeling took hold that the lessons learned from the outbreak would enable companies to cope with similar outbreaks, should they occur.

The problem is that history does not always repeat itself. Unpredictable crises have hit Asia, and the world at large, with increased frequency. The year 1997 seemed to usher in a new period of turmoil. The devaluation of the Thai baht in July of that year sparked the first economic crisis that spread throughout East Asia. Since then we have had to cope with events such as the anti-Chinese riots in Jakarta, the subsequent fall of President Suharto, the bursting of the dot-com bubble that led to the longest decline in US stocks since the 1930s, the September 11 attacks on the World Trade Center and Pentagon, and the terrorist bombings in Bali and Jakarta. Viewed in this context, the SARS epidemic was simply the latest in a series of unpredictable events that had the potential to cause serious economic and business disruption.

> **HRM should have communication plans and checklists ready before the crisis even begins. This requires advanced planning and preparation even when a crisis is not even in sight.**

HRM professionals must be prepared for crises no matter when, where, or how they occur. During these crises, HRM has four critical roles:

1. contingency planning;
2. advising management;
3. coordinating the response; and
4. communicating to employees.

Contingency planning

Planning is a critical part of crisis preparation. HRM must consider and assess the range of risks that might confront the company and its employees. HRM practitioners need to be ready with responses to possible scenarios as they play out. It needs to identify potential critical audiences that will become the focus of communication and it needs to put into place a team of crisis communicators that will coordinate responses with all parts of the organization. Related to this, every company needs a plan for developing and distributing information. In turn, an established approval path for rapid release of information is essential to ensure the smooth and quick dissemination of information.

Advising management

By bringing a different perspective to the situation, one that focuses on the human aspects of the crisis, human resource managers can provide valuable advice to management. During a crisis, it is the responsibility of the HRM manager to represent the interests of employees and show how employees may react to any proposed actions. When it comes time to explain what needs to be done, HRM should ensure that leadership communicates effectively with all levels of employees.

Coordinating the response

Once the decisions have been made and the plan is in place, HRM should have a primary role in activating the plan. It should be the one to coordinate the communication and to monitor the reaction. When employees raise issues, HRM has to be prepared to deal with those concerns in an effective manner.

Communicating to employees

Effective crisis management means developing communication tactics and infrastructure. Time is of the essence during a crisis. HRM should have communication plans and checklists ready before the crisis even begins. This requires advanced planning and preparation, even when a crisis is not in sight. Furthermore, HRM staff should have undergone training in crisis communication and counseling long before such skills are actually required.

As part of the crisis communication preparation, HRM staff need to get to know what emergency benefits and assistance is available and know how to get these benefits quickly into the hands of employees and their families.

HRM's crisis management questions

- Are we properly prepared for the next crisis?
- Will we have the ear of leadership when it occurs?
- What should be our role during times of turmoil?
- What advice should we provide in a time of crisis?
- Does HRM have the necessary crisis management skills to play a central role in responding to a crisis?
- Who are the critical audiences that will become the focus of communication?
- Who should be part of our team of crisis communicators?
- Do we have an effective plan for developing and distributing information?
- Do we have in place an established approval path for rapid release of information?
- Have we trained our HRM staff to handle communications and our response to a crisis?

WHAT DOES HRM NEED TO KNOW?

The pressures on the HRM professional are great and will continue to grow. A new set of competencies, beyond those needed in the past, are required to meet current-day challenges. The HRM manager still needs the skills, knowledge, and experience to efficiently manage the day-to-day activities of the HRM functions. But, the successful HRM professional in Asia must also have:

1. a solid grounding in economics and politics;
2. business mindedness;
3. analytical capabilities; and
4. communication skills and assertiveness.

The economic knowledge is important as external factors increasingly affect the HRM professional's ability to deliver. A HRM professional who blithely performs day-to-day activities without being aware of the potential risks to tomorrow's operations may be blind-sided by events that appear to have come out of nowhere. The ability to interpret economic signals and identify the impact on one's own operations is extremely valuable in an uncertain environment.

> " **The successful HRM professional must have the confidence and conviction to act as an equal business partner to top management.** "

Business-mindedness is necessary not just to cope with issues in the local environment, but also to understand the global forces that will impact on the organization and its employees. The HRM professionals must have the ability to identify and implement changes that are necessary due to these global forces. Plus, HRM professionals need to understand and be able to use the technology that is increasingly available to deal with the ever more complex issues of a global organization.

Analytical skills are required, as the solutions are not often readily apparent. For example, long-term demographic trends indicate that labor shortages will become more pronounced; however, short-term economic and business conditions may mean that cost control is of paramount importance. The effective HRM professional will analyze the situation and develop solutions that are appropriate for the immediate future while preparing the organization for future eventualities.

Even if the HRM professional has all of the knowledge and skills cited above, these capabilities are meaningless without assertiveness and the ability to communicate. The successful HRM professional must have the confidence and conviction to act as an equal business partner to top management. They must be able to articulate and explain the issue and its ramifications to top management, communicate the response to employees, and proactively follow through with implementation of any approved actions.

▶▶ CONCLUSION

While the challenges are great, the obstacles in the way of delivering world-class performance are equally as high. The legacy of the past can often haunt the HRM professional that wants to transform the HRM function. Senior management can be highly skeptical and resistant to ideas that emanate from HRM. The HRM function may lack credibility since previously it may not have proposed and delivered innovative and future-oriented solutions. Furthermore, the HRM staff themselves may lack the skills to move from a purely transactional role to one that is a full partner with the business.

The implications of these challenges and obstacles are profound. The role of HRM will undergo a transformation. HRM must learn to balance its role as an advisor to management in business strategy and an expert in functional operations. It needs to align HRM policies and practices with the business, then ensure that those policies are carried out in an efficient and effective manner.

The experience of the past has done little to prepare many HRM professionals in Asia for the challenges of the future. In the past functional expertise in the transactional elements of the HRM function was enough to spur a HRM professional into a successful career. Such experience is woefully insufficient now. Experience, skills, and knowledge in economics, business, crisis management, leadership, consulting, and communications have become necessary prerequisites for success in the future.

The question is: "Are you truly prepared?"

---

[1] Sources: United Nations World Population Prospects (1992); OECD Social Policy Studies (1994).

11

Leadership in Asia

Regional PMR and Jack Lim

*G*lobally, the imperative to manage talent and create leadership capability effectively is more urgent than ever. Many companies are experiencing a shortage of top leadership talent as well as greater competition for critical skills. New technologies, rapidly changing business models, and globalization of markets have all increased demand for new workforce capabilities and continuous improvement in workforce performance. Meanwhile, aging high-performing workers are leaving the workforce faster than crucial new talent is entering it. While shortages of technical skilled staff are often corrected by the forces of demand and supply, shortages of leaders is more difficult to tackle as leadership capability needs to be nurtured through experience. In this chapter we explore the leadership trends and cultural forces that have shaped some of the leadership values in Asia. We also explore the interrelated variables of Asian values, motivation, and make a case for distinguishing between management and leadership as we try to understand leadership models. A better understanding of leadership development will provide HRM and business leaders with a clearer perspective of what works in Asia and suggest a way forward. There is no doubt that raising the quality of an organization's leadership can directly impact employee motivation, retain customers, and improve shareholder value.

TREND SPOTTING

The average duration of a CEO's tenure is just a little bit lower than what it has been. The big trend is that firms are much more likely to hire replacement CEOs from the outside than from the inside. This clearly demonstrates a shortage of leaders in organizations. Incidentally, the number of CEO failures has also increased by a similar rate.

In Asia, the leadership and talent issues are often compounded by economic, social, and political uncertainties. The recent slowdown exposed many organizations' lack of discipline in managing their talent:

- some were caught with many performers that were hired during spurts of significant growth;
- others that had acquired or displaced talent in a knee-jerk response to market volatility were left without the people they needed to stay competitive;
- many lost experienced talent due to poor management of human capital following privatization and poorly managed mergers and acquisitions.

HRM and business leaders are being forced to address previously ignored realities of leadership development. Increasingly this will determine the sustainability of the organizations. Business leaders are asking and answering these critical questions:

- What workforce capabilities, behaviors, and attitudes do we need in order to implement our business design successfully?
- Are we developing the workforce capabilities we need to succeed in the future?
- Do we know who our current top contributors are?
- Can we clearly identify those with the highest potential for leadership growth, as well as technical mastery?
- Are we attracting, selecting, and retaining "A-grade" players?
- Do we have the ability to remove underperformers continuously, as well as recognize exceptional and effective performers?
- Do our pay, performance, and career development programs align with our business strategy? Do they increase retention and inspire commitment?

REALITIES OF ORGANIZATIONAL LEADERSHIP

In Asia, leadership development has been an ad-hoc exercise that involves sending a select group of individuals to training programs. Often, these programs are technical in nature and are in response to employee requests for greater development opportunities. They do not develop talent or address a strategic need in the organization. Such ad-hoc efforts often yield a poor return as the effect from the training is short-lived. This in turn has an adverse effect on funding for future programs, as the perceived value of the training to the organization and the individual is minimal.

This unstructured approach to leadership development is practiced by many organizations in Asia. Organizations in the West have experimented with leadership development practices for several years, and have invested millions of dollars in consulting fees in an attempt to develop a formula for creating leaders. They have designed systems and processes, some of which have worked better than others. Their experience and ours have revealed three realities that will set the tone of this chapter.

Reality 1: Leadership and management are two sides of the same coin

Leadership and management are distinct, yet complementary. Management is necessary for creating order in a complex internal and external operating environment. Leadership is necessary for motivating and navigating an organization toward a shared vision. Just as there are many managers who cannot lead, there are many leaders who cannot manage. In time, both strip the company of valuable resources in the form of high employee turnover or a workforce that does not perform at its full potential. It is important to understand the differences and the role of leadership and management in organizations so that competencies in both areas can be consciously developed.

Reality 2: A CEO cannot be the sole leader of a large organization

There are simply so many leadership tasks that must be accomplished effectively. A CEO cannot do all of them single-handedly. Smart companies develop leaders at all levels in the organization. All good managers are leaders to various degrees. They need to carry out their leaders' visions by creating their own visions that support the larger vision, and then getting their workers to believe in and accomplish them.

Leadership at every level is also necessary to ensure that a pool of leaders is available for deployment in various existing positions, as well as to lead new business units. In the long run, leadership at every level will lead to an engaged workforce and enhance the firm-specific value of its human capital.

Reality 3: CEO owns the outcomes of leadership development, but HRM owns the process

Leadership development is the responsibility of all managers in an organization. The human resource department plays a vital role in ensuring that the leadership pool the organization is nurturing is aligned with the requirements of the organization. In order to do so HRM needs to take a seat at the strategic table and understand the people requirements from a business perspective.

Clearly defining the required leadership behaviors will give supervisors and subordinates a clear picture of what is required for success. HRM can then develop the systems and processes that will provide opportunities for regular assessment and development of leaders.

MANAGEMENT AND MOTIVATION

As has been stated in several chapters of this book – Asia is diverse and so are its people and management philosophies. Asian management philosophy is grounded in business networks such as the Indian business houses (for example, The Aditya Birla Group), Japanese *keiretsu* (for example, Mitsubishi), the Korean *chaebol* (for example, Daewoo), the overseas Chinese groups (for example, Wah Chang Group), and the Chinese state-owned enterprises. To an outsider these networks look like unfathomable environments where stakeholders are difficult to identify and decision-making seems to be shrouded in mystery. In reality, each organization functions within a set of written and unwritten rules derived from the culture of the geography and the value system of its people.

For example, overseas and mainland Chinese behaviors are deeply rooted in the legacies left by the Chinese philosopher Confucius (551–479 BC). For more than 2000 years, Confucius' disciples have worked to assure that his legacies have become an integral part of the Chinese social, economic, and

> " The most important thing is to listen to people and figure out what is motivating them. "
>
> CARLOS GHOSN, NISSAN MOTOR COMPANY

cultural inheritances. When dealing with authority figures the Chinese, as a rule, fulfill their obligations by being obedient without questioning the decisions of their superiors. They emphasize vertical relationships and would not risk offending authority by cutting horizontally across function or business lines to resolve an issue. They see themselves as following correct protocol and demonstrating correct behavior, which in fact have been clearly described in Confucian principles. Correspondingly, an exemplary leader in a Confucian value society must demonstrate kindness toward the feelings of others, much like the head of a household.

Leadership in a Chinese SOE

Within China's state-owned enterprises (SOEs), where businesses are run like a centrally planned economy, great emphasis is placed on "collectivism." These decisions tend to be made by a group of managers or committees.

The decision-making process is relatively slow. Managers typically spend a lot of time in meetings. They also tend to hold the group rather than an individual accountable for the consequence of any decisions. There is a tendency to follow "policies" rather than for any manager to take personal risks when he or she undertakes a project.

Leadership in a privately held Chinese company

In Chinese private companies, there's always a "core leader." He or she functions like "a god" in the company. This leader plays the central role as the figure head. One example is Zhang Ruimin, CEO of Haier, a global white-ware manufacturing company. Typically, the core leader is the owner and the entrepreneur who started the company. Such a leader:

- is the epicenter of power in the organization;
- tends to lead or manage by business acumen rather than by management systems;
- typically has very strong capability to "lead," inspire, or motivate employees; and
- is weak in terms of setting up procedures or systems to manage employees.

Leaders at private companies operate very well when their businesses are small because they can make decisions quickly to respond to the market's needs. But when the business grows to a certain scale, these leaders typically encounter difficulties in management because of the absence of effective and efficient management systems.

Although there is no common definition of Asian management, there are some common characteristics in the way business is conducted in Asia.

- *Business networks – kereitsus, chaebols* or overseas Chinese groups. Asian firms are organized around business networks that are based on individual or organizational cross-ownerships or relationships. Trade is often carried out with organizations where relationships have long been established or with individuals where managers have developed a level of comfort
- *Collectivism* – this is a result of Confucian legacy. Organizations and individuals act for the benefit for the society rather than for self-gain. The Asian culture requires all participants to reach

a consensus before moving forward. Goals merge in the common interest of a long-term destiny of the society.

- *Mutual trust* – this is between organizations and individuals. Asians use and develop long-term personal connections. This is a contrast to the Western planning inclinations and their short-term orientation to goals. Their decision-making process is often not easily understood by Westerners. One example is the behind-the-scene decision-making process practiced by the Japanese, or the Chinese emphasis on relationships-building in getting business done.

Renault–Nissan merger

The Nissan merger masterminded by Renault is a clear reflection of the weaknesses in the Japanese management system, which not so long ago had been revered by Western business gurus. Take *keiretsu*, for example, that circle of related stockholders that has encapsulated business relations in Japan for two or three decades. The purpose of *keiretsu* is multiple. Its system of cross-holding of stocks had been devised during the period of rapid economic growth in the 1950s and 1960s, when Japan was obliged to remove restrictions on the holding of Japanese stocks by foreigners, as a condition of entry to the OECD. Typically, 30–50 percent of stocks were cross-held by companies in the same *keiretsu*, as a means of preventing takeovers by outside investors.

In a sector such as automobiles, for example, *keiretsu* fostered long-term relationships between buyers and suppliers of parts and components. *Keiretsu* members worked together to carry out joint R&D projects, to ensure a stable supply of parts, and to provide mutual help when needed. The senior managers of the *keiretsu* companies of the Nissan Group were former Nissan employees, and usually senior ones at that. This made it very difficult for Nissan to refuse to buy from these *keiretsu* companies, even when they were not competitive. This cohesive and longstanding supplier–buyer relationship has been one of the most important ingredients of both the Japanese corporate governance system and management.

Chris Patten, the former governor of Hong Kong, blamed Asia for corruption, nepotism, and self-aggrandizement. Patten believed that Asian management should not be any different from its Western counterpart. Asian organizations and leaders have long been experimenting with new management practices that have improved corporate governance and global acceptability. The *kereitsus* and the *chaebols* are reducing reliance on each other and divesting from non-core assets to improve competitiveness.

NEED FOR BETTER UNDERSTANDING OF BEHAVIOR

Globalization has meant that the Asian employee now works and competes with his or her Western counterpart more directly than before. Misunderstandings among Asians and Westerners are the common result of a lack of cultural understanding, and management actions are often misconstrued for the same reasons. Thus, when Carlos Ghosn drove Nissan out of its near-bankruptcy state, he did so because of his sensitivity to the Japanese culture and his understanding of the values that the Japanese hold dear. Carlos Ghosn adapted Western management principles and adopted leadership traits that appealed to Japanese values. His commitment to achieving the objectives of the Nissan Revival Plan or resign was akin to the centuries-old practice of hara-kiri – a traditional form of honorable suicide. In order to motivate the workforce, it is necessary to have a clear understanding of the values of the society.

A clear understanding of on-the-job-behaviors will provide a key to the value system in Asia. Leaders are likely to experience greater success in their roles by adapting their leadership style to their followers.

LEADERSHIP: BUY OR BUILD

The Commonwealth countries in Asia, with English as a common second language, have for some time exported human capital to the West with great success. One country that is highly successful at exporting human capital is India. An Indian press report, citing figures from the United Nations Development Programme (UNDP), said that

India loses about US$2 billion per year due to migration of its IT professionals. Several Asians who migrated to the West have succeeded both as entrepreneurs and in the corporate world.

Not all talent seeks better fortune in the West. Asian leaders in Asia have the benefit of understanding the Asian culture and several have succeeded in Asia. A look at *Fortune Magazine Asia's Businessmen of the Year* editions had several prominent names. Dr Cheong Choong Kong, CEO of Singapore Airlines, was the winner in 1999; Keihi Tachikawa, CEO of NTT DoCoMo, was the winner in 2001; and Narayan R. Murthy, Chairman of Infosys, won the award in 2002. Each of these individuals has led and managed their organizations successfully.

While several Asian leaders have fully understood the cultural requirements of leading in Asia, few have mastered the management skills to drive organizations to new levels. As a result, foreign nationals are now found at the helm of several prominent Asian businesses. Most come to Asia with specific tasks that need to be achieved and more often than not these have to do with improving management systems and procedures, or providing a specific technical capability. The acceptability of foreign leadership of local business offers a sensitive test of the true depth and acceptance of globalization. If we look, what do we see? Carlos Ghosn, who is Brazilian-born and French-educated, leading the Nissan Motor Company. In Singapore, Philippe Paillart was recruited to lead the Development Bank of Singapore out of the island and into the world. He has since left the job. In 1999, the Singapore government did the same for Neptune Orient Line, which was once run by Prime Minister Goh Chok Tong. To this job they recruited Flemming Jacobs, a partner in Danish industry leader, AP Moller/Maersk. In Indonesia, the boss of James Riady's Bank Lippo is Australian Ian Clyne, who was brought in from ING Barings. In India, Coca-Cola has had a string of expatriate CEOs since its reentry into the Indian market in 1993. Such appointments are very high profile. There will be others.

Leader profile: Carlos Ghosn, Nissan Motor Company

Background
- Born in Brazil; raised in Beirut; citizen of France.
- Developed the highly ambitious Nissan Revival Plan and exceeded its goals.

Key leadership actions
- Used cross-functional teams to develop the Nissan Revival Plan.
- Showed commitment to the objectives of the Nissan Revival Plan stating that if they were not achieved the president of the company and the members of the Executive Committee would resign.
- Defied Japanese management etiquette by shaking hands with every employee he met, not just top managers.
- Dispensed with impersonal executive meetings and chose to meet face-to-face with hundreds of managers, sales staff, and technicians to get a frontline perspective.

Not all have succeeded. Carlos Ghosn (profiled above) has gone from strength to strength to become the most frequently interviewed and most often-quoted businessman in Japan. He has also become the unlikely star of a Japanese comic strip. The others have not done as well. Flemming Jacobs, Philippe Paillart, and other Western CEOs have departed after a short stint at their positions. Often their early departures leave the organization worse off than when they first came in.

Most leaders have mastered the principles of management but few have mastered leadership. The success of a Brazilian-born Frenchman in Japan and the failures of other leaders indicate that leadership is not about management ability alone, but also about aligning to the values of the people in the organization.

LEADERSHIP IN ASIA

Leadership is a universal phenomenon – no society has existed without leaders. Whether you subscribe to the theory that leadership is bound by cultural settings or that good leadership traits can be transported anywhere, there is no doubt that Asia is faced with a leadership gap at this juncture in history.

The leadership gap in Asia can be attributed to the social-economic development path undertaken by various countries in Asia. In Japan, in the days of lifelong employment, powerful unions, and protected economies, the imperative to develop talent through career paths was not a priority for the employer or the employee. Japanese models of leadership have worked in Japan because Japanese leaders were largely interacting with other Japanese who understood their behaviors and actions. The same is true for Indian or Chinese leadership models.

> I am the type who consults his staff and asks for their wisdom. I have found that people are generally more willing to cooperate when you solicit their advice than when you try to tell them how to do everything.
>
> KONOSUKE MATSUSHITA, FOUNDER OF MATSUSHITA

Coke in India

Since its reentry into the Indian market in 1993, Coke has faced challenge after challenge in India. Not the least of which has been its revolving door in the executive suite. In 10 years it has had five expatriate heads with one of them at the helm for just three months. The first task of the last expatriate CEO, Alex von Behr (appointed in 2000), was to rebuild trust with the business community and employees in Coca-Cola India (CCI). He localized the organization's structure to make the system more entrepreneurial. To support this he introduced a detailed career planning system for its 530 managers. Von Behr initiated two training programs: the Pegasus and Way Forward. Pegasus was to develop middle managers, Way Forward was aimed at identifying future business leaders within the company. He also put in place a succession plan. In 2001, Sanjiv Gupta was appointed deputy president. This was also the first year that CCI recorded a profit. In 2003, Sanjiv Gupta became the first Indian CEO and President of Coca-Cola India.

Leader profile:
Konosuke Matsushita, founder of Matsushita

Background
- Born in 1894, youngest of eight children to a farmer.
- Devoted his entire career to the promised new electric industry of post-1905 Japan.

Key leadership actions
- Among the first ever Japanese companies to enter into a technical alliance with a European partner (this was with a difference – he paid a royalty to the European partner for technical know-how, who in turn paid a royalty to Matshushita for managerial expertise).
- Set for the following codes in 1933:
  - Spirit of service through industry
  - Spirit of fairness, harmony, cooperation
  - Spirit of courtesy, gratitude, and humility
  - Spirit of accord with natural laws.

In traditional cultures that exist in most parts of Asia, interpersonal relationships have been considered to be the hallmark of effective leaders. The command and control models of leadership, which were successful in the past, are no longer working and a more participative and globally acceptable leadership style is emerging in Asia. This has been brought about by several factors, including a large number of Asians educated in business schools modeled on Western management and leadership philosophies. The change has been triggered by several factors, some of which are as follows:

- A new generation, educated in the leading universities of the West, is entering the workforce. This is particularly true for family-run businesses in Asia.
- After years of neglect, corporate governance has come to the forefront in Asia. Maturing regulatory systems are forcing organizations to disclose relationships that previously would not have raised suspicion.

- Outside equity and capital is more freely available than in earlier days. This reduces the need for funding from a *keiretsu* or other networks.

Our view is that new leadership models are evolving in parts of Asia. These leadership models combine the best of East and West, and can be found in companies such as India's Infosys, Singapore Airlines, and Japan's Toyota and Sony, among others. The forces of globalization demand that organizations are agile, flexible, and can compete beyond national boundaries. Leaders of organizations in Asia who are keen to compete in a global market need to acquire new management and leadership competencies. Similarly, global organizations of non-Asian origins will have to tune their leadership styles so that they are aligned with the values of the countries in Asia that they operate.

MAKING A LEADER

Many leaders don't see themselves as such. Organizations train executives to be task-oriented. Task accomplishment and meeting short-term profit goals are rewarded in the form of an annual bonus in Asia and in the West. The increase in the size of the contingent workforce results in short-term thinking. Some leaders are fearful of letting go of task accomplishment as this would mean letting go of the concrete. The task of leadership that deals with the more abstract issues has made people uncomfortable.

However, all is not lost for Asia. Multinational enterprises have realized the potential of the Asian market and as a result they are investing heavily in Asia. Not only do they bring the much-needed foreign direct investments, but also the well-established performance management and leadership development practices. Global corporations expect the same from their leaders regardless of whether they are based in India or Ireland. A review of the leadership competency frameworks developed by Mercer for clients in Asia shows certain leadership characteristics that are consistently repeated across countries.

Common leadership characteristics

- Coaching
- Positive
- Motivational
- Decisive
- Confidence-builder
- Communicator
- Excellence-oriented

- Trustworthy
- Just
- Honest
- Team-oriented
- Intelligent
- Problem-solving
- Cultural awareness
- Cultural adaptability

HRM AND LEADERSHIP

Asian organizations are feeling the leadership gap. HRM departments are often tasked with developing leaders for the future. They have, in turn, gone on to hire consultants who they believed held the magic formula for leadership development. More often than not, consulting firms leave the organization with a generic performance and talent management system that does not align with the strategy, values, or culture of the organization. The appeal is lost in implementation as the new system is rarely the answer that organizations are seeking.

Potential leaders often lie dormant in organizations, as they do not have the systems and processes in place to identify and develop leadership talent. The current thinking on leadership development essentially evolves around the following:

- identifying competencies relevant to leadership;
- identifying potential leaders; and
- offering programs and systems that facilitate the development of these competencies.

Enhancing leadership effectiveness: Mercer's point of view
Colleen O'Neill

The pursuit of leadership effectiveness is not a quick fix. It is a steady, ongoing labor that requires discipline, data, and decisiveness. Five guiding principles reflect the point of view of leadership experts in both Mercer HR

Consulting and its sister company Mercer Delta Consulting. They are as follows:

Leadership is critical

Leadership is a key driver of large-scale organizational change and effective business performance. The volatility of today's environment places greater urgency on developing leaders who can handle change. Effective leadership is the critical factor for sustainable profitable growth.

CEO involvement is required

Leadership development, like most critical organizational priorities, requires the top executive to invest personal time and energy. The CEO can't delegate his or her role in setting the strategic talent agenda and building leadership capability.

Unique context matters

Mercer's research and experience tells us that the effectiveness of any human resource practice depends on its fit with the broader system in which it operates. The most powerful leadership practices respond to an organization's unique business and human capital context. Finding the right fit with strategy, structure, and culture will allow an organization to reinforce the messages it wants to send about performance, rewards, advancement, and careers.

Align and integrate solutions

To maximize high performance and encourage leaders at all levels to "pull in the same direction," leadership solutions should be aligned and integrated. Business strategy drives the performance and development requirements for leadership. Talent acquisition, development, performance management, and rewards processes for leaders should operate as an integrated and cohesive system and be tightly linked to the strategic goals of the company.

Measure business impact

It is possible to get the facts about the personal and business impact of leadership solutions. A combination of qualitative and quantitative diagnostic tools can identify optimal practices that will build leadership capability and create economic value. Leadership development is an important "internal labor market" dynamic in organizations. Leadership behavior and organizational practices can be observed through statistical modeling of workforce dynamics and statistical modeling of links between leadership practices and business outcomes. Facts about business outcomes provide the best evidence for assessing the ROI of leadership solutions.

Mercer case study: Leadership development

Situation

ABC Holdings, an investment company in Thailand, had recently acquired a government-held logistics organization. An internal leadership struggle ensued. A recently established corporate strategy division, headed by a newly hired MBA, fought for control with the existing stalwarts. HRM facilitated a temporary truce and embarked on developing a roadmap to transform the organization from a not-for-profit operation to a profit-driven one. The transformation was spearheaded by the development of a leadership competency framework. The framework would instill new values and requirements for leaders in the organization. Mercer worked with it to define a Leadership Competency Framework that was aligned with the strategy of the business. Additionally, we defined a Managerial Competency Framework. ABC Corporation further commissioned Mercer to design and manage development centers for all its managers. At each development center managers went through psychometric tests and several strenuous simulations to identify their strengths and developmental needs. The process involved assessing the managers on the two competency frameworks and providing them with actionable development feedback that would be built into their personal objectives.

Learning

The uniqueness of this project lay in defining the role of the leader in terms of both leadership behaviors and management practices. As the competency development process revealed, the members of this organization had personal values that were guided by their desire to work for a non-profit organization. Some of these values were also hard-coded in the competency frameworks. By clearly separating and defining the two it became easier to identify developmental opportunities for the managers that would allow them to develop both their leadership (how) and management (what) capability, and at the same time respect the values of the organization and its people.

> " Leadership, therefore, is all about raising the aspirations of followers. It is about making people believe in themselves; it is about making them confident; and it is about making people achieve miracles. "

NARAYAN MURTHY IN A TALK TO THE
WHARTON MBA CLASS OF 2001

BUSINESS TIP

Best practices in talent management and leadership development

Here are some items for Mercer's Talent Management Quotient (TM-Q) Survey. Checklist your company's talent quotient based on the issues we raised.

Talent strategy and systems

- We have a clear, articulated talent strategy in place.
- We have a clear employment brand or value proposition articulated.
- We have integrated systems and programs in place to identify and manage high performers and high potentials.
- We have developed a culture that attracts and retains high-potential and high-performing people.
- We have aligned our talent strategy and employee brand to our business strategy and objectives.
- We have implemented and tracked a specific set of metrics to measure the success of our talent strategy.
- We have systems and programs in place to identify and manage low performers.

Talent profiling and identification

- We use clearly defined competencies and success criteria for identifying and assessing our leaders.

- A sound process is in place to ensure that a variety of data sources are used to assess high potentials.
- A structured process is in place to identify our future leaders.
- We have an in-depth understanding of the profile of the people in our talent pool(s).
- A CEO-led, structured process is used to review top leadership talent at least annually.
- We have a structured process in place to identify talent at every organizational level.
- We use a system to select people based on their "fit" with organizational values.

Talent retention and commitment
- We have a strategy in place to retain our high performers and high potentials.
- Managers at all levels in our organization are effective coaches and mentors.
- We implement specific practices to continuously motivate high performers and high potentials toward better performance.
- We track the retention rate of high and low performers/potentials.
- Our HRM practices and systems are tailored to retaining high performers and high potentials.
- We have a process in place to ensure that high potentials and high performers receive regular feedback and personal guidance.
- High potentials/high performers are asked about their aspirations and interests.
- Talent development and deployment.
- Career paths are clearly defined, mapped, and communicated in our organization.
- We have a structured program in place to accelerate the development of high potentials.
- We have various competency-based tools and initiatives available to develop people; for example, action learning, job rotations, learning resource guides, executive coaches, development advisors, high-profile developmental assignments, and so on.
- We map and categorize our talent pool according to certain criteria (for example, performance level and potential level) and develop them accordingly.

- Career movements/progressions are well planned according to the development needs and potential of individuals.
- We invest more in the development of our high potentials than in general staff.
- We have a process in place to regularly review and follow-up on the implementation of development plans of our high potentials.

MANAGERS AND LEADERSHIP

The word "leader" has its root in the word meaning "to travel" or "show the way." It appeared in the English language in the early fourteenth century. The term "leadership" followed some five centuries later. Values and culture, on the other hand, have existed since civilization. Different cultures deserve respect. Too much has been made of the negative aspects of traditional societies and too little of the positive. The West can learn much from these. Modern management thinking in the West has unconsciously promoted cultural biases and an ethnocentric view of management and leadership. Assumptions about people's and organizations' sole concern of maximizing economic reward contradict important values held by people in Asia.

> " The ultimate test for a leader is ... whether he or she teaches others to be leaders and builds an organization that can sustain its success even when he or she is not around. "
>
> NOEL TICHY – THE LEADERSHIP ENGINE 1997

Similarly, most modern published notions of leadership have their origins in the West. Such notions have been propagated by the Western management education industry and the Western media. Most leaders' common failing is not understanding how they must use management and leadership together.

Infosys has taken the lead in leadership development. This process starts from the recruitment of the correct person. Each year Infosys receives over 250,000 applications from potential employees. Infosys runs regular workshops to propagate leadership values. Its recruitment process is stringent.

> " Leadership is all about courage, courage to dream big, the ability to raise the aspirations of people and to accept great ideas from different countries and cultures across the world. "

NR NARAYAN MURTHY, FOUNDER OF INFOSYS

Leaders in Asia: NR Narayan Murthy, Infosys

Background
- Started Infosys Consultants in 1981 along with five partners.
- Currently employs over 10,000 people and has revenues in excess of US$500 million.

Key leadership actions
- Set up a 50-acre campus in Bangalore, India (a replica of a college campus) with extensive infrastructure.
- Set up a leadership institute in Mysore to train Infosys leaders.
- Rated best employer in India by Business Today-Hewitt Associates
- Best Annual Report award from the Indian Institute of Chartered Accountants from 1995 to date.
- Strong on relationships, Narayan Murthy continued to work closely with the five partners who set up Infosys in 1981, in a style of participatory management that has been described as "intellectually and values driven."

> " I believe in a kind of psychic law of management here: that workers, customers, everyone involved with a management can tell when it is just mouthing the right words. "

MINTZBERG

Leadership development at an SOE in China

Background

XYZ Group is one of the biggest SOEs in China, dealing in commodity manufacturing. It also has a diverse range of businesses, including IT, trading, financial services, and real estate, among others. We were invited to help build a leadership competency model for managers at the headquarters. We started by clarifying and analyzing the company's short-term and long-term strategies, facilitating workshops to discuss the desired culture, and to conduct interviews on what behavior shaped the company's high-performing managers.

Key learning and issues

Although the Chinese government is focused on leadership development, and wants SOEs to put more emphasis on competency and leadership development, most Chinese companies don't really have a system or the technology to build competency models. So for managers within the XYZ Group, it was really a totally new concept. Part of our challenge was getting the Behavior Event Interviews done. (These interviews are to help us find out critical behavior or values that make the person succeed in his or her job). Some managers in SOEs are not familiar with Western thinking styles of methods of working, such as brainstorming or behavior analysis. This makes it difficult to make comparisons between high performers in the company and the rest.

At this stage, China's SOEs still lack the freedom to adjust their compensation structures, or to remove headcount. One of our major tasks is bringing the company up to speed on what developments are shaping HRM. Most SOEs and private companies in China are still at the phase where their priority is setting up market-oriented HRM systems. Leadership modeling typically falls at the second phase of their development.

▶▶ CONCLUSION

Leaders now need to have the cultural sensitivity and experience tha will allow them to lead organizations regionally and globally. Asiar managers do not have to wait for the future. They can shape i themselves. Leaders cannot choose their styles at will. What is feasible depends on the cultural conditioning of one's subordinates.

Merely mimicking a Western approach to management will no motivate the employees to follow. Creative adaptations of Westerr management practices are needed to reflect Asia's unique cultura heritage and to motivate the Asian employee. Simultaneously, leadership that appeals to the basic Asian values needs to be developed.

---

[1] "Brain Drain Can Be Harnessed, Not Controlled," Rina Chandran, The HinduBusinessOnline.Com <http://www.thehindubusinessline.com/2002/01/12/stories/2002011201470200.htm>, January 12, 2002.

CHAPTER

12

Capturing the Illusive HRM Numbers

Norman Ramion

*D*eveloping precise measures for investments in people to ascertain how they directly impact on business outcomes is complex and difficult. However, with advancement in measurement methods, the mysteries of the "people factor" are beginning to unravel. In fact, at the cutting edge of measurement practice, direct causal links between people practices and the bottom line have already been established. What's the case for investing in good people measurement practices? Quite simply, companies that do it best will be able to fine-tune their investments to achieve maximum returns. This will be true regardless what they do, and where and how they operate. Good measurement of people investments and practices will be a key competitive advantage for Asian companies, just as it will be for companies everywhere. Are Asian companies ready for this? Ready or not the time is ripe to put the building blocks in place to deliver numbers, rather than anecdotes, to push the case for HRM investment. Many companies in Asia already use various metrics as a way of building ROI scenarios. Those that lag behind will soon be left behind. Once HRM can bring to the table the direct link between human capital investments and the impact on bottom-line, there will be perfect alchemy between HRM and the wider business.

WHY FUNDING AN ORGANIZATIONAL "BLACK HOLE" WITHOUT QUESTION IS THE CURRENT STATE FOR MANY

Here is a paradox: The investments companies make in human capital – recruitment, salaries, benefits, training and development, etc. – are some of their largest expenses. Yet they are also the investments that corporate executives typically know the least about with respect to financial returns. Because these investments are substantial they can and do have significant impact on the bottom line. Even so, human capital is often just accepted as an organizational 'black hole' that must be funded without clear expectations for return on the investment (ROI). To use a balance sheet metaphor, the "liabilities" (read, the costs) of human capital investments are well accounted for and understood, but the "assets" that are developed as a result, and the returns that will be generated in the future, are often accepted a divine mystery.

Why do even the most financially hard-nosed CEOs and CFOs so readily acquiesce when it comes to measuring human capital investments? The fact is that "soft" or "people" factors, such as compensation and benefits or training, are often just accepted as being necessary but immeasurable. At best, the available measures are thought to be too imprecise to be very useful.

Take for example a relatively pervasive people measure, the employee opinion survey. Many management teams eagerly collect the data and study the results, but then allow them to "wither on the vine," feeling that they lack the time, resources, and/or know-how to build and manage an effective follow-through program. In other words, this reasonably robust people measure is often grossly underutilized.

Even with wide-scale adoption of performance management systems such as the balanced business scorecard, the greatest weight is usually placed on the financial quadrant – meeting revenue targets, net operating income (NOI), return on investment (ROI), and so forth. "Balanced" is not (and perhaps should not be) synonymous with "equal" in the scorecard context. However, the people quadrant is all too often relegated to last position in terms of importance, or else it contains vague objectives that do little to drive positive change in people's behavior.

Given the perceived and the actual weaknesses of measuring the people aspects of business, it is no wonder that HRM professionals face an uphill battle to convince top executives that allocating new budgets for HRM measurement programs will be worthwhile. If Western organizations are finding it difficult to get the necessary funding, what of the tough-minded business environment in Asia?

HRM practitioners in Asia often work across many languages and jurisdictions compared to their counterparts in the West. Until recently, most HRM practitioners in Asia have had little formal education or training in HRM or Human Resource Development. The "professional" HRM community in Asia is a young one. Furthermore, the operating size of many Asian companies is a constraining factor. The fixed costs to set up and implement HRM systems are substantial. For small- and medium-sized enterprises, budgets for HRM are necessarily smaller. That being the case, budget monies for HRM are put to the most fundamental and pragmatic aspects of the function: recruiting programs, payroll systems, benefits administration, and basic training and development. Some companies, especially foreign multinationals, also invest in salary benchmarking if significant competition for labor exists in their operating market.

The culture of many Asian organizations may also be a constraining factor for introducing many progressive HRM practices. For example, operation heads may consider the basic support functions HRM provides to be its sole purpose, and therefore that HRM is strictly administrative in nature. In order to be maximally efficient, they believe, HRM service should be transactional, and any information requested by HRM from the operations should be for compliance purposes only. Because of mindsets such as these, most Asian HRM professionals still have a long road to travel before top managers treat them as strategic partners in running the business.

So, just how long is this "long road"? It certainly varies from organization to organization, but advances in measurement tools and processes are helping to speed up the travel time regardless of the distance. Executives in Asia can and will be persuaded by reliable data and analyses, and credible and powerful measurement systems will enable HRM to compile such information. Measurement of the "immeasurable" has taken great strides in the last decade, and measures of human capital practices that are quantitative in nature and linked to business strategy and key business outcomes are already grabbing the attention of the C-suites in the West.

This chapter will illustrate how the HRM function can play a vital role in shaping corporate strategy by knowing what to measure with respect to human capital, and how to get the measures done. Measurement can be salvation for those who want to be a real business partner and earn a seat at the executive table.

> " The better they understand which human capital investments yield the greatest ROI, the more opportunity Asian organizations will have to make the most effective investments in human capital. "

WHY IS HUMAN CAPITAL MEASUREMENT SO IMPORTANT?

Labor cost[1] is a significant part of the national economy, between 50 and 60 percent of GDP in the United States, depending on industry and the sector. Considering this and that the GDP of the United States is more than US$10 trillion per year, even small improvements in effectiveness can have substantial payback. A 1 percent reduction in cost (or improvement in productivity) in an economy of this size represents US$100 billion. Even in an economy the size of Singapore's, labor costs are more than 40 percent of GDP.

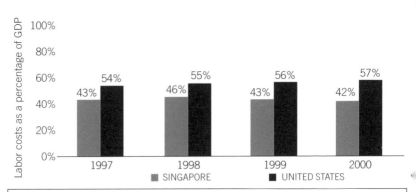

Given the sheer size of labor costs even modest gains in labor productivity through HRM improvement would yield significant returns to firms.

Exhibit 12.1 Labor costs

At present, most economies in Asia have an advantage with respect to labor costs. This cost advantage in turn is the principal means by which countries in the region can price their goods and services competitively and make them attractive to consumers in the major Western markets of Europe and North America. In emerging economies the percentage of a company's total revenues spent on labor costs averages between 10 and 20 percent, and for some industry sectors with large populations of unskilled workers the percentage dips into single digits. Nonetheless, companies in emerging economies still have substantial challenges with respect to investments they must make in human capital. At the most basic level, their challenge is to raise workers' literacy rates and ensure that they understand basic workplace health and safety. Even Singapore – which has largely shed basic industries such as textiles and assembly-type manufacturing and is evolving toward high value-added services such as banking, education, and healthcare – is challenged by the investments it must make in the training and development required to continuously upgrade and re-skill its workforce. As companies evolve, their human capital expenditures will still need to be substantial, despite the lower basic labor costs than in more mature economies.

Therefore, Asian organizations that best understand which human capital investments yield the best ROI for their business will have the greatest opportunity to make the most effective investments and will be the most successful.

WHERE ARE WE NOW, AND WHERE ARE WE HEADED WITH MEASURING HUMAN CAPITAL?

It is conventional wisdom among managers that various people factors, often referred to as "soft" factors, are linked to business outcomes. These are factors such as satisfaction, motivation, commitment, and organisational culture. The service–profit chain model, described and supported in detail by Heskett, Jones, Sasser, and Schlesinger in their 1997 book, demonstrates how employee satisfaction leads to better customer satisfaction, which in turn leads to better business outcomes.[2]

This study has since been adapted in various forms but the fundamental theory put forward is that employee behavior can influence a company's business performance. Exhibit 12.2 illustrates how an employee's satisfaction can impact on a company's bottomline.[3]

The authors of the exhibit above have also ascribed precise quantitative relationships between employee behavior, customer impression, and revenue growth variables in a *Harvard Business Review* article, "Putting the Service-Profit Chain to Work."[4] Their view is that a five unit increase in employee attitude can lead to a 1.3 unit increase in customer impression and a resultant 0.5 increase in revenue growth.

Perhaps the most famous study to date that illustrates the service–profit chain is that conducted by the US retailer, Sears, in the 1990s. The outcome of that study ascribed precise quantity relationships between employee behavior, customer impression, and revenue growth variables (see Exhibit 12.2).

The linkage here is that a "happy" employee tends to be a more motivated employee. His or her improved motivation results in higher productivity and improved "organizational citizenship." Improved productivity and value-added behaviors lead to better business performance without having channeled through the customer's experience (see Exhibit 12.3).

Exhibit 12.2 Direct linkage between employee satisfaction and business outcomes

The continuing wide-scale adoption of performance management systems, such as the balanced business scorecard (BBS), also gives rise to increased interest in quantifying the human capital contribution to business success. The "People" quadrant of the scorecard needs clear goals and objectives, just as the other quadrants do. However, despite the advances made in studies such as that conducted by Sears, precision in quantifying "People" goals and objectives are still lacking. In order for people factors to be given more weight in judging performance, quantification will have to become more precise and reliable. But how and when will better precision and reliability be possible?

POWER OF MEASUREMENT TOOLS AND THE PRACTICE OF BENCHMARKING

The challenges of measurement in the "People" realm are many, but one of the fundamental issues is the relative power of the measurement tools versus those used in other parts of a business. Many aspects of production, sales, and finance, for example, are all quantifiable and objective, but this is much less true for human capital. As the discussion of Sears and other such research indicates, it is true that human capital practices are directly linked to business outcomes. Although growing in number over time, high-quality research studies that demonstrate linkage are still relatively few and most of the evidence is still anecdotal. Although anecdotes are abundant, they are not very powerful in terms of proving cause and effect, let alone in quantifying the relationship.

The most powerful measurements establish true causation between practice and outcome. For example, one type of evidence used to demonstrate training effectiveness is the "impact" of the training reported by the employees; that is, trainees' ratings of how much the course helps them do their work. Such self-report ratings do not establish causation, however. In order to show causation, a significant and reliable impact on some important outcome would have to be demonstrated. For example, sales training could be said to cause improved sales volume if trained employees generated significantly greater sales than a group of employees who had not been trained. Furthermore, this effect should be demonstrated repeatedly over time.

Once a causal relationship such as this has been established, it can then be used to simulate future states, such as revenue growth

goals, and to forecast human capital requirements to achieve them.
Currently, very few companies have achieved this level of measurement
sophistication. Most linger at the level of benchmarking and correlational
evidence as illustrated in the measurement "power curve" in Exhibit
12.3.

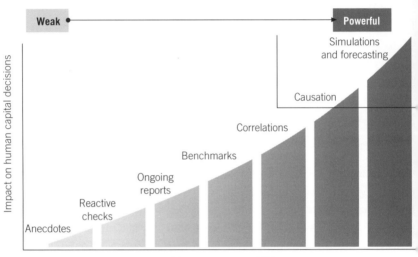

Exhibit 12.3 The "power curve"

Let's consider benchmarking for a moment. Although benchmarking
can provide evidence of what is possible to achieve in terms of outcome
and process, it does little to inform as to how effective (if at all) the
practice will be in any given company, even when considering companies
within the same industry. The context (for example, the type of
business, where it operates, its leadership style, culture, and so on)
that a company operates in is crucial to deciding which combination
of human capital "best practices" is going to yield maximum value for
it. In fact, where the practice of benchmarking is concerned, the leading
thought is that it can actually be counterproductive to a business.

In a recent article, Becker and Huselid[6] argue that "relying on
external benchmarks as a measure of HRM's performance is
fundamentally wrong." Benchmarking is appealing simply because it
is quantitative, objective, and reasonably quick and painless. "Reliance
on benchmarking…allows HR professionals to report measures of HR
performance without fundamentally changing their perspective on

HR or developing any new competencies around HR measurement or strategy execution."

What's needed instead of benchmarking data is the comprehensive development of a unique and robust HRM scorecard that links people practices, strategy, and performance. Becker, Huselid, and Ulrich in their popular book *The HR Scorecard*[7] describe a seven-step process for achieving this. According to the authors, in order to transform an organization's HRM architecture into a strategic asset it must:

- clearly define the business strategy;
- build a business case for HRM as a strategic asset;
- create strategy maps;
- identify HRM deliverables within the strategy map;
- align the HRM architecture with the HRM deliverables;
- design the strategic measurement system; and
- implement management by measurement.

Such a measurement system and scorecard can yield the conceptual and operational tools HRM practitioners need to demonstrate the value of the function that other executives find convincing.

Mercer's thinking and consulting practice aligns with Becker, Hudelid, and Ulrich. In fact, Mercer is working with many leading companies around the world with ambitions to develop and utilize HRM measurement systems of this type. *Play To Your Strengths*,[8] Mercer's recently published book on the same topic shares numerous case studies of the experiences our clients have had improving their HRM measurement systems. Mercer works with clients to first create statistical models of their "internal labor markets" (ILM); that is, the entire range of management practices that govern transactions between employer and employees inside the organization. These ILM models are then used to build links to specific business outcomes such as productivity, revenues, and profitability. Once such links are established, the client's executive team can see, in precise quantitative and causal terms, which elements of their human capital management practices have created or destroyed value for the organization.

This causal linkage is indeed vital because global thinking on the measurement of the ROI of human capital converges on the need to gain a better understanding of precisely how human capital practices add to or detract from positive business outcomes. Companies with the most precise measures will be able to fine-tune their investments to achieve maximum returns, and this will be a key competitive advantage for them moving forward.

WHERE IS ASIA RIGHT NOW WITH RESPECT TO HUMAN CAPITAL MEASUREMENT?

To the latter part of the twentieth century, most Asian companies had been successful using traditional business trading models. The nature of much of the business they did required few skilled workers (that is, plantation agriculture, basic and low-tech manufacturing, general import/export trading, shipping, and so on) and the labor supply was plentiful. Furthermore, labor laws were nonexistent or weak, and with the exception of a few countries, such as South Korea, labor unions were few in number (if permitted at all) and poorly organized. Because many businesses were family owned, organizational cultures were built around the founders and their extended families. Management teams and boards of directors were more like "cults of personality," rather than strategic architects and governance bodies. Employment "contracts" were based around simple rules of trust and reciprocity, fair wages for a fair day's work and loyalty to the organization. In many companies, staff were treated more as extended family, and in return they were guaranteed employment for life provided the company stayed in business.

Of course today most successful Asian companies, and certainly the leading ones, have modernized their approach to human resource management. Many utilize salary benchmarking in order to stay competitive with the market and to maintain a level of "fairness" with regards to the wages they pay. The most progressive Asian organizations are beginning to break away from standard bonus pay-outs by position or seniority to rewarding performance based on key performance indicators. Also, competency-based talent management systems are being introduced to ensure the "right" people are placed in the "right" roles doing the "right" things to make the company successful. Even practices that focus on "soft" areas such as employee satisfaction and organizational culture are being used more and more. To use a broad term, use of employee research techniques such as focus groups, climate surveys, and culture audits is growing rapidly. Although business leaders in Asia prefer quantitative and objective information they also recognize that employee satisfaction and motivation are linked to the bottom line. The use of employee research is evolving together with HRM practice in general.

Employee research is evolving in Asia

- salary and benefits benchmarking
- focus groups, small-scale fact-finding
- exit interviews
- employee surveys: climate, culture, engagement/commitment, alignment, effectiveness/quality
- performance management (for example, Balanced Scorecard)
- talent management (multi-source feedback surveys/360 degree surveys)

Coming soon…
- HRIS database mining, modeling of internal labor markets
- business impact modeling (that is, cause and effect between human capital investment and business outcomes)

While the relative sophistication of HRM practice in Asia is progressing, a significant limiting factor is the size of many Asian companies. Large spends on HRM activities beyond the basics are prohibitive. Furthermore, HRM professionals are still largely viewed as "administrators." Their opinions relating to operational or business strategy matters are not sought after, nor would they be respected by senior executives and operational heads. A "catch 22" is effectively created: additional funding for HRM measurement and programs that would raise the profile and value-add of HRM will not be approved because HRM does not produce "business relevant" (read financial) justification for it. Yet, HRM requires additional funding to produce these sought-after "business relevant" data for justification.

What are some common experiences of HRM professionals around Asia with respect to measurement of human capital? They run a wide range for sure. Many of the pitfalls are the same anywhere in the world, but perhaps still happen more frequently in Asia. A brief list is presented:

Head against the wall: Common experiences of organisations trying to implement HRM measurement tools

- lack of time devoted to implementation
- lack of funding for training and or follow-through
- lack of mechanisms to track success
- lack of buy-in from senior managers to fully adopt the systems
- lack of trust from senior managers in the reliability/veracity of the outputs

HRM MEASUREMENT IN ASIA: TALES FROM THE FRONT

Since the dawn of humanity, nothing tells and sells as well as a good story. At this point in the chapter you may be asking, "What are some actual experiences of Asian companies with HRM measurement and research? What are the steps to success and pitfalls to avoid? How have these organizations extracted maximum value, or not, from their measurement forays?" The following vignettes will provide some insights from the corporate "front lines" in Asia.

CASE STUDY

ChemCo: The employee survey that worked, for a change

This Malaysia-based manufacturing facility of a global chemicals company struggled with leadership churn over an extended period of time with four plant managers in as many years passing through the operation. Although production quotas were being met, the manufacturing operations staff endured exceptionally low morale. The work environment became so unpleasant it led them to vote for organized representation by a national industry union. Although management was willing to accept the union if that was the true wish of the employees, it felt it unnecessary and that it would work against the employees' interests in the long term. As a last-ditch effort, management moved quickly to diagnose and try to address the key concerns. Although a global employee survey process existed, the next cycle for it could not come quickly enough.

Mercer was brought in to conduct a special "off-cycle" research program that included senior leadership interviews and employee-focus groups. These were then followed by an opinion questionnaire administered to all employees. The broad-based questionnaire did not focus exclusively on "hygiene" factors like working conditions and pay and benefits, but rather on important business outcome-linked issues, such as information and knowledge-sharing, leadership, teamwork, company image, and commitment.

The research uncovered clear drivers of dissatisfaction, which highlighted above all else a debilitating lack of trust between employees and plant management. This lack of trust had driven the employees' vote for union representation because they felt it was their only remaining alternative to get management to listen to them.

In light of the survey findings, management moved quickly to deliver the results of the survey to all employees. Results were presented by the plant manager. Mercer was there to lend objectivity and answer employee questions when necessary. As part of the presentation, coming actions were announced to address the most serious and volatile issues the employees were concerned with. For example, the end-of-year bonus system was to be reevaluated and brought into line with local, rather than corporate practices, and management agreed to additional formal communication channels being established through which employees could offer confidential feedback. Satisfied that they had been heard (at last!), employees agreed to postpone unionization.

What worked? An external third party (in this case Mercer) implemented a rigorous research process that made employees feel safe enough to offer their true opinions. Senior plant management visibly supported the initiative and took ownership of the results publicly, sharing them in person with all employees. "Quick win" changes were implemented within six weeks of the survey results being announced.

The moral of the story – Although previous employee surveys had been conducted at the plant, the "revolving door" of the plant manager position meant results had never been shared with employees, let alone any meaningful changes taking place. A measurement effort such as an opinion survey needs the full support of, and active participation by, senior leadership. Just going through the motions of a corporate sponsored research initiative in this case the annual global employee satisfaction survey, is not helpful.

InfoCo: A 'skin-deep' survey that wasn't enough

A prominent Asian blue-chip information and entertainment company faced growing concern over poor employee morale and dissension among the executive team. At the same time, the company faced new challenges as it expanded its business portfolio into new lines of entertainment and e media. Although a new CEO was brought in to help the company transform itself, the chairmanship was retained by a very elderly and very traditional "patriarch" who insisted on continuing to take part in most important management decisions. In addition, most of the business unit and corporate function heads had been in their jobs for 15 years or more. Although the executive management team were all in agreement to conduct an employee opinion survey, different executives had very different private agendas for utilizing the survey data.

These differences became apparent in the pre-survey management interviews. What also became apparent was a strong and enduring "turf mentality" among the leaders and a universal dislike for the new CEO's management style.

Results verified low levels of satisfaction and morale among the staff in general. Employees were especially bothered by what they considered bureaucracy in the organization. Many employees believed it to be a substantial driver of the lack of success of the new business arms. Among the senior managers, "communication" was tagged as the most important area of concern, the root cause of which they believed to be the CEO's unwillingness to listen to them. At the same time, the CEO felt that the executive team members were so entrenched in their traditional ways of operating, and so fearful of ceding any precious turf, that they were not open to his ideas for change.

What worked? The survey was a success in verifying issues and bringing them to "plain view" for the entire team. Results communication was managed well with substantial openness at all levels. However, the deep divisions in the executive team remained, and therefore action planning and follow-through was severely hindered. A year after the survey and with only several years in the job, the CEO resigned. His replacement entered the organization in almost the exact same circumstances.

The moral of the story – A deeply divided, disjointed management team cannot make effective use of survey data. The employee survey in and of itself was not a bad idea, but it was an attempt to put a Band-Aid over a gaping wound. Upon entering the organization the CEO really needed to embark on a journey of total transformation. He needed to insist that the "patriarch" step down, and he needed a completely free hand to build his own management team, even if that meant the departure of some of the tried and true "old guard." The criticisms of senior management team about the CEO were not completely off-base, however. He indeed needed coaching on improving his own listening and interpersonal skills, and he needed to work harder to change his interpersonal style and earn the respect of his senior colleagues.

ResourceCo – The tale of a beautiful Balanced Business Scorecard

A pan-Asian integrated natural resource company did not have a unifie
way of managing organizational results across its diverse entities. Acros
all of the business groups, there was no formal alignment of objectives an
targets with the overall strategic plans, and the performance managemer
system lacked effectiveness. Mercer was brought in to align corporate
group, and individual activities with the company's long-term strategic pla
and one group was chosen to pilot the project.

The balanced business scorecard model was used to first take the to
management team of the pilot group through a process to develop strategi
thrusts, critical success factors, and key performance indicators for eac
of the four quadrants: financial, customer, processes, and people. The
further workshops were run to develop scorecards for four individual busines
units and performance contracts for the top 100 managers.

What worked? The development process went smoothly. Scorecard
and personal performance contracts were successfully developed for fou
business units and 100 managers.

What was lacking? The timeline for the project was pushed back furthe
and further due to the management team's difficulties in finalizing the overa
scorecard for the organization. For starters, the team was too large an
unwieldy to gain consensus. Second, the diversity of the businesses pose
substantial difficulties in finding enough measures that worked across a
the groups. Implementation of the scorecards proved the final and mo
difficult hurdle. While ownership for developing the scorecards was share
the process for implementation sat primarily with one individual, and th
person was not up to the task.

The moral of the story – Management adequately funded and supporte
the development phase of the initiative, and using a single group to pil
the effort was very smart, given how new and different the process wou
be for most managers. However, when the critical time arrived fo
implementation, the senior leaders stepped into the background as if th
process would virtually implement itself. Implementation was woefully unde
resourced. The beautiful BBS system was like a Formula One race car wi
a rookie driver – too little fuel and no pit crew for support.

ManuCo: Multisource feedback implementation

A large multinational manufacturing organization setting up a new operation in Singapore faced challenges on multiple fronts, including the physical capital side, facility design, and construction; and on the human capital side the attraction and retention of high-caliber people. The human capital strategy was to build a robust HRM infrastructure, which included market-based salary structures and performance management programs. Because "people development" was a key corporate core value it was decided that an integral part of the performance management system should be to use multiple sources of feedback to assess an individual's competencies and aid in his or her development.

From the beginning, there were serious concerns about implementing a multisource feedback (MSF) system. It would be the first attempt at MSF at any of the company's Asian operations. If a 360-degree process was to be used, many expatriate senior managers with experience in Asia were concerned about employees subordinate to the manager being reviewed not wanting to give feedback, and therefore using only favorable or neutral rating scale points. For peer-level reviews, concerns also were raised about the potential of "sabotage" of unpopular colleagues where raters would collude to give only negative feedback, or the complete opposite where raters would collude to manipulate ratings to help popular colleagues look better.

However, the potential benefits of MSF were viewed to be greater than the potential risks, so the company embarked on developing a system. Because this facility would "pioneer" MSF in Asia for the company, the overall design principle was simplicity and user-friendliness. To help gain employee "buy-in" a pilot project was run involving only the most senior managers. The message was simply that the leadership would take the "first plunge."

To prepare for the pilot, the company trained all potential feedback providers on the theory and rationale of MSF, as well as how to observe competencies, how to write effective feedback, and what typical issues were likely to arise. The training sessions were filled with case examples and exercises.

The outcome of the pilot test was positive. The amount of participation and the quality of feedback exceeded expectations. Feedback-providers had no trouble understanding and using the system. The senior managers in turn felt they were given an accurate "mirror" reflecting their strengths and areas for development. As a final outcome of the feedback exercise, personal development plans were created for each of the participants.

What worked? Initial concerns about willingness of employees to participate and provide balanced feedback proved unfounded. The employees and managers being reviewed found the process easy and engaging to use. The process and results were validated by the fact that the managers could easily relate to both the complementary as well as the challenging outcomes.

What was lacking? To date, no problems with the system have surfaced nor have there been any negative outcomes from the system. However successful as the initiative is so far, even the best designed and implemented measurement systems need to be tracked and evaluated regularly. Over time, and as the MSF process works its way down the hierarchy, different issues can and probably will arise. As new employees join the organization they too will need the same depth and quality of training on the system as the initial groups of participants received.

The moral of the story – If the cultural stereotype of Asians being reluctant to give direct feedback, especially to a superior, is at all based on fact, this case proves that such a system can work very well. Substantial investment may be required to instill confidence in the users of the system (perhaps especially in the employees doing the rating), but great outcomes can be achieved. To realize substantial returns from this type of measurement investment, it will need continuous monitoring and refinement, and the commitment to stay on course and allow it to take root over time.

Useful tips for starting a measurement initiative

Planning a major measurement initiative in your organization in Asia? The following tips can help you avoid some of the most common pitfalls.

- **Get the process and the personnel right** – Any initiative worth doing needs a clear process and implementation plan. And once that's done make sure you have the people with the right experience and skills working on it. If you don't have the right people in-house, industrial/organizational psychologists often have a suitable educational background and many HRM consulting companies have professionals with experience in measurement.

- **Measure the right things** – It may sound obvious but many companies have false starts in measurement endeavors because they have not precisely identified what they wanted to measure and why. What you measure should be linked to your strategy and to what's right for your organization. There is no "top 10 must have" list of metrics. What worked for other companies won't necessarily work for yours.

- **Involve senior management** – It is not enough just to gain budget approval from the senior management, they also need to believe in the initiative and be involved throughout.

- **Think "user-friendly" and "action oriented"** – In due course, it is likely that managers at all levels will need to use the measures. Make sure the results from the measurement program are practical enough to be put to use by them. If managers can't figure out how to drive changes based on the data, they won't use it at all. Without follow through, it will remain just an academic exercise. Put simply, measurement initiatives should be treated as "change" initiatives.

- **Brand it** – Initiatives can gain immensely from the recognition factor that branding can bring. An employee opinion survey can become the "Feedback – survey of employee views." A 360-degree survey might be "Broadview – developmental survey." Brands can lessen confusion when multiple and new initiatives are happening in an organization.

- **Communicate throughout** – Set the context for the measurement initiative with a formal communication plan that includes strong management endorsement. But, don't believe you can get away with one announcement! A message typically needs to be repeated at least three times, and by different people or through different media.

- **Avoid fatigue** – Recognize that measurement initiatives are only one among a myriad things managers have to pay attention to. Too many measures, or too many measurement initiatives at the same time, can overwhelm the users. Remember the adage, "less can be more."

▶▶ CONCLUSION

The field of measurement in the people domain is advancing quickly. It is being pushed by top management wanting better information with which to make decisions and lead the company to success, as well as by corporate boards and the investment community wanting to know with greater accuracy what investments yield the best return and what the real "value" of people is to the overall value of the company.

Quantification of, and subsequent precision in, measuring people factors lags behind other areas of business, such as production and finance, but headway is being made. The assumption that people do matter to the bottom line is beginning to be borne out with evidence that is more powerful than anecdotes. More robust research methods have produced correlational evidence of linkage between employee satisfaction, customer satisfaction, and business outcomes. Cutting edge methodology that utilizes data collected in HRM information systems, payroll records, and financial databases can be used to establish cause–effect relationships and even to model future business scenarios.

The quantity and quality of people measures used by companies will continue to grow and evolve. Asian enterprise has followed this trend and in all likelihood will continue to do so. Measurement practices from salary benchmarking to employee opinion surveys to balanced business scorecards and more have all been used successfully by Asian companies, and their use continues to spread. Although cultural diversity drives differences in how they are implemented, there is no evidence to suggest that they cannot work or that fundamentally different measurement techniques must be developed. If anything, the proclivity of Asian executives to prefer quantitative over qualitative evidence may drive development and implementation of sophisticated measurement techniques more quickly than in other parts of the world.

Globally speaking, why is the use of HRM metrics, and the idea of measuring "people phenomena" in general, going to be different from other developments in HRM practices? Because it already has a natural "fit" to the executive mindset. Once the more stringent practices of measuring and tracking the ROI of human capital attains a critical mass of acceptance and use, it will be talked about and utilized as commonly as financial and production measures. Virtually every business will do it in order to compete and because financial markets will demand it.

For those companies that are able to realize the full potential of measuring human capital, they will be the leaders in their respective industries, have the best earnings and profits, the highest market valuations, and be considered the best places to work. This will be possible, not because they successfully mimic the past "best practices" of prior or existing blue-chip companies, but because they will find the optimal formula for attracting, retaining, and motivating their employees, which in turn will produce optimal strategy execution, sterling product and service quality, and previously unimagined levels of productivity. Measuring people practices and human capital has arrived and the time to get started is now.

Star-gazing: What will be some of the "must haves" for HRM measurement in five to 10 years time?

- Robust, integrated, and user-friendly human resource information and talent management systems.
- Strategic metrics that track strategy implementation and demonstrate HRM's contribution to the organization (for example, percentage of employees trained on product/service knowledge, dollars invested in training, and incentives/percent increase in customer satisfaction).
- Basic metrics for the chief human resources officer (CHRO) to track HRM function effectiveness within the organisation (for example, HRM FTE/total headcount, HRM expense/total headcount, cost per hire, time to fill positions).
- Basic metrics to track HRM outsource vendors' effectiveness (for example, cost of service/HRM budget, employee satisfaction with service).
- HRM teams with new and expanded competencies in operations, finance, sales and marketing, and strategic planning and implementation.
- Valuation of human capital in the organization to be used by the Board, as well as customers and stock analysts

[1] Labor cost is defined as employee compensation; gross domestic product (GDP) is calculated by adding consumption, government expenditures, investment, and net exports.

Data sources: *National Income and Product Accounts in Survey of Current Business* (US), August 2001 and April 2002, Wong, Soon Teck and Ong Lai Heng (2002), "First World Per Capita Income But Third World Income Structure? Wage Share and Productivity Improvement in Singapore," *Statistics Singapore Newsletter*. The annual labor shares for Singapore are approximations because they are read off Chart 6 in Wong and Heng (2002), p. 9

[2] *The Service–Profit Chain*, James L. Heskett, Thomas O. Jones, W. Earl Sasser Jr. and Leonard A. Schlesinger, 1977, The Free Press: New York.

[3] "Putting the Service–Profit Chain to Work" by James L. Heskett, Thomas O. Jones, W. Earl Sasser Jr. and Leonard A. Schlesinger. *Harvard Business Review*, March/April 1994.

[4] Heskett, Jones, Sasser, Schlesinger 1994.

[5] Heskett, Jones, Sasser, Schlesinger 1994.

[6] "Measuring HR?: Benchmarking is NOT the Answer!," by Brian Becker and Mark Huselid. *HR Magazine*, December 2003, pp. 57–61.

[7] "The HR Scorecard: Linking people, strategy, and performance," by Brian Becker, Mark Huselid, Dave Ulrich. Harvard Business School Press, 2001, pp. 36–52.

[8] *Play To Your Strengths: Managing Your Internal Labor Markets for Lasting Competitive Advantage*, Haig Nalbantian, Richard Guzzo, Dave Kieffer, and Jay Doherty, 2003, McGraw Hill, New York, 2003.

Index